BRITISH WOMEN FICTION WRITERS

1900-1960 ❧ VOLUME ONE

BRITISH WOMEN FICTION WRITERS 1900 – 1960

VOLUME ONE

Edited and with an Introduction by

Harold Bloom

CHELSEA HOUSE PUBLISHERS

Philadelphia

ON THE COVER: Romaine Brooks, *Self-Portrait*, 1923. National Museum of American Art, Washington, DC/Art Resource, NY

CHELSEA HOUSE PUBLISHERS

EDITOR-IN-CHIEF Stephen Reginald
MANAGING EDITOR James D. Gallagher
PRODUCTION MANAGER Pamela Loos
PICTURE EDITOR Judy Hasday
ART DIRECTOR Sara Davis
SENIOR PRODUCTION EDITOR Lisa Chippendale

WOMEN WRITERS OF ENGLISH AND THEIR WORKS:
  British Women Fiction Writers, 1900–1960: Volume One

SERIES EDITOR Jane Shumate
CONTRIBUTING EDITOR Henna Remstein
SENIOR EDITOR Therese De Angelis
INTERIOR AND COVER DESIGNERS Alison Burnside, Terry Mallon
EDITORIAL ASSISTANT Anne Hill

First Printing
1 3 5 7 9 8 6 4 2

Library of Congress Cataloging-in-Publication Data

British women fiction writers, 1900-1960 / edited and with an
  introduction by Harold Bloom.
        p.   cm. — (Women writers of English and their works)
  Includes bibliographical references.
  ISBN 0-7910-4483-1 (v. 1). — ISBN 0-7910-4499-8 (pbk. : v. 1)
    1. English fiction—20th century—History and criticism. 2. Women and literature—Great Britain—History—20th century. 3. English fiction—Women authors—History and criticism. 4. English fiction—Women authors. 5. English fiction—20th century.
I. Bloom, Harold. I. Series.
PR888.W6B75 1997
823'.91099287—dc21   97-20282
                                                                                    CIP

CONTENTS

BRITISH WOMEN FICTION WRITERS

1900-1960 & VOLUME ONE

The Analysis of Women Writers

HAROLD BLOOM

I APPROACH THIS SERIES with a certain wariness, since so much of classical feminist literary criticism has founded itself upon arguments with that phase of my own work that began with *The Anxiety of Influence* (first published in January 1973). Someone who has been raised to that bad eminence—*The Patriarchal Critic*—is well advised that he trespasses upon sacred ground when he ventures to inquire whether indeed there are indisputable differences, imaginative and cognitive, between the literary works of women and those of men. If these differences are so substantial as pragmatically to make an authentic difference, does that in turn make necessary different aesthetic standards for judging the achievements of men and of women writers? Is Emily Dickinson to be read as though she has more in common with Elizabeth Barrett Browning than with Ralph Waldo Emerson?

Is Elizabeth Bishop a great poet because she triumphantly meets the same aesthetic criteria satisfied by Wallace Stevens, or should we evaluate her by criteria she shares with Marianne Moore, but not with Stevens? Are there crucial gender-based differences in the representations of Esther Summerson by Charles Dickens in *Bleak House*, and of Dorothea Brooke by George Eliot in *Middlemarch*? Does Samuel Richardson's Clarissa Harlowe convince us that her author was a male when we contrast her with Jane Austen's Elizabeth Bennet? Do women poets have a less agonistic relationship to female precursors than male poets have to their forerunners? Two eminent pioneers of feminist criticism, Sandra Gilbert and Susan Gubar, have suggested that women writers suffer more from an anxiety of authorship than they do from influence anxieties, while another important feminist critic, Elaine Showalter, has suggested that women writers, early and late, work together in a kind of quiltmaking, each doing her share while avoiding any contamination of creative envy in regard to other writers, provided that they be women. Can it be true that, in the aesthetic sphere, women do not beware women and do not suffer from the competitiveness and jealousy that alas do exist in the professional and sexual domains? Is there something in the area of literature, when practiced by women, that changes and purifies mere human nature?

I cannot answer any of these questions, yet I do think it is vital and clarifying to raise them. There is a current fashion, in many of our institutions of higher education, to insist that English Romantic poetry cannot be studied in the old way, with an exclusive emphasis upon the works of William Blake, William Wordsworth, Samuel Taylor Coleridge, Lord Byron, Percy Bysshe Shelley, John Keats, and John Clare. Instead, the Romantic poets are taken to include Felicia Hemans, Laetitia Landon, Charlotte Smith, and Mary Tighe, among others. It would be heartening if we could believe that these are unjustly neglected poets, but their current revival will be brief. Similarly, anthologies of 17th-century English literature now tend to include the Duchess of Newcastle as well as Aphra Behn, Lady Mary Chudleigh, Anne Killigrew, Anne Finch, Countess of Winchilsea, and others. Some of these— Anne Finch in particular—wrote well, but a situation in which they are more read and studied than John Milton is not one that is likely to endure forever. The consequences of making gender a criterion for aesthetic choice must finally destroy all serious study of imaginative literature as such.

In their *Norton Anthology of Literature by Women*, Sandra Gilbert and Susan Gubar conclude their introduction to Elizabeth Barrett Browning by saying that "she constantly tested herself against the highest standards of male-defined poetic genres," a true if ambiguous observation. They then print her famous "The Cry of the Children," an admirably passionate ode that protests the cruel employment of little children in British Victorian mines and factories. Unfortunately, this well-meant prophetic affirmation ends with this, doubtless its finest stanza:

XIII

They look up with their pale and sunken faces,
    And their look is dread to see,
For they mind you of their angels in high places,
    With eyes turned on Deity.
"How long," they say, "how long, O cruel nation,
    Will you stand, to move the world, on a child's heart,—
Stifle down with a mailèd heel its palpitation,
    And tread onward to your throne amid the mart?
Our blood splashes upward, O goldheaper,
    And your purple shows your path!
But the child's sob in the silence curses deeper
    Than the strong man in his wrath."

If you read this aloud, then you may find yourself uncomfortable, on a strictly aesthetic basis, which would not vary if you were told that this had been composed by a male Victorian poet. In their selections from Elizabeth Bishop, Gilbert and Gubar courageously reprint Bishop's superb statement explaining her refusal to permit her poems to be included in anthologies of women's writing:

> Undoubtedly gender does play an important part in the making of any art, but art is art and to separate writings, paintings, musical compositions, etc., into sexes is to emphasize values in them that are *not* art.

That credo of Elizabeth Bishop's is to me the Alpha and Omega of critical wisdom in regard to all feminist literary criticism. Gender studies are precisely that: they study gender, and not aesthetic value. If your priorities are historical, social, political, and ideological, then gender studies clearly are more than justified. Perhaps they are a way to justice, or at least to more justice than women have received throughout thousands of years of male domination and aggression. Yet that is a very different matter from the now vexed issue of aesthetic value. Biographical criticism, like the different modes of historicist and psychological criticism, always has relied upon a kind of implicit gender studies and doubtless will benefit, as other modes will, by a making explicit of such considerations, particularly in regard to women writers.

Each volume in this series contains copious refutations of, and replies to, the traditionally aesthetic stance that I have advocated here. These introductory remarks aspire only to a questioning, and not a challenging, of feminist literary criticism. There are no longer any Patriarchal Critics; they are all dinosaurs, fabulous beasts fit for revival only in horror films. Sometimes I sadly think of myself as Bloom Brontosaurus, amiably left behind by the fire and the flood. But more often I go on reading the great women writers, searching for the aesthetic difference that yet may prove to be there, but which has not yet been found.

OF THE WRITERS DISCUSSED in this book, Elizabeth Bowen clearly was the most eminent, surpassed in her own generation only by Virginia Woolf. Her fiction is much more in the mode of Henry James than of Woolf, though, particularly the middle James of *The Awkward Age* and *What Maisie Knew*. Like James, Bowen became a master of subtle evasions, a chronicler of the unlived life. Also like James, Bowen distinguished herself in the representation of fantasy, especially as it affects the lives of sensitive women. In this regard, she anticipated aspects of Iris Murdoch's art in the next generation.

Though she wrote remarkable novels—most notably *The Death of the Heart* and *The Heat of the Day*—Bowen's great achievement is her *Collected Stories*, the best of which challenge James Joyce and D. H. Lawrence in that crucial genre. Joyce indubitably influenced Bowen; from Lawrence she derived a few nuances at most. If one asks for the highest art in the short story, Bowen suffices as well as any other titan of the form. Her most characteristic stories are precisely akin to great lyric poems; they are economical, poignant, inevitable, and astonishingly memorable.

I have written, a decade ago, about three of my favorite Bowen stories: "Sunday Afternoon," "Mysterious Kôr," and the magnificent "Ivy Gripped the Steps," perhaps her masterpiece. Here I want to comment only upon the very brief but endlessly haunting "The Demon Lover," in which a prosaic, middle-aged, upper-middle-class London wife and mother is carried off, in the midst of the Blitz, by the apparent ghost of the slain lover to whom she had pledged herself a quarter century before. We might be in the world of medieval Romance or of the Border Ballads, and yet we are in wartime London, where Bowen worked at the Ministry of Information while enduring, with her fellow citizens, the German bombardment. That London is uncannily evoked in the silences and spaces of "The Demon Lover." Life, unlived and evaded, makes a demonic return upon the anxious and empty Mrs. Drover (whose married name intimates her passive existence and ultimate fate). Her demon lover's note accurately and ominously remarks, "In view of the fact that nothing has changed, I shall rely upon you to keep your promise." Attempting in vain to flee her occult destiny, Mrs. Drover steps into what she assumes is a taxi, only to discover that indeed she has kept her promise:

> The driver braked to what was almost a stop, turned round and slid
> the glass panel back: the jolt of this flung Mrs. Drover forward till
> her face was almost into the glass. Through the aperture driver and
> passenger, not six inches between them, remained for an eternity eye
> to eye. Mrs. Drover's mouth hung open for some seconds before she

could issue her first scream. After that she continued to scream freely and to beat with her gloved hands on the glass all around as the taxi, accelerating without mercy, made off with her into the hinterland of deserted streets.

This is the story's conclusion, at once enigmatic and definitive. Bowen is not interested in telling us more; we know what we need to know. Perhaps the demon lover is taking the terrified Mrs. Drover to some precise location, where his long-deferred lust will be gratified. More likely, the drive never will end, as in Emily Dickinson's great lyric "Because I could not stop for Death" or in Kafka's grand fragment "The Country Doctor." Bowen's story, at once drab and sublime, sustains itself even in the realms of such visionaries and their visions.

ELIZABETH BOWEN

1899–1973

ELIZABETH DOROTHEA COLE BOWEN was born on June 7, 1899, in Dublin, Ireland, into a family of financial and social privilege. Her father, Henry Charles Cole Bowen, was a barrister who had inherited the 800-acre family estate, Bowen's Court. When Elizabeth was seven, her father's mental health declined and her mother, Florence Colley Bowen, retreated with her to England. By 1912, Henry Bowen had recovered, but, while plans progressed for a return to Ireland, Florence Bowen died of cancer. Thereafter, Elizabeth was cared for during the school year by one or another unmarried aunt and later was sent to a boarding school in Kent, though she summered in Ireland at Bowen's Court. There she and her cousin Audrey often occupied themselves with storytelling, a practice Bowen continued through her teens to entertain herself as much as her girlfriends.

World War I, during which Bowen helped care for shell-shocked soldiers in a Dublin hospital, became the first of many world conflicts that would emerge in her writing. Most significantly, the Anglo-Irish War (1919–1921), or the War of Independence as it is called in Ireland, and the Irish Civil War (1921–1923) directly affected the lives of her family and neighbors. During this period, the Sinn Fein political party won in the general elections and refused to recognize the British Parliament, instead establishing their own Irish Parliament (Dail), which, in turn, England would not acknowledge. These events entrenched the bitter division between North Ireland, a British province, and South Ireland, a self-governed state. For Bowen, it would also set the stage for many of her novels, including *The Last September* (1929), populated by young Anglo-Irish officers who socialize among the Irish elite.

In 1918 Bowen briefly attended the London County Council School of Art, marking the beginning of a five-year period of restlessness. Her search for a purpose ended with the publication of her first collection of short stories, *Encounters* (1923), and her marriage to Alan Charles Cameron, assistant secretary for education in Northamptonshire. The couple moved to Oxford, England, where Cameron became secretary for education and where Bowen found a nurturing intellectual environment and the support of fellow novelist Rose Macaulay; she was soon publishing volumes of short stories and her first several novels at a prolific rate. Strongly influenced by Henry James and her friend Virginia Woolf, yet defying categorization,

Bowen earned praise from critics, and by 1934 her literary reputation was assured.

In 1930 Bowen became the first woman to inherit Bowen's Court, though she and Cameron continued to live in England and later moved to London after the publication of *The House in Paris* (1935). Her rigorous pace of writing continued with regular contributions to the *Tattler* and other publications, work for the BBC, and the completion of her sixth novel, *The Death of the Heart* (1935). Bowen was elected to the Irish Academy of Letters in 1937, and other honors followed throughout her life: she was made a Commander of the British Empire in 1948; she was awarded an honorary Doctor of Letters from Trinity College, Dublin, in 1949, and one from Oxford in 1956; and she received a Royal Society of Literature Award in 1965.

After Alan Cameron's death in 1952, Bowen resided full time at Bowen's Court. By 1965, however, she had returned to Hythe, Ireland, where she wrote her last novel, *Eva Trout* (1968), which received the James Tait Black Memorial Prize in 1970. On February 22, 1973, Elizabeth Bowen died of lung cancer, leaving behind one work in progress, *Pictures and Conversations*, published posthumously in 1975.

CRITICAL EXTRACTS

GRAHAM GREENE

⟨Elizabeth Bowen's⟩ novel, *The House in Paris*, covers a period from before the birth of an illegitimate child until he has reached the age of nine. The popular novelist would have described every one of these years, however dull to the reader the accumulation of trivialities. Miss Bowen has simply left them out with the merest glance backward; we may believe that she has been forced to omit, but she has made of her omissions a completely individual method, she has dramatized ignorance. How with so little known of the 'backward and abysm' can she convey her characters with any clearness? It is impossible, but her consciousness of that impossibility proves her great value as a novelist. She makes it the virtue of her characters that they are three parts mystery; the darkness which hides their past makes the cerebrations which we are allowed to follow the more vivid, as vivid as the exchanges of people overheard talking on a platform before a train goes out. It is an exquisite sleight of hand: the egg was in the hat, now it is being removed from the tip of a robust woman's nose. We must fill in for ourselves what happened between; the burden of that problem is passed to the reader. To the author remains the task of making the characters understand each other without our losing the sense of mystery: they must be able to tell all from a gesture, a whisper, a written sentence: they have to be endowed with an inhuman intuition as James's characters were endowed with an inhuman intelligence, and no writer since James has proved capable of a more cunning evasion. Unable to convey the passage of time, she has made capital out of the gap in the records; how can we doubt the existence of a past which these characters can so easily convey to each other?

 —Graham Greene, "The Dark Backward: A Footnote" (1935), *Collected Essays* (1969), excerpted in *Twentieth-Century British Literature*, ed. Harold Bloom (New York: Chelsea House Publishers, 1985), 213

LOUISE BOGAN

Modern fiction of the subtler kind when written by women is likely to depict at length the trouble resulting from unsuitable and complicated people falling in love. The stays and obstacles once provided by difference in social position, family feuds, missent letters, and trumped-up misunderstandings have narrowed into drama arising from the fact that the lovers have neuroses that do not match, are in love for the wrong reasons, in love too late or too soon, or are incapable of love at all. Elizabeth Bowen in her previous novels has described such combinations, and Madame Colette has worked with them for years. Miss Bowen has also probed with great thoroughness into the reaction of sensitive children, sometimes the offspring of mismatings, thrown into situations of which they hold only one or two clues. *The House in Paris* successfully brought off an atmosphere of emotional tension, resulting when the past, present, and future converged on such a child, who was caught, between journeys, in rooms full of the tragedy to which he owed his being. *The Death of the Heart* turns on a girl of sixteen, the product of a misalliance, who, when introduced into the "edited life" of her half-brother's smart London household, throws upon it the full glare of her innocence, breaks through its surface, and shows the lack of human feeling on which it is based. ⟨. . .⟩

Miss Bowen has elsewhere spoken of "the limitations of English narrative prose, with its *longueurs* and conventions dangerous to truth." In her novels she has taken every precaution to reduce these conventions to a minimum. The strokes come close, and every stroke tells. Miss Bowen is particularly good at reflecting one character in another, always making it clear that some people see things partially while others take in every detail. Matchett, the self-contained upper servant, with her toughened sympathy and snobbery and her pride of the good artisan, sees everything. Eddie sees everything—in his way—and himself, "at once coy and insolent," only too well. Matchett can sum people up. Of the "sacrificing" first Mrs. Quayne she says: "I couldn't care for her; she had no nature"; of Anna: "Oh, she has her taste and dearly loves to use it. Past that she'll never go." Eddie says of Anna: "She loves to make a tart out of another person. She'd never dare to be a proper tart herself." Thomas has an occasional moment of insight into the society about him: "self-interest, given a pretty gloss." But Portia, not yet absorbed into "the guilty plausibility of the world," sees more than everything. She detects the impossibility of a natural human relationship between these people who write letters, go to dinner parties, talk at tea—always "stalking each other." She watches "thoroughly"; she tries to shake some human response out of Eddie; she importunes; she nags with the implacable fury of first love. At the end she gives the show away to simple, kind Major Brutt. "Anna's always laughing at you. She says you are quite pathetic. . . . And Thomas thinks you must be after something. They groan at each other when you have gone away. You and I are the same."

Miss Bowen's talent is so rich and so searching, and this novel stands so far outside the class of novels which resemble packaged goods put up for the trade, that one is tempted to give her nothing but praise. She sees deeply, but not widely enough. Corruption has not lately entered the class of which she writes; the heart is not dying in these people; it never lived in them. And her tone, too keyed up, never lets down for a moment; the *longueurs* are deleted to such an extent that they are missed. Beautifully-done descriptions of times of day and the weather edge the action—to a tiresome degree. The backgrounds for emotions are chosen with care; one, an empty seaside boarding-house on a Sunday morning, is almost unbearably appropriate. Miss Bowen can cook the vulgar English to the same crispness to which she treats their betters. But *The Death of the Heart* is too packed, too brilliant, for its own good. What Miss Bowen lacks is a kind of humility. She has forgotten more than many novelists ever knew, but what Turgenev, for example, knew, and was chary of expressing, she cannot quite deal with. Once in a while the reader hears the accent of self-satisfaction, if not display, in the novelist. But for all that, *The Death of the Heart* deepens our view of the horrors experienced by open innocence up against a closed world.

—Louise Bogan, "The Pure in Heart" (1939), *Selected Criticism* (1955), excerpted in *Twentieth-Century British Literature*, ed. Harold Bloom (New York: Chelsea House Publishers, 1985), 214

EDWARD SACKVILLE-WEST

In her latest novel, *The Heat of the Day*, Miss Bowen achieves by subtlety what a male novelist, treating a similar subject, would have tried to achieve by power. For the first time since *The Last September* she has chosen a theme which takes her outside the bounds of private life. Yet she avoids, with extraordinary adroitness, the threats to her scope offered by an international plot to sabotage the Allied war effort during the autumn of 1942. In creating the figures of the traitor, Robert Kelway, and the counter-spy, Harrison, the temptation to strain her imagination beyond bearing must have been considerable. For the world in which these men move, when they are off the stage—the world behind the life, public and private, of Stella Rodney—is that which writers like Simenon and V. S. Pritchett and Graham Greene do not have to invent because they know it. Miss Bowen does not attempt to invent it: as Jane Austen would have done, she takes it for granted, but without losing sight of its effect on character and behaviour. She loads her three central figures with the heaviest possible responsibility: the fate of nations is assumed to depend, at least to some extent, on the good faith and intelligence required by the work in which they are engaged; and their 'reality', as characters of fiction, is to be measured by our awareness of the ways in which their humanity is modified by what they are compelled to do.

This bringing of public to the bar of private life gives weight and solidity to a story which is painfully dramatic, but never merely sad. Finer and subtler in the analysis of complex feeling than *The House in Paris*, wider in range than *The Death of the Heart*, *The Heat of the Day* is cunningly built up in scenes each of which concentrates the light upon a portion of the displayed canvas. Time plays—is meant to play—little part in the drama, which is superficially laid out in the first few chapters. All that is left is for us to discover, through Stella's eyes, what is really there. The characters do not change: what changes is our attitude towards them. In the process of gradually stripping her people Miss Bowen shows a control that only occasionally falters—though when it does falter, in the case of Robert Kelway, the result is nearly disastrous. Her portrait of the counter-spy, Harrison, is her most brilliant feat. We end by feeling something like affection for this unbearable creature whose unlovability is the clue to his comfortless self. (Incidentally, this figure is an ironic comment on the possible results of a complete victory of character over personality.) It was clever of Miss Bowen to have seen Harrison, not as sub-, or super-, but as pseudo-human—provisional—mechanical—sinister and rigid as a being invoked by a sorcerer's spell.

> His concentration on her was made more oppressive by his failure to have or let her give him any possible place in the human scene. By the rules of fiction, with which life to be credible must comply, he was as a character 'impossible'—each time they met, for instance, he showed no shred or trace of having been continuous since they last met. His civilian clothes, though one could be remotely conscious of alternation in suit or shirt or tie, *seemed* to vary much less than Robert's uniform; the uninterestingly right state of what he wore seemed less

> to argue care—brushing, pressing, change of linen—than a physical
> going into abeyance, just as he was, with everything he had on him,
> between appearances.

Perceived with the acuteness of extreme distaste, but not entirely without sympathy, Harrison is much more convincing than Robert Kelway, who suffers from Miss Bowen's inability to invest him with any charm. Apart from the fact that he is alleged to be good-looking, tall, and lame in one leg, it is difficult to see why Stella (whose attractiveness we never for a moment doubt) should have been drawn to so null a man. There are signs of fumbling here: astonishment that Robert should be capable of treachery somehow gets confused with a more general wonder that men should be the odd creatures they are. 〈. . .〉

Nevertheless, *The Heat of the Day* is literature: as a whole it will stand up to serious criticism of detail because its effect, as a work of art, is homogeneous and impressive. Miss Bowen has gone to school with Henry James, but in order to learn how best to express an original vision. The result is an analytical prose continually enlivened by deft allusion and clever imagery. And her idiom is poetic because it is sustained—like that of James and Conrad—at the level of drama.

—Edward Sackville-West, "Ladies Whose Bright Pens . . . ," *Inclinations* (1949), excerpted in *Twentieth-Century British Literature*, ed. Harold Bloom (New York: Chelsea House Publishers, 1985), 214–15

ELIZABETH HARDWICK

The opinion, or sentiment, that occurs again and again in Elizabeth Bowen's fiction and which seems to have commanded the labors on her ancestral chronicle, *Bowen's Court*, is that to know *who* you are, to be close to your past, to feel the pride and obligations of family and place, are, if not the most exquisite and difficult attainments, a great source of personal and national virtue. These warm, sustaining emotions are found most frequently in the gentry and upper class; the disloyal, the insincere and unreliable are the homeless, the shapeless nobodys, the complacent, vapid middle class, the mysterious foreigner, the restless, self-loving *arriviste*. In the case of very young girls, such as Lois in *The Last September* and Portia in *The Death of the Heart*, the pattern is reversed and the family betrays. However, here the reversal is necessary for pathos, the thundershowers of pity that are the main weather of these two novels. By whom can a young girl be more miserably misunderstood, since she has little freedom of movement, than by her family? To be sure, Portia in *The Death of the Heart* has a more democratic fate: she is victimized impartially by all classes and with such supererogatory heartlessness that one yawns, occasionally, and suspects Portia really may be the nuisance her selfish betrayers believe. Even in this book, with its villainous cast, the real sewer of corruption is a young man, Eddie, who has overdrawn himself socially. ⟨. . .⟩

The most striking thing about Miss Bowen's novel is that the attitudes and generalities which establish the tone, the more weighty reflections on status and character, either contradict or have nothing to do with the action. This author, as Mme. de Sévigné said of herself, is often very far from being entirely of her own opinion. Her typical heroines (Karen in *The House in Paris*, Emmeline in *To the North*, Stella in *The Heat of the Day*) are described as well-bred, calm, honest and attractive; they represent class and family virtue, and yet we can understand their actions only in terms of bohemia, that land no parent, relative or property owner ever enters. The girls are unconventional and daring, not in the manner of artists or intellectuals, but in the more starchy, unprogrammatic way of independent, competent business women. In love they lack caution and, to some degree, conscience; with fanatical dogged-ness they deceive their parents and friends, have illegitimate children, open affairs with men they know little about, and even commit murder, or at least that is the way I interpret the ending of *To the North*. All of the neat, loving domestic purity of the heroine's background does not keep her away from the sordid scenery of weekend cottages and hotel rooms. And it is almost always the heroine who passes beyond the expected and discreet in love; indeed, the man's "betrayal" is simply his embarrassment, his disabling reasonableness, his unwillingness to "live on the top of the Alps."

The main characteristic of the heroines is incuriosity. We can sympathize with the traitor Robert Kelway when he tells Stella he thought she knew of his secret activities. "How could she not have suspected *something*?" he and the reader wonder. Markie in *To the North* tells Emmeline, as they take off for a weekend in Paris, that he doesn't wish to marry her, but for some reason she discounts his frank admission; Eddie in *The Death of the Heart* is understandably astonished that Portia should have imagined he loved her. The heroines are bemused, credulous, and humorless; their high-mindedness is often only a fan-tastic, unrelenting literalness; we can seem to hear their desperate pleading going on long after the disaster, "But I thought you said—" and "How could you when—?" or "But you promised—."

The men are complex, ambiguous, dissatisfied—qualities Miss Bowen looks upon with finicky contempt. At the best, this contempt gives a structure to the story and a resolution to the plot. Elizabeth Bowen's novels *end*, usually in the death of the man (*The House in Paris, The Last September, The Heat of the Day, To the North*). One cannot help but see these concluding immolations as the "woman's revenge," condign punishment for male weakness, hesitation and disingenuousness. And if there is something chilling and merciless in these finales, no one can doubt they give prodigal relief to both feminine sentiment and womanly outrage.

Since Miss Bowen's purest talent is for the simple love story, she seems to me at her best in *To the North*, a harsh, terrifying and unaffected book. Even the title avoids the sentimental disguise of the other novels and candidly indicates the zero temperature at which these love affairs end. Emmeline, the heroine, has the charm of an admission; she is in the flesh what you have felt the other heroines really were, no matter what the author pretended. Fresh, competent (a business of her own), myopic, always reaching for her glasses or seeing the world through a pleasant, deceptive haze, exorbitantly insensitive to the true character of her lover, unwilling to countenance his frantic warnings, idealistic, cruel when disabused, she hounds the fleeing man, and finally, when she can no longer avoid facing the truth, gets him into a car and drives so fast they are both killed. This book has the finished, clean and moving success the others merely hope to achieve by considerable cant about taste and manners.

I cannot share E. Sackville-West's statement in *Horizon* that "Elizabeth Bowen is already assured of a superior place in any civilization capable of appreciating, say, *Middlemarch*." This critic might have gone through the whole of *The Cambridge History* without finding a comparison more unflattering to Miss Bowen. But I wonder if these comparisons are meant to be taken seriously. They are apparently an accepted form of discourse and whenever the subject under discussion is a woman writer we can always expect to pass the time of day with chatter about Jane Austen, Charlotte Bronte and George Eliot.

Just where Elizabeth Bowen "belongs" I cannot say. Readable, gifted, the very equanimity of her work makes criticism difficult. In a relaxed mood, she offers one the satisfaction of unabashed tears, an emotional evening in which love retains all its old sovereign rights, and the final pleasure of witnessing the bad end to which the inconstant come. As in an opera libretto you must take the roles on faith—a grunt of satire or a shiver of commonsense on the spectator's part would be enough to disrupt the performance and bring the pretty scenery down upon the soprano's head.

—Elizabeth Hardwick, "Elizabeth Bowen's Fiction," *Partisan Review* (November 1949), excerpted in *Twentieth-Century British Literature*, ed. Harold Bloom (New York: Chelsea House Publishers, 1985), 219–21

ANTHONY BURGESS

When Elizabeth Bowen's name is mentioned, other women novelists are mentioned too—often ineptly: Mr. ⟨V. S.⟩ Pritchett's comparison with Virginia Woolf won't really work. To fit Miss Bowen into a group is one thing, to find her origins quite another. Having subscribed ⟨. . .⟩ to the big male-female opposition, I am not really reneging if I bring in Henry James as her true progenitor. James is the unique example of a writer who (and there is no Western substitute for these terms) allowed the *yin* principle to overcome his *yang* when he settled in Europe. Those endlessly qualified sentences with their spinsterish scruples were a bequest not only to Edith Wharton, but to a whole line of woman novelists, of whom Miss Bowen is one ⟨. . . .⟩

The involutions of James's prose, the torturings of natural syntax to avoid the cliché, the enthroning of the cliché where the cliché is not even enlightening—all this was James's substitute for poetry. But, paradoxically, if there had been more poetry in him there would have been a less massive image of a civilisation. In Miss Bowen there is a great deal of poetry: it is what lightens her involutions, and if it sometimes drops to mere fancy (the French clock 'busy . . . on the chimneypiece, amid idling china'), that is appropriate—it serves her concern with 'atmosphere.' Where James articulates a whole culture, Miss Bowen conserves a particular place at a particular time; this is a feminine gift. ⟨. . .⟩

The Little Girls is Miss Bowen's first novel for nine years. She hasn't, apparently, been using those nine years to plot new departures, though her observation of the contemporary world is, as we expect, very sharp: 'atmosphere' is still her business. But the contemporary world is only part of it. Three women of sixty—Dinah, Clare and Sheila—were schoolgirls together in 1914 (Dicey, Mumbo and Sheikie). Dinah, an ageless beauty, summons her friends from the past by means of newspaper advertisements. A great burier-for-posterity, she wants to know what's happened to a box the three of them buried at St. Agatha's all those years ago ('We are dead, and all our fathers and mothers. You who find this, Take Care. These are our valuable treasures, and our fetters . . . Here are Bones, too . . .'). This gives Miss Bowen an opportunity for a delicious recall and a fine scenic set-piece on what's become of the school's site now:

> . . . The revenants stood back, backs to the balustrade—above them,
> ten or a dozen nice-looking houses, spaced out over the hill's face,
> harmlessly contemplated the Channel; garages, their doors painted
> pastel colours, sat on ledges surrounded by landscape gardening. . . .
> In general, the gardens were veiled in the thinly dusky yellows and
> coppers and bronzy purples of mid-autumn. . . .

And so on. This, I think, is authentic flavoursome Bowen.

The box, when they find it, is empty. The warning comes too late for the three, but not for the reader; the story is, in fact, an easy morality: 'Gently dip, but not too deep.' The intensities of a childhood relationship are invoked in middle age at one's own peril. Never choose to call back past time: choice, anyway, is dangerous. 'We were entrusted to one another, in the days which mattered,' Clare thought. 'Entrusted to one another by chance, not choice. Chance, and its agents time and place. Chance is better than choice; it is more lordly. In its carelessness it is more lordly. Chance is God, choice is man.' Moral profundities swirl about, among the aubergine jerseys and the coloured scenery-motifs on cups and bowls. They are of much the same order as the discrete elements of the sensuous world that Miss Bowen proves, so lavishly, to exist. What James made terrifying is here rather charming.

Confronted by so much technical brilliance, even when not awed by reputation, the reader may well blame himself for being, as he thinks, insufficiently moved. But what Miss Bowen has achieved is less the peopling of time and place with entities which, like Emma Bovary or Charlus or Bloom, have a human validity which bursts their literary bonds, than the furnishing of time and place with the conditions which might enable such beings to exist—and this means not only 'atmosphere' but the texture of skin and hair and bags under the eyes. There are times when, seduced by the miraculously caught cadences of feminine speech, one wakes to the shock of thinking it all a contrivance—a device for moving spheres (if one may use the old metaphysical imagery) which in themselves have no intelligence. Perhaps all this is going too far: the book is, after all, a comedy, a pleasant warning against the dangers of nostalgia, a demonstration of the allure which informs a sensuous world uncoloured by nostalgia. It is a wonderful artefact, a triumphant Female Novel by one whose gifts release her from the more male duty of being just among the Just, among the Filthy filthy too, and of suffering dully all the wrongs of Man.

—Anthony Burgess, "Treasures and Fetters," *Spectator* (12 February 1964), excerpted in *Twentieth-Century British Literature*, ed. Harold Bloom (New York: Chelsea House Publishers, 1985), 210–11

LIONEL STEVENS

Having presented her testament of war-time London (in *The Heat of the Day*), the gist of which is that no intelligible connection between personal feeling and external reality could subsist under such chaotic conditions, Miss Bowen returned in her next novel, *A World of Love*, to Ireland, where the destructive crises of a generation previous have been succeeded by inertia. Hence the effect of hallucination, already disturbingly perceptible in *The Heat of the Day*, becomes more conspicuous. The title of the book is derived from the mystical meditations of Thomas Traherne: "So is there in us a world of Love to somewhat, though we know not what in the world that should be." This combination of emotional yearning with intellectual uncertainty is the theme of the whole novel. The setting is a crumbling, isolated country-house that seems to be totally detached from the living world; and the landscapes, while described with all Miss Bowen's customary poetic vividness, are suffused with an unearthly light. As in her preceding novel, the preciosity of style enhances the effect of illusion: a reader will scarcely accept occurrences as objectively real when they are suspended in an opalescent medium of metaphors, alliteration, double negatives, inversions, and literary echoes.

As in *The House in Paris*, an ingenious device is employed to convey a complex relationship of past and present. The events of the novel occur in a span of three days, but their motivating impulses date back a full generation. The heroine, typical of Miss Bowen's romantic young rebels against tedious conformity, discovers a package of love letters written by a former owner of the house, who was killed in the First World War, long before she was born. She falls in love with her image of the seductive young man, and when her secret is discovered it infects the two older women of the household, who both loved him and whose dormant passion and antagonism are thus revivified. The spell of the past is not exorcised until the end of the story, when the two women begin to find themselves purged of their unresolved tensions and the young girl abruptly transfers her romantic ardor from her dream of the long-dead letter-writer to a normally alive man whom she has never seen until he steps off an aeroplane in the last paragraph of the book.

In *The Little Girls*, published nine years later, the study of obsessive fantasy is carried much further and the past which is spectrally resuscitated is not thirty but fifty years gone by. Though the theme is still the disparity between the romantic will and the harsh realities, the protagonist is now not a self-centered girl but a widow past sixty, whose comfortable life has enabled her to remain emotionally an adolescent. The imminence of old age impels her to sentimental nostalgia and a compulsion to construct some sort of objective memorial of her existence. She fills a cave in her garden with assorted odds and ends that she has accumulated, and then decides to seek out two school friends who shared with her a similar escapade half a century before. The gradual disclosure of their intervening lives combines the fascination of a detective story with the morbid interest of psychiatric case-histories. The author's technical skill is undiminished in the handling of the evidence, but the total effect is not wholly satisfactory in its precarious balance between whimsy, sentiment, and serious psychology. In reviving juvenile nicknames and games, Mrs. Delacroix is more silly than charming, and the reader remains uncertain as to whether the picture of the three women is sly satire or sympathetic insight. The reunion, in which the three display jealousy, suspicion, and all uncharitableness, is contrasted with the gaiety of their childhood pranks, presumably to indicate time's malevolent deforming of branches that should have grown full straight; but the contrast is almost too violent to be credible. The conclusion, when the long-buried chest is found to be empty and the

instigator of the quest suffers an inexplicable trance and bruising, seems point-
lessly mystifying. The whole story, indeed, is crammed with details which may
possibly have symbolic import but which are more likely to appear merely
grotesque; and the author's involution of style sometimes approaches unintel-
ligibility.

Elizabeth Bowen's fiction has always been strangely hard to classify. An
expert craftswoman, she tends to bedazzle readers with her verbal virtuosity
and opulence to the point of obscuring other qualities. While her novels are
deceptively simple—even trivial—in incidents, they must be considered as
something more than domestic comedy. She is frequently ironic but seldom
quite satiric, since satire requires a more specific target than she seems to aim
at. The persistent implications of symbolism and the poetic exquisiteness of
style set her work apart from realism, yet no metaphysical significance can be
confidently recognized. Somewhere close to the surface of the everyday life
that she depicts there is an elusive vein of fantasy, and the fantasy is apt to be
redolent of evil. She is perhaps the most representative novelist of the hyper-
civilized modern intelligence, aesthetically sensitive and morally concerned,
but inadequate for coping with the blind forces and mechanisms of twentieth-
century existence.

   —Lionel Stevens, "A Group of Able Dames," *The History of the English Novel*, vol. 11 (1967),
   excerpted in *Twentieth-Century British Literature*, ed. Harold Bloom (New York: Chelsea House
   Publishers, 1985), 216–17

HARRIET BLODGETT

Miss Bowen's young heroines must learn to be adults of emotional vitality and
moral integrity. Twenty-two-year-old Sydney of Miss Bowen's first novel *The
Hotel* (1927) masters the proper nature of woman, as do the comparable heroines of *The Last September* (1929) and the much later *A World of Love* (1955).
Sydney will eventually become the sixtyish heroines of *The Little Girls* (1964),
but whatever her age, "Sydney" will sustain Miss Bowen's central myth of the
Fall: growth into higher consciousness with gain in Paradise lost. In a pointed
clue to the myth which is the embodiment of her cherished moral and spiritual values, Miss Bowen chooses "A Rev. J. D. L. Milton—*John?*"—the
Protestant clergyman James Milton—as lover of the first Sydney. A tempter's
role goes to Sydney's adored Mrs. Kerr, a serpent of regressive attraction to the
unconscious. Since psychic integration and redemption through trial, or maturation and moral crisis, presage all the Bowen novels, *The Hotel* is an important harbinger. ⟨. . .⟩

Hymning love rather than urging vocation, the late *A World of Love* strikes
a less duteous note than the earlier novels. It had taken Miss Bowen some time

to realize in fictive translation the large role love played in her philosophy: how tragic was the death of the heart among men when so generous was the gift of God's love to them. The major social consciousness now is concern for the civilization which, having brought itself through error to war, must restore itself through love, assimilating its losses of persons and of faith better than it did after World War I. The book is quietly recalling the disturbed past from its very first sentence in which the sun rises "on a landscape still pale with the heat of the day before." *The Heat of the Day* is Miss Bowen's wartime novel. Two world wars with their unnatural deaths lie behind this novel's action so that now two generations of "unlived lives" crowd "the living's senses"; and Jane Danby, its twenty-year-old heroine seeking the attachments of maturity, has "grown up amid extreme situations and frantic statements" while "altogether the world was in a crying state of exasperation." But Jane, auguring "a new world," discovers a world of love accessible to all. Miss Bowen's aptly chosen epigraph from Traherne reminds us that "There is in us a world of Love to somewhat, though we know not what in the world that should be . . . Do you not feel yourself drawn by the expectation and desire of some Great Thing?" (*Centuries of Meditations*, I.2). For Traherne, as for Miss Bowen, man's desire for Truth derives from the soul's memory of Paradise; the world of love, stemming from the same divine memory, is an expression of *amor dei*.

Miss Bowen saw this book as being "of Ireland, but not specifically Irish" perhaps because it is really a universal legend of a house in decay ever since the young lord of the manor died in war, but now to be renewed through faith in love. Mysteriously summoned Jane becomes a mythic quester who not only matures into perfected womanhood and love, but also within three days conducts the stifled souls at Montefort farm back from the land of the dead. Jane's pursuit of love, renewing memory and desire, is a sanctified quest; the book, a modern grail legend. Begun in a period of near-drought, it culminates with rain falling as Jane, her Montefort mission completed, meets the youth Richard Priam, a rain god descended at Shannon Airport, and (in the novel's last sentence) "they no sooner looked but they loved." Even Shakespeare's Rosalind, who scoffed at Celia and Oliver's precipitousness, fell in love, and love remains the fructifying ascensional force that defines the truest self.

The young heroine of *A World of Love* is assigned a redeemer's role. This narrative translation of the Christ aspect of the myth of the Fall is a concentrating of theme which Miss Bowen develops only after *The Hotel* and *The Last September*. The more simply conceived early books are concerned rather with what the heroine can make of herself.

—Harriet Blodgett, "Gain in Paradise Lost," *Patterns of Reality* (1975), excerpted in *Twentieth-Century British Literature*, ed. Harold Bloom (New York: Chelsea House Publishers, 1985), 221–23

ALFRED CORN

On the basis of her fiction alone, Bowen is as good as Evelyn Waugh, better than Ivy Compton-Burnett, Graham Greene or Henry Green. Her novels yield to Woolf's in visionary intensity but are superior to them in formal construction, variety of subject, and moral force. Bowen said she liked the work of her younger contemporaries Iris Murdoch and Muriel Spark, and she shares some characteristics with them ⟨. . . .⟩

Bowen is below the greatest novelists—Flaubert, George Eliot, Tolstoy, James, Proust—but like them she reflected constantly and profoundly on the nature of fiction. ⟨. . .⟩

⟨. . .⟩ Bowen's brilliant "Notes on Writing a Novel" have a poetic, almost an allegorical quality. She can say, for example, "Characters must *materialize*—*i.e.*, must have a palpable, physical reality. . . . Physical personality belongs to action. . . . Eyes, hands, stature, etc., must appear, and only appear, *in play*." Discussing dialogue, she says, "Speech is what the characters *do to each other*." And, in general, "The presence, and action of the poetic truth is the motive (or motor) morality of the novel."

It would be wrong, however, to regard Bowen as a rulebook novelist. The rule she most often waives is the one proscribing authorial comment. Rather like one of the "innocents" in her own novels, Bowen can't keep quiet about what she sees and knows. The proportion of comment to narrative is much higher than Flaubert, say, would have tolerated. Yet Proust commented even more freely than Bowen, and her rushes of insight are often as good as his. In both cases you feel that some principle of genius is at work, so that the propensity must be indulged, and the rules broken—all the more since the results are so startling. As much by their weaknesses as by their strengths do artists come into their own.

Much of the moral energy of Bowen's novels resides in just these passages of authorial comment. In them, she renews for English fiction the tradition of the French *moralistes*—La Rochefoucauld, La Bruyère, and the great women diarists and letter-writers of the eighteenth century. But she is still squarely within the precincts of fiction: these passages arise directly from the action presented, and they illuminate what comes after them. Moreover, Bowen isn't deficient in the way many moralists are, so intent on the meaning, purely, of human action they lack sensory awareness. Bowen is all perception. Reading her you realize you have never paid close enough attention to places or persons, the mosaic of detail that composes the first, or the voices and gestures that reveal the second. Her novels invariably take the point of view of an omniscient narrator; and, if omniscience means all-seeing as well as all-knowing, the term is especially apt for Bowen. Of course, this very knowingness can be a fault: the reader may feel as though Bowen is always too far ahead, running circles around reader consciousness. This is an unpleasant sensation if only because it gives, inevitably, an impression of unreality: no one feels that life is told by an omniscient narrator; and that point of view in novels is most effective when least obtrusive. For the most part, however, Bowen strikes the right balance between the transparence and opaqueness of reality.

As a prose stylist Bowen is elegant but quirky. She casts for the short sentence, the clipped epigram. We don't normally associate delicacy of observation with a percussive syntax like Bowen's, but that is her compound. Reading her is like being pelted with feathers, occasionally the quill end. Critics have sometimes complained about her inversions. Habitually she puts the most important word of a sentence in attack position at the beginning or tonic position at the end. By turns, the sentences can seem mannered or forceful. Certainly they contribute to the Anglo-Irish flavor of her writing. Sentences like hers can only be written by someone who has grown up with a special speech-music in the ear.

R. P. Blackmur noted that in Henry James's last novels there was always "a plot which does truly constitute the soul of the action, which does truly imitate the conditions and aspirations of human life as seen in the actions of men and women of more than usual worth and risk." Bowen would certainly have acknowledged these ideals as her own; and she realized them well—except for the last phrase, "more than usual worth and risk." Consistently she made it a part of novelistic plausibility not to invent larger-than-life characters. The figure, so common in her novels, of the innocent young girl forging toward experience leaves an impression less of "worth and risk" than of the destructiveness of innocence, to self and others. Other kinds of characters in Bowen tend to be all too human; we always look a little down at them. Yet if we are in fact experiencing an "ironic" phase in literature, as understood by Northrop Frye, in which fictional characters are typically marginal, hindered, or "low," Bowen can't be called to special account—she is only doing as other moderns do. Larger-than-life characters in modern fiction? There are none; but their absence is felt more keenly in Bowen's novels because in all other ways they exhibit the characteristic strengths of the nineteenth-century classics. The brilliant, humane analysis, the patient, even heroic notation of physical detail remind us of the older books, and, so conditioned, we scan Bowen's pages with an unconscious expectation of finding heroes there. Their failure to appear, then, disappoints. On the other hand, Bowen has created many magnetic and memorable characters—Stella in *The Heat of the Day*, Emmeline in *To the North*, and (perhaps the nearest Bowen came to inventing an heroic character) the housemaid Matchett in *The Death of the Heart*. All of these go readily into that stock everyone keeps of fictional persons—Mr. Casaubon, Pierre Bezhukov, Mrs. Dalloway, and so forth—characters that have caught special human qualities or attitudes toward experience and come to stand for them. In a fictional world made actual and palpable, Bowen's characters move and make their discoveries, comic or tragic or both together. These novels themselves will soon be rediscovered; new biographical and critical studies would help clarify Bowen's place among English novelists. Weighing real issues, and with a small readjustment of the sights, readers ought to reach a fair view of Elizabeth Bowen—as one of the few masters of modern fiction.

—Alfred Corn, "An Anglo-Irish Novelist," *Yale Review* (Summer 1978): 619–22

HERMIONE LEE

Elizabeth Bowen is clear about the responsibility of the short story. It must be *'necessary'*, it must have a 'valid central emotion', as with a lyric poem.

> However plain or lively or unpretentious be the manner of the story, the central emotion—emotion however remotely involved or hinted at—should be austere, major. The subject must have implicit dignity.
> ⟨Introduction to *The Faber Book of Modern Stories*, 1937, 14⟩

Writing about Irish and American short stories in the Introduction to her own 1936 selection, she praises the 'semi-poetic' art of enforcing 'amazement' through understatement. This she calls the 'extraverted' short story, 'bare of analysis, sparse in emotional statement', which provides 'general significance' through the particular. For the short story to justify itself, it must mean seriously or, as she puts it, 'must raise some issue'. It's a severe rubric, resting as it does on words like 'necessary' and 'austere', and recommending 'exact and impassive' narration ⟨11⟩. ⟨. . .⟩

The control and the focus of her stories arises initially, she says, from their settings. This is true of the novels too, of course, and she is scathing about the 'negative apathy' which she repeatedly encountered in thesis writers and interviewers about 'Bowen terrain'. 'Am I not manifestly a writer for whom places loom large?' ⟨"Pictures and Conversations," 34⟩. It is places, far more often than faces, which have 'sparked off' stories; some 'arose out of an intensified, all but spellbound beholding on my part, of the scene in question' ⟨Preface to *Stories by Elizabeth Bowen*, 78–79⟩.

There are obvious examples of this, like the story set in a garden blazing with roses, first seen from a car by a bored couple driving back to London; the story set in suburban woods full of families out for the day, providing no shelter for a pair of lovers; or the story set on a bleak new housing estate which drives a middle-aged woman to the point of madness. As their title suggests ('Look at All Those Roses', 'A Walk in the Woods', 'Attractive Modern Homes') the effect of these places *is* the story. But that interrelationship between place and plot is almost always discernible, even when the stories are less obviously about a particular location. It is a moral interrelationship in the tradition of Jane Austen, Henry James and E. M. Forster, and 'raises the issue' of inheritance and continuity. 'Bowen terrain' is not a wild uninhabited countryside. She is not interested in the aesthetic effects of landscape nor in a Wordsworthian contemplative solitude. The characteristic position of her people in relation to the sea is, like Gavin in 'Ivy Gripped the Steps', to stand with their back to its 'heaving mackerel vacancy', longing to be with the crowd on the promenade. The tendency of her settings is towards a social diagnosis, and she likes nothing so much, in the stories as in the novels, as to put groups of people into the place they deserve. The moral interrelationship between places and people, already seen to be crucial in the Anglo-Irish work, is very acute in the short stories.

Places are used repeatedly to expose a deficiency in the people who inhabit them, either because they have been built or landscaped for a diminished quality of life, or because their decline presents a challenge that can't be met by the occupants. Many of them, therefore, are not fulfilling their intended function. There are family houses which have fallen into disuse, seaside hotels and esplanades which have become scenes of desolation. The moral scheme of the places quickly becomes recognisable. Certain locales are always bad for the soul, and recur in the stories, which chart an opposition between experience and innocence, or a withdrawal from a pointless surplus of experience, or a social group so anaesthetised that it's not aware it has lost anything.

—Hermione Lee, "The Life Room," *Elizabeth Bowen* (1981), excerpted in *Twentieth-Century British Literature*, ed. Harold Bloom (New York: Chelsea House Publishers, 1985), 226

ALEXANDER G. GONZALEZ

One of Elizabeth Bowen's earliest published Irish short stories, "Her Table Spread" (1930), merits serious attention for two central reasons: not only is it an engrossing and rewarding work of art but it also reveals yet one more Irish fiction writer contemporary with James Joyce who was clearly influenced by him. Moreover, Bowen's story demonstrates surprisingly similar aesthetic and social attitudes—despite obvious differences in the authors' social classes and general cultural upbringing—which are a testament to how strong an influence Joyce was. Bowen's Court and the streets of Dublin are as strikingly diverse raw materials of experience as one may imagine in Ireland. At first "Her Table Spread" would appear to have nothing Joycean about it, since it involves Ireland's Protestant upper class during the twenties; Dublin's slums and middle-class neighborhoods are nowhere in sight. However, further connections do exist once we consider certain significant subtleties of symbol, theme, and technique—all of which Bowen successfully adapts to suit her own purposes.

Not much has been written on Bowen's short stories, and precious little is dedicated to the study of her *Irish* stories. Antoinette Quinn, the only recent scholar to focus specifically on Bowen's Irish stories, unfortunately restricts herself to the period 1939 to 1945. Heather Jordan ⟨"The Territory of Elizabeth Bowen's Wartime Short Stories," 1989⟩, however, not only lists Joyce among those authors Bowen most admired but also reminds us that Bowen's first published book, a volume of short stories, was titled *Encounters*— a fact of some significance for two fairly obvious reasons: it echoes the title of Joyce's second *Dubliners* story, "An Encounter," and it suggests Joyce's epiphanic method in his collection, a method utilized by Bowen in "Her Table Spread" to imbue the story with significant depth and poignancy. Mary Jarrett ⟨"Ambiguous Ghosts," 1987⟩ has noted Bowen's use of paralysis as spiritual metaphor in another of her stories, "The Dancing Mistress," likening it to something out of *Dubliners*; the same metaphor is clearly at work in "Her Table Spread," whose protagonist has much in common with Gabriel Conroy of "The Dead" both in terms of character traits and in the narrator's rhetorical stance toward the protagonist.

Bowen makes it very clear throughout her story that she is criticizing not only a handful of upper-class individuals, and one in particular, but also the remnants of Ireland's formerly powerful ascendancy as a whole. In fact, Bowen's story seems the logical ending point of a tradition in Irish fiction concerned with exposing the ascendancy's ailing spiritual condition. Beginning with George Moore's *A Drama in Muslin* (1886) and continuing through Seumas O'Kelly's *The Lady of Deerpark* (1917) and various short stories by Daniel Corkery, Brinsley MacNamara, and others, this tradition has always emphasized the ascendancy's paralysis in parallel fashion to the better-known tradition that criticizes Ireland's other classes for having the same disease—as manifested in *Dubliners*, its most salient example. Even though Valeria Cuffe may own her palatial home while Joyce's Misses Morkan merely rent their sprawling second-floor middle-class apartment, considerable similarities exist between the dinner parties in the two stories, especially since the events presented at each party occupy the bulk of each story. The party in Bowen's story is something of a reduced version of the one in Joyce's, for it involves far fewer participants. Still, when the story's protagonist, Mr. Alban, plays the piano, no one listens; Mr. Rossiter, Bowen's version of Mr. Browne, drinks to excess and has some ridiculous flirtation—or worse—going on with the parlor maid; and the general veneer of good manners hides only temporarily the underlying indelicacies of human nature. ⟨. . .⟩

Mary Jarrett has argued that in all of Bowen's best stories "there is a refusal to pronounce on the validity of the worlds her characters create for themselves." This is most certainly true for Alban—and Valeria for that matter—in "Her Table Spread." What we have, then, is an ambiguity very similar to that at the end of "The Dead." Is Alban to change as a result of his epiphany? Is Gabriel? Is either capable of change? Are they too old, chronologically or emotionally? Or is each man terminally paralyzed and now painfully aware of it—and of what each, somnambulistically, has missed in his life? Such ambiguity is both meaningful and intended. As is the case at the end of Joyce's story, multiple perspectives emerge as possibilities. Those of us who are optimists would hope that significant change will occur in each protagonist.

Harold Bloom ⟨Elizabeth Bowen, 1987⟩ finds Bowen's stories to be "even . . . more remarkable than [her] novels" and he places Bowen only after Joyce and Lawrence as possibly "the most distinguished writer of short stories in our time." Once again we have Bowen and Joyce linked, this time in terms of quality. "Her Table Spread" is by no means on the level of "The Dead," but then not many stories are. Bowen's story is, however, qualitatively comparable to other Dubliners stories that demonstrate both spiritual paralysis and then the use of epiphany as the means by which a character becomes acutely aware of his or her affliction. This level of quality acts to reinforce the argument that Bowen, perhaps idealizing Joyce's work as a level of art to which to aspire, read him carefully and—probably subconsciously—imitated some of the effects he had perfected, especially in "The Dead." When she applied her considerable talents to writing the story of Mr. Alban and Valeria Cuffe, what emerged was a thoroughly Joycean story—except for the merely surface differences of setting and social class. The imitation may possibly have been a conscious effort, but it seems to me more likely that it was a subconscious phenomenon that Bowen could not have helped noticing soon after the composing process had begun. The aesthetic stance and the multiplicity of connections between Bowen's story and "The Dead"—on the level of character, theme, symbol, and technique—make the case for influence considerably strong.

—Alexander G. Gonzalez, "Elizabeth Bowen's 'Her Table Spread': A Joycean Irish Story," *Studies in Short Fiction* 30, no. 3 (Summer 1993): 343–44, 347–48

BIBLIOGRAPHY

Encounters: Stories. 1923.
Ann Lee's and Other Stories. 1926.
The Hotel. 1927.

Joining Charles and Other Stories. 1929.

The Last September. 1929.

Friends and Relations. 1931.

To the North. 1932.

The Cat Jumps and Other Stories. 1934.

The House in Paris. 1935.

The Death of the Heart. 1935.

Look at All Those Roses: Short Stories. 1941.

Bowen's Court. 1942.

English Novelists. 1942.

Seven Winters: Memories of a Dublin Childhood. 1942, 1943.

The Demon Lover and Other Stories. 1945. Republished as *Ivy Gripped the Steps.*
    1946.

Anthony Trollope: A New Judgement. 1946.

The Heat of the Day. 1949.

Collected Impressions. 1950.

The Shelbourne: A Center of Dublin Life for More Than a Century. 1951.

A World of Love. 1955.

Stories by Elizabeth Bowen. 1959.

A Time in Rome. 1960.

Afterthought: Pieces about Writing. 1962.

The Little Girls. 1964.

A Day in the Dark and Other Stories. 1965.

The Good Tiger. 1965.

Eva Trout, or Changing Scenes. 1968.

Pictures and Conversations. 1975.

AGATHA CHRISTIE

1890-1976

AGATHA MARY CLARISSA MILLER was born on September 15, 1890, in Torquay, Devon, England, the youngest of three siblings. Raised primarily by her mother, she remembers being a lonely child isolated in a self-created fantasy world. In early childhood she dreamed of becoming a concert pianist, but fear of public performance led her to writing. As a teen, she attempted to publish short stories under pseudonyms, though all were rejected.

At 24, Agatha married a member of the Royal Air Corps, Archibald Christie, and for the remainder of World War I she worked as a Red Cross nurse. During quiet periods in the hospital dispensary, Christie refined her first detective story, *The Mysterious Affair at Styles*. Published in 1920, it introduced readers to Hercule Poirot, the fastidious little detective who would become the protagonist of 33 Christie mysteries. Around the same time, she gave birth to her only child, Rosalind.

With two other novels published by the time *The Murder of Roger Ackroyd* was released (1926), Christie was already an established author. The family moved to the suburbs, but Christie was unhappy, often alone while her husband indulged his passion for golf. Growing increasingly distressed, Christie disappeared for 10 days, instigating a nationwide search. Circumspect reporters and police questioned Archibald; finally, a hotel chambermaid connected newspaper photographs to a hotel guest and Christie was returned home. Doctors diagnosed amnesia, although others suggested a publicity stunt, revenge against her husband, or a plot enactment for a forthcoming book. Regardless, the obvious distress foreshadowed her divorce from Archibald Christie in 1928. Two years later, she married archaeologist Max Mallowan, traveling with him throughout the Middle East on expeditions that inspired many of her well-known books, including *Murder in Mesopotamia* (1936) and *Death on the Nile* (1937).

Christie created several other archetypal detectives who solved the conundrums put before them with idiosyncratic flair, among them, Parker Pyne and Miss Jane Marple, the gray-haired amateur sleuth who starred in 12 novels. In addition, Christie wrote *Come, Tell Me How You Live*, a nonfiction account of rugged life on archaeological digs (1946); 150 short stories; poetry; romances under the pseudonym Mary Westmacott; and 20 plays, including history's longest-running play, *The Mousetrap*. On the stage, in film, or on television, Christie's

stories are entertaining puzzles structured by the most human of emotions—greed, hate, lust, jealousy. Though critics like Edmund Wilson
accused her of "mawkishness and banality," her books continue to sell
into the billions and have been translated into 63 foreign languages.

Agatha Christie received many honors: the Grand Master Award
of the Mystery Writers of America in 1954; an LL.D. from the
University of Exeter in 1961; a Commander of the British Empire in
1956; and a Dame Commander of the British Empire in 1971. She
died on January 12, 1976, in Wallingford, England.

CRITICAL EXTRACTS

H. DOUGLAS THOMSON

⟨Agatha Christie⟩ believes in a clean, slick murder and plenty of swift, exciting, low-brow action. Her detective, Poirot, belongs to the old school of
super-detectives who keep things pretty much to themselves, and spar inces-
santly with the arrogant tribe of police inspectors. In Captain Hastings she has
held the mirror up to Dr. Watson. The dedication shows that she is an advocate of the most unlikely person theme. As a final example of her orthodoxy,
she is the perfect matrimonial agency in pairing off the right couples.

But granted that Mrs. Christie writes "down" rather than "up," that she
keeps her crow a crow—in Mr. St. John Ervine's phraseology—and does not
seek to make it a flamingo, that she does not cast about her for spurious
effects, it is not difficult to discern a delicious vein of satire in her stories. Even
before she essayed the burlesque of *Partners in Crime*, she had a hankering to
poke fun at the various schools of detective fiction. She is certainly well read
in the Classics, as the adventures of Tommy and Tuppence show. It is almost
as if she had set herself to learn all she could about the methods and technique
of "How to Write a Detective Story for Profit"—and had then proceeded to
pull legs.

Mrs. Christie is not a criminologist. She is not even a first-rate detective.
Compared with Mr. Crofts she is in this respect a babe-in-arms. For the group-
ing of data, for the building up of a case from "purposeful" *minutiæ*, for the
effects of belladonna on rabbits she has no time. And evidently she has felt
unequal to the strain of assiduous bluffing. Her description of the data is,
therefore, of the sketchiest. In lieu thereof she gives us a plethora of motives.
Most of her *dramatis personæ* have quite a few motives concealed on them—

motives white and black, motives satisfactory and unsatisfactory, so they be only motives. Mrs. Christie's skill lies in playing off motive against motive, and thus character against character; for her characters are often merely pegs on which to hang these motives.

Neither does Mrs. Christie usually bother her head with character study. The recognised types are quite sufficient to be going on with; big-game hunters of the Ethel M. Dell variety; hard-boiled Americans after Mr. Edgar Wallace; fencers and blackmailers of the Oppenheim School; private secretaries and so forth. ⟨. . .⟩

In *The Mysterious Affair at Styles* Mrs. Christie evolved a scheme which she evidently felt would bear repetition. The murder was postponed for a few chapters to allow the reader to play the eavesdropper to conversations inevitably heated and inevitably interrupted. The murder out, she will probably toss a coin to decide on whom first to turn the searchlight of suspicion. It's really in a way immaterial, as they've all got to go through it. The plot gathers speed from the discovery of at least two significant incidents big with motives for the murder. This means that suspicion will rest in turn on all those implicated in these events. During this time Poirot flits about like a Tchehov character, casting the pearls of his innuendo before the pigheadedness of Hastings. The inquest will quicken Poirot's steps, for it means the veering of suspicion from the first star suspect to the second (the second being equally guiltless). All this time you will be feeling a shade uncomfortable. Two love affairs will be going in full swing; not of the type, however, to arouse Evoe's nausea, for at least two of the lovers will be under a cloud. By a process of elimination, the field will be reduced to one or two "favourites." Then comes Poirot's hour. Not all the king's horses will prevent him from holding a salon. Certainly it is impressive, with all the characters as his audience, to begin his exegesis with a *Messieurs, mesdames*. Impressive, too, is the grand climax when he points his finger to the villain, and the chair is overturned in the confusion.

The Mysterious Affair at Styles is a very good example of our old friend the "double bluff"; but it is different from the ordinary species in that the very person responsible for directing suspicion at the start on the real criminal is actually an accomplice of the latter. Thus we have the amusing situation of the villain wishing to be arrested as soon as possible. He relied on securing an acquittal while the evidence was fragmentary and while he had, through the male impersonation of his accomplice, an unobjectionable alibi. Poirot was equally anxious in the circumstances to delay his arrest. ⟨. . .⟩

—H. Douglas Thomson, "The Orthodox Detective Story," *Masters of Mystery* (1931), excerpted in *Twentieth-Century British Literature*, ed. Harold Bloom (New York: Chelsea House Publishers, 1985), 336–37

EDMUND WILSON

I have been told by the experts ⟨that the⟩ endless carrying on of the ⟨Sir Arthur Conan⟩ Doyle tradition does not represent all or the best that has been done with the detective story during the decades of its proliferation. There has been also the puzzle mystery, and this, I was assured, had been brought to a high pitch of ingenuity in the stories of Agatha Christie. So I have read also the new Agatha Christie, *Death Comes as the End*, and I confess that I have been had by Mrs. Christie. I did not guess who the murderer was, I was incited to keep on and find out, and when I did finally find out, I was surprised. Yet I did not care for Agatha Christie and I hope never to read another of her books. I ought, perhaps, to discount the fact that *Death Comes as the End* is supposed to take place in Egypt two thousand years before Christ, so that the book has a flavor of Lloyd C. Douglas not, I understand, quite typical of the author. ("No more Khay in this world to sail on the Nile and catch fish and laugh up into the sun whilst she, stretched out in the boat with little Teti on her lap, laughed back at him"); but her writing is of a mawkishness and banality which seem to me literally impossible to read. You cannot *read* such a book, you run through it to see the problem worked out; and you cannot become interested in the characters, because they never can be allowed an existence of their own even in a flat two dimensions but have always to be contrived so that they can seem either reliable or sinister, depending on which quarter, at the moment, is to be baited for the reader's suspicion. This I had found also a source of annoyance in the case of Mr. ⟨Rex⟩ Stout, who, however, has created, after a fashion, Nero Wolfe and Archie Goodwin and has made some attempt at characterization of the people that figure in the crimes; but Mrs. Christie, in proportion as she is more expert and concentrates more narrowly on the puzzle, has to eliminate human interest completely, or, rather, fill in the picture with what seems to me a distasteful parody of it. In this new novel, she has to provide herself with puppets who will be good for three stages of suspense: you must first wonder who is going to be murdered, you must then wonder who is committing the murders, and you must finally be unable to foresee which of two men the heroine will marry. It is all like a sleight-of-hand trick, in which the magician diverts your attention from the awkward or irrelevant movements that conceal the manipulation of the cars, and it may mildly entertain and astonish you, as such a sleight-of-hand performance may. But in a performance like *Death Comes as the End*, the patter is a constant bore and the properties lack the elegance of playing cards.

—Edmund Wilson, "Why Do People Read Detective Stories?" (1944), *Classics and Commercials* (1950), excerpted in *Twentieth-Century British Literature*, ed. Harold Bloom (New York: Chelsea House Publishers, 1985), 333–34

DOROTHY B. HUGHES

There was yet another Christie whom nobody knew, or so few as to amount to almost nobody. This was Mary Westmacott. Even today, and even in book circles, there are more who do not know than who do know her true identity.

The Westmacotts bear as little relation to women-type novels as to Winnie-the-Pooh. One cannot but wonder if any of those who proffered opinions had ever read her work. Had they, they would know that in its own way, each of these books, whose heroes lead lives of quiet desperation and whose villains are villainous only in that they do not understand, presents a fragment of the human comedy. Each tells a tale of the procession of days which add up to the years, and which resolve not in a crashing dissonance but in a whimper. And life goes on, but down a different lane and to a different bird call.

These are works in which Christie is trying to fathom herself and those who were a part of her world. The stories are the revelations of a woman of perception, a woman who is searching human emotions to preserve and heighten moments which must be remembered. She is writing of men and women whose dreams bleed when pricked, who are not beset by the gods or the fates, but who are made bereft by human frailties and a wanton expenditure of the loving heart.

Not by any catch-phrases can Westmacott be put into a Christie category. The books are not concerned with 'breathless romance, intrigue and suspense . . . tangled lives and star-crossed passions . . . dangerous secrets', as has been written of them. Westmacott was a distinctly different person from the mystery writer, Agatha Christie.

The six books are actually all a part of the same book. In the whole they are the fictionalized autobiography of Dame Agatha. Properly the autobiography begins with the second, *Unfinished Portrait* (1934). Christie could not have given many interviews before that time, at least not about her childhood and youth, or the Mary Westmacott identity would have been revealed immediately. In *Unfinished Portrait*, Larraby, a portrait painter, frames the story, thus making the pretence that it is a story, not a personal revelation. Yet there can be no doubt that Celia, the unknown woman he presumedly met and spoke with, is Christie, so much younger than others of her family that she is in effect an only child, the beloved of her mother.

—Dorothy B. Hughes, "The Christie Nobody Knew," in *Agatha Christie: First Lady of Crime*, ed. H. R. F. Keating (1977), excerpted in *Twentieth-Century British Literature*, ed. Harold Bloom (New York: Chelsea House Publishers, 1985), 335

LeRoy Panek

Few of Christie's novels, if any, when examined with any sort of objectivity, can be considered as puzzles which the readers are supposed to solve. They do not yield the solution to the enigmatic circumstances until the final chapters when Christie chooses to present it herself. Otherwise they would lose all of their force.

Consider the case of *And Then There Were None*. In this novel ten people die while they are trapped on an isolated island to which they have been lured by person or persons unknown. At the end of the book readers hear the musings of police officials who cannot solve the murders. The police continue at sea until a note in a bottle washes ashore and outlines the truth about the events on the island (which exemplifies the readers' position—or the position which Christie would like her readers to be in). If this is a puzzle story, where are the clues which should lead the readers to a logical interpretation of the facts and events which have been presented? There is no material evidence, there are no meaningful alibis, and the crimes have no internal similarities (poisoning, sandbagging, pistol shot, hanging, drowning, and stabbing all appear). The physician who pronounced the deaths could have been in cahoots with any one of the victims. All of the characters are in the same circumstance: each is accused of having committed a murder in the past by a mysterious recording. The psychological evidence is useless; the narration penetrates the consciousness of some people (including the murderer) but this does nothing to reveal the truth. Any of the victims could have feigned death and done the murders. Most of the characters have vocations which might lead them to this sort of mass judgment and execution, but this is moot, since each of us judges countless people daily, and this hardly makes us murderers. Upon what clues ought we to base our solution if we try to figure it out before the book provides it? There is, given retrospect, one clue—Christie describes one death (the fake one) in figurative language while she depicts the others in physical detail. Ought we to see that? I would like to say of course not, but I will waffle and say I think not. We don't see the miniscule, isolated clue for any number of reasons, but chiefly because the novel is three quarters thriller. It this were a *bona fide* puzzle detective novel, there would be ten deaths to be thought through and solved; instead, here, there are ten episodes in a thriller plot which pushes the readers on to the end even if they would otherwise incline to look for and analyze the events and facts in the story. With only one hundred and seventy-one pages in the book, divided into extremely short chapters, we know that we can finish the book tonight if we go on, and that she'll give us the answer at the end without making us think, and the chapters fly by so quickly, why bother? Not many people really do try to puzzle out the answer. It is the psychology. It is the thriller psychology and not that of the puzzle story: all of the facts are not in our possession. ⟨. . .⟩

⟨. . .⟩ As a prose stylist Christie is hardly distinguished. From the beginning she wrote in a neutral, simple fashion using short sentences and brief paragraphs which do not tax the reader. Occasionally, however, she uses her lack of a prose style to spring traps on the readers: this is the case with the intrusion of figurative description in *And Then There Were None*, as well as the irritatingly simple-minded style adopted for *Easy to Kill*. If Christie has any particular claim to literary originality, though, it is because of her use of point of view. The important lesson which she learned early and well was that detective stories work chiefly because of the way in which they are told. Using Hastings as the narrator in *The Mysterious Affair at Styles* shows that from the beginning she liked Conan Doyle's method of hiding the obvious from the reader by using an obtruse narrator. She also realized, in the early twenties, that this technique was old hat and she started to poke about for alternate styles of narration which would obscure the facts which needed to be withheld until the conclusion. In *The Man in the Brown Suit* she mixed straight narration with extracts from two diaries, covering the facts by switching the point of view. This mixture of points of view, although it is not always so obvious, appears in most of the non-Hastings novels—and in *The ABC Murders* which Hastings narrates—written subsequently. The point of view of a typical Christie novel of the period usually shifts among 1) straight third person narration describing people and events from the outside, 2) third person narration over the shoulder of a particular character following him or her around, 3) selectively omniscient narration which probes some of the characters' minds, and 4) dramatic presentation of dialogue with little more than speech tags supplied. By switching from one point of view to another, Christie manipulates her readers in several ways. First, she gives the readers the false confidence that they can sympathize with and trust the judgments of the character whom the narrative follows. Almost equally important is the impression which the readers receive from the omniscient passages: they falsely believe that they receive insight into all of the characters' thoughts, while this never happens. By tossing together these different points of view, Christie can keep her important facts back and fool her readers almost every time.

—LeRoy Panek, "Agatha Christie," *Watteau's Shepherds* (1979), excerpted in *Twentieth-Century British Literature*, ed. Harold Bloom (New York: Chelsea House Publishers, 1985), 334, 336

PATRICIA CRAIG AND MARY CADOGAN

Agatha Christie has taken a common term of criticism applied to women novelists in the Victorian era—narrowness of experience—and shown how the deficiency can be turned to good account. Miss Marple's own experience of life is neither wide nor deep, but she has a very productive familiarity with other people's. She has spent a lifetime observing the untoward in St Mary Mead. Her method of detecting works by extension—applying the principles that got to the bottom of a small contretemps like the disappearance of a quantity of shrimps from the fishmonger's—and analogy: '"I always find one thing very like another in this world," said Miss Marple.' This is presented as an endearing mannerism:

> 'And perhaps he reminded you of someone?' prompted Sir Henry, mischief in his eye.
>   Miss Marple smiled and shook her head at him. 'You are very naughty, Sir Henry. As a matter of fact he *did*. Fred Taylor, at the fish shop. Always slipped in an extra I in the shillings column . . .'
> (*A Murder is Announced*, 1950)

Miss Marple attributes her successes to specialized knowledge, by which she means knowledge of the characters involved; she has just sufficient gumption to repudiate the term 'feminine intuition' which is bandied about on several occasions. It is not intuition but accuracy of thought which leads her, time and again, to a pertinent conclusion. Otherwise she behaves with impeccable femininity, according to the popular and pejorative definition of the term: she simpers, flutters, flatters, dithers, and is subject to apparently meaningless digressions in conversation. Invariably she exasperates the bluffer and more stolid type of policeman: 'For about ten seconds Inspector Neale stared at Miss Marple with the utmost bewilderment. His first idea was that the old lady had gone off her head. "Blackbirds?" he repeated.' But the old lady's confusion is on the surface only, to amuse the reader who knows what is coming. Miss Marple's thoughts are always in order and the significance of her remarks will soon strike the Inspector with appropriate force: 'Craddock caught his breath. She'd got it! She was sharp, after all.'

In fact Jane Marple is both sharp and fluffy, intelligent and muddle-headed, timid and resolute, inquisitive and fastidious, self-effacing and persistent, unworldly and cynical. Her character is composed of contradictory elements for maximum effect. If she had a counterpart in real life it was the author's Victorian grandmother who was continually surprised by human gullibility. But the requirements of detective fiction supervened before a note of realism could be transcribed. It is well-known that Agatha Christie was not so much a novelist as the inventor of a novelty, a peculiarly intricate and entertaining type of puzzle. All the complexity and originality she could muster went into the construction of the story; her characters, apart from a handful of principals, are rarely more than cyphers. The principals—Poirot, Jane Marple,

Mrs Oliver, Tommy and Tuppence Beresford—have a greater number of personal characteristics and mannerisms and this causes them to stand out although they lack substance. They have, however, exactly the right degree of presence to fulfil the function enjoined to them.

—Patricia Craig and Mary Cadogan, "Grandmotherly Disguise," *The Lady Investigates* (1981), excerpted in *Twentieth-Century British Literature*, ed. Harold Bloom (New York: Chelsea House Publishers, 1985), 334–35

DAVID I. GROSSVOGEL

Writing in the years immediately after the end of the first world war, Agatha Christie was instinctively striving for a delicate balance, but one that was still possible at that time. It consisted in an intrusion upon the reader's ideal world, but an intrusion not so intense as to cast doubt on its eventual dissipation. She achieved this balance by identifying accurately her middle-class audience and its hankering for an Edwardian gentility. Dame Agatha offered these readers recognisable posters of a world which they had experienced only through posters: they were offered a journey to a land that they knew well, but only in the world of their social fantasising and bygone dreams of empire. Poster and book served the selfsame purpose: they preserved the awareness of a world that must have existed for someone; it was a far better world than the known world and doubly comforting because of a suspicion that if it had indeed existed once, its days were now numbered. ⟨. . .⟩

Murder within this English pastoral was not so much an evil act as one whose consequences would be unfortunate for a prescribed moment. Whereas a Mike Hammer or a Sam Spade might right their little piece of the corrupt, urban jigsaw puzzle while the complex itself remained corrupt and awaited the private eye's attention to the next area of his concern, murder upon the mead was more in the nature of a washable and cathartic stain. For a while, these good people would become each and every one suspect (Agatha Christie, who built her reputation early on a disregard for established rules, showed as little unwarranted sentimentality here: however much tradition might have endeared a particular type to the reader, none was above suspicion). Within this dream of rural England, murder was trivial enough; the corpse upon which Philip Marlowe stumbled might not have had quite the stench of Laius', but in St Mary Mead or Styles St Mary the murder itself was antiseptic—already a part of the cleansing process (there were always half a dozen compelling reasons to kill the victim—and as many evident suspects). It was the wake of the murder that made things momentarily disagreeable: the country inn would lose its ruddy bonhomie; the vicarage might be pressed uncomfortably close to moral quandaries; and, worst of all, aliens would walk the pristine land. For just as the reader was able to people fully a world to which he aspired, the reader would temporarily jeopardise through his own malaise the harmony of the world he had conjured from his fiction. And here again, Dame Agatha remained supremely aloof, giving the reader only such few and accurate stimuli as were needed. ⟨. . .⟩

It was within a world distracted only momentarily by this kind of curable malaise that was born the detective destined to become one of the most famous of the genre: Poirot was able to dissipate the uneasiness, but he was also created and shaped by it to a great extent.

Like his prototypes, Dupin and Holmes, this sort of detective demonstrates a perfect intelligence within a multitude of flaws. The structural reason for this contrast results from a fundamental identity between the fictional detective and his circumstances: that detective is the reader's assurance that his expectation of an end to a number of small annoyances will be met—the detective's acuity is therefore absolute; but the reader's concession in that contract requires that a semblance of doubt be maintained for as long as it takes to tell the tale—all else in the detective is therefore flawed.

However, the strangeness of Dupin and Holmes confirmed their intelligence even as it removed them from the common world of mortals; Dupin and Holmes dwelt in remote worlds, isolated by books, drugs, laboratory or musical instruments—all awesome objects that extended the awesomeness of their brains. Poirot's flaws, on the other hand, represented a compendium of what marred the idyllic landscape once it became the temporary site of the sombre event that brought Poirot into it. When Agatha Christie first described Poirot, he was in fact a part of the negative consequences that followed the transgression of the bucolic dream.

To start with, Poirot was a foreigner, another alien note within the pastoral harmony. The evidence of his foreignness was multiple, but because of the specific area of Poirot's first trespass, it was peculiarly unEnglish. Starting with his ridiculously short stature, most of his obvious traits were intended to amuse, but also to annoy, his English reader ⟨. . . .⟩

Poirot's very intelligence, before even his unseemly boasting about it, was yet another exaggeration, and one which he displayed with equal lack of tact in his all too apparent egghead. Aloof as ever, but knowing full well from which vantage point *she* observed her creation, Dame Agatha named him after the least favoured of vegetables (*poireau*: the leek, which also means 'wart' in French) and then stressed the dismissiveness by pairing it with a singularly grandiloquent Christian name, Hercule—itself turned into still another overassertion by the diminutive size of its bearer. ⟨. . .⟩

Why then her continuing popularity? A part of the answer was intuited by the directors (Sidney Lumet, Don Guillermin, Guy Hamilton) who have recently turned into films *Murder on the Orient Express*, *Death on the Nile*, *The Mirror*

Crack'd, peopling them with old-time actors now seldom seen on the screen—
Lauren Bacall, Richard Widmark, Bette Davis, David Niven, Angela Lansbury,
or, in a new, Queen-Motherish avatar, the enduring Elizabeth Taylor. These
actors represent the cinema of a shinier moment, over a third of a century ago,
before they were swept aside by the new forms of the present cinema. Seeing
them once again on the screen, we re-enter that world briefly. This is especially felicitous casting for Agatha Christie, since we now regress through her
books to something more real than the times she described: the period pieces
that those descriptions themselves have become now attract us. There may
have been a time when Agatha Christie mediated for her reader unattainable
worlds: now her archaic books have become those worlds. We acknowledge
our present discontent in retrospections that make us smile at what once constituted the measure of our passing cares, the sense of how comfortable we felt
in a world of referable absolutes (after all, Dame Agatha herself tells us in her
autobiography that she came to the detective story out of a comforting sense
that Evil could be hunted down and that Good would triumph—an avowal
that explains not a little her sombre mood within, and tenuous gap on, the
world that followed the second world war).

    In that world, our present one, a residual pull of pyschological gravity
draws us to the evidence that we once had faith in the possibility of control,
of knowledge and of the power of reason against the irrational. We are still
drawn to the old writings of Agatha Christie.

    —David I. Grossvogel, "Death Deferred," in *Art in Crime Writing*, ed. Bernard Benstock
(1983), excerpted in *Twentieth-Century British Literature*, ed. Harold Bloom (New York: Chelsea
House Publishers, 1985), 338–39

EARL F. BARGAINNIER

In her autobiography Agatha Christie wrote, "The creative urge can come out
in any form: in embroidery, in cooking of interesting dishes, in painting, drawing and sculpture, in composing music, as well as in writing books and stories.
The only difference is that you can be a great deal more grand about some of
these things than others." Christie was never "grand" about her detective fiction, and was even less so about her poetry. Yet in 1973, three years before her
death, she permitted a small volume of her "collected" poems to be published.
Christie's position as the most popular British writer ever deserves some analysis of her poems and their relationship, though slight, to her fiction. ⟨. . .⟩

    In form Christie's poems are traditional. There are sonnets and various
stanzaic patterns, as well as freely metered works. Except for seven ballads, the
poems are brief lyrics, nearly all between twelve and forty lines. She was fond
of refrains, alliteration, and incremental repetition, and her favorite type of

rhyme was the couplet. She was equally adept at both short and long lines, but usually used tetrameter and pentameter. The general tone of the poems is reminiscent of such poets of the 1890s and early twentieth century as Ernest Dowson, Arthur Symons, Alfred Noyes, Walter de la Mare, and James Elroy Flecker—the last of whose "Gates of Damascus" provided the title of her last written novel: *Postern of Fate*. The ballads resemble those of G. K. Chesterton. With only one or two exceptions, Christie's poems could have been written before 1920. They are Romantic and Georgian in spirit: modernism is absent. ⟨. . .⟩

It would be an exercise in futility to try to find many implicit or explicit relationships between ⟨her⟩ essentially personal poems and Christie's fiction. That poems such as "Dark Sheila" or "Down in the Woods" deal with mysterious fear, an element often present in detective fiction, is hardly enough evidence on which to draw parallels, nor is the fact that there are poems on Baghdad, the Nile, and Dartmoor and also novels set in those places. "Hymn to Ra" in Volume I shows her early interest in ancient Egypt, but *Death Comes as the End* (1944), her mystery novel set in that world was first suggested to her by one of her husband's colleagues nearly twenty years later. The poems are filled with her interests, likes, and dislikes, and some of the same are bound also to appear in her fiction; that is all that need be said.

There is one major exception, however, and that is the obvious connection between "A Masque of Italy" and the Harley Quin stories, for both have the same source: her childhood attendance at Christmas pantomimes. The characters of the Italian *commedia dell'arte* developed into stylized stage characters of English pantomime in the eighteenth century, and by the end of the nineteenth, Harlequin, Columbine, and their cohorts were standard figures of the annual Christmas pantomime: fairy-like creatures not bound by time or space. Thus the pantomime–"A Masque"–Quin link is clear. The immortal Harlequin of "A Masque of Italy" loses Columbine to the mortal Pierrot, but she in turn loses her immortality and dies. Pierrot is last seen as an old man living with an elderly Pierrette and awaiting his own death. The ten songs which recount the story are Christie the poet at her best, and it is not surprising that she won prizes for them. The songs are simple, direct, yet individualized for each character; that typical melancholy is everpresent; and the supernatural is accepted as a given without explanation or apology. Similarly, Harley Quin is a figure of the supernatural. He acts through the mortal Mr. Satterthwaite to help lovers and solve mysteries. In such stories as "Harlequin's Lane" and "The Harlequin Tea Set," Quin is presented as the messenger—if not the personification—of death, but death as a kind of ultimate fulfillment of life. The shadowy, all-knowing Quin, who like his stage counterpart can appear or disappear at will, is a deliberately enigmatic figure. He is, without question, Christie's most unusual detective; she wrote in *An Autobiography* that the Quin stories were her favorites and that she only wrote one when she felt like it, and added that Quin "was a kind of carryover for me from my early poems in the Harlequin and Columbine series" (420). Perhaps the Quin stories were her own favorite detective works because in them she came closer than in any others to writing like a poet.

Poems is the least known of Agatha Christie's some eighty books. Few of the billions of readers of her fiction are even aware of its existence. Yet one can imagine her pleasure on its publication, a pleasure probably greater than that on the appearance of her fiftieth or sixtieth novel, for it is a distillation of her most private thoughts and emotions, as lyric poetry always is for its writer. Christie was a very private person, and this little volume, whatever its faults, provides a new perspective on her personality—one quite different from the public image of "mistress of mystery."

 —Earl F. Bargainnier, "The Poems of Agatha Christie," *Journal of Popular Culture* 21, no. 3
 (Winter 1987): 103–4, 109–10

MARY LOEFFELHOLZ

Like most of the relatively popular women detectives in the genre, Miss Marple is an amateur, not a detective in the strict sense at all. A village gossip and a spinster, she has learned what she needs to know in order to solve crimes simply by watching what passes under her nose in St. Mary Mead. Miss Marple by and large solves crimes by simple knowledge of human nature, not through professional expertise, and she need not poke around, climb trees, or peer over windows to do it; indeed she can find the villain while doing her after-dinner knitting (and does so several times, in *The Tuesday Club Murders*, 1932).

In some senses Miss Marple could be called a feminist heroine. She quietly challenges the notion that women's sphere, the stereotypically private sphere of the home and garden, contains nothing that could possibly foster deductive intelligence. At the same time, however, she never openly fights with the boundaries of that sphere; and her ability to solve crimes simply by knitting and nodding her head can make her seem more a fictive dea ex machina, the fantasy of an all-seeing mother, than a rounded character.

The Moving Finger (1943), a Miss Marple novel, exemplifies both the strengths and the limitations of Christie's writing. Like Dorothy Sayers's *Gaudy Night*, which it postdates, *The Moving Finger* is plotted around a poison-pen case, anonymous notes that initially seem noxious but trivial, only to bring genuine violence in their wake. As in *Gaudy Night*, the problem of trying to find the writer of the notes is partly shaped by Freudian assumptions—that sexually frustrated women (but not men) are likely to do these things—that are at least partly disproved by the novel's end, appropriately enough with Miss Marple's help. Also like *Gaudy Night*, *The Moving Finger* ends with a marriage between two of the characters. But this marriage is far more conventional than in Sayers's novel, and the village's sexual norms are never fundamentally called into question. Christie's Miss Marple operates from a special but comfortable place within things as they are, rather than imagining things as they might be.

—Mary Loeffelholz, *Experimental Lives: Women and Literature, 1890–1945* (New York: Twayne Publishers, 1992), 147–48

GLENWOOD IRONS AND JOAN WARTHLING ROBERTS

The idea of a spinster involved in solving a mystery is on the surface paradoxical. Of course she pokes and pries, but then what good can come of it? What could she do with those bits and pieces of information she gets? The cliché is that the spinster is woolly-headed, has no logical methods of examining things, and worst of all, has no experience with passion or power, both of them in the domain of the young. How could she ever understand the murky motives behind a crime? But the spinster's potential lies more in her formidable intelligence and ability to connect seemingly insignificant details—indeed, in her existence outside the normal society of heterosexual couples—than in the repression which the term often implies.

And on the surface Christie seems to corroborate the stereotypically negative definition of the spinster. She gave the world Jane Marple seven or eight years after she had started writing detective fiction with Hercule Poirot as her first detective in 1920. *The Murder at the Vicarage*, in 1930, is often cited as Miss Marple's début, but actually she entered the world of fiction in 'The Tuesday Night Club,' which appeared in 1928. In this first appearance, Miss Marple is about sixty-five years old, caught in the fashions and manners of the turn of the century. We see her through the eyes of her nephew, Raymond West, seated in his Aunt Jane's house: 'The room was an old one with broad black beams across the ceiling and it was furnished with good old furniture . . . His Aunt Jane's house always pleased him as the right setting for her personality . . . She sat erect in the big grandfather chair, wearing a black brocade dress, very much pinched in around the waist. Mechlin lace was arranged in a cascade down the front of the bodice. She had on black lace mittens; a black lace cap surmounted the piled-up masses of her snowy hair' (*Tuesday Club Murders* 2). Christie was adept at presenting her sleuth through the lens of condescending characters, in all her fuzziness (a narrative device allowing at least one male observer, someone of keener perception than most, to come to a new and startlingly revised appreciation of Miss Marple), and seen through the eyes of her fond but always condescending nephew, Jane Marple seems like a relic of a time past, functioning in the present world only as a bit of family background for her nephew's cleverness. Miss Marple never looked older and was never more of a sibyl than in that first story, seemingly 'out of time' and consulting with a host of inner voices—those of experience and memory—to find answers. ⟨. . .⟩

However, as she wrote more stories, Christie seemed to sense the too stereotypical nature of the character: Miss Marple kept getting younger, bustled about St Mary Mead in a more energetic, quotidian way, and dressed in a more country-tweedy fashion than in the earliest story. In the 1950s, for example in *A Pocket Full of Rye*, Jane Marple is a 'tall, elderly lady wearing an old-fashioned tweed coat and skirt, a couple of scarves, and a small felt hat with a bird's wing' (78). An aged but good-quality suitcase reposed by her feet. 'Aged but good quality' is the operative idea here. What does remain the same through the years is the implication of value. Jane, her house, and her belongings all embody those two shibboleths of English worth and gentility: age and fine quality. It is essential that there is absolutely nothing 'nouveau' about Miss Marple. Her quality has little to do with sexuality but a great deal to do with gender, and her experience, organized by a fine mind, makes her age an asset. She has not dried up like an unpicked apple, existing solely as a relic of fertility unused. Jane Marple has observed, thought, compared, and understood a great deal. Her interest in other human beings is natural, kindly, but never sentimentalized and fluffy, even though she finds it useful to keep a façade of fluffy knitting between herself and observers. Instead of mouthing sentimentalities, she is startlingly clear-eyed about the possibilities of human weakness and evil.

Jane Marple makes no lists but examines the evidence internally, and then brings out her observations in a flurry of apparent irrelevancies which snap together with the firmness of a steel trap. Her portrayal is the forthright and respectful portrayal of the older unmarried woman. She is still about sixty-five and is dismissed as useless and pesky by various bystanders in the novels, though the reader knows better. ⟨. . .⟩ In *The Body in the Library*, Clithering characterizes Jane Marple as a detective so good that she is better at the job than he is. The reader has been led to see that recognition of Jane Marple's worth depends on a character's ability to perceive people clearly for what they are, and not through the fuzzy but comfortable lens of stereotype. Henry Clithering is happy to acknowledge the worth of his spinster sleuth. Still, coming as it does from a patriarchal authority, the recognition shows Miss Marple as needing the backing of men in order to be effective.

—Glenwood Irons and Joan Warthling Roberts, "From Spinster to Hipster: The 'Suitability' of Miss Marple and Anna Lee," in *Feminism in Women's Detective Fiction*, ed. Glenwood Irons (Toronto: University of Toronto Press, 1995), 65–67

BIBLIOGRAPHY

The Mysterious Affair at Styles: A Detective Story. 1920.

The Secret Adversary. 1922.

The Murder on the Links. 1923.

Poirot Investigates. 1924.

The Secret of Chimneys. 1925.

The Road of Dreams. 1925.

The Murder of Roger Ackroyd. 1926.

The Big Four. 1927.

The Mystery of the Blue Train. 1928.

Partners in Crime. 1929.

The Under Dog. 1929.

The Seven Dials Mystery. 1929.

Giant's Bread (as Mary Westmacott). 1930.

The Murder at the Vicarage. 1930.

The Mysterious Mr. Quin. 1930.

The Floating Admiral. 1931.

The Sittaford Mystery. 1931.

The Thirteen Problems. 1932.

Peril at End House. 1932.

The Hound of Death and Other Stories. 1933.

Why Didn't They Ask Evans? 1934.

Murder on the Orient Express. 1934.

Unfinished Portrait (as Mary Westmacott). 1934.

Parker Pyne Investigates. 1934.

Black Coffee. 1934.

The Listerdale Mystery and Other Stories. 1934.

Murder in Three Acts. 1934.

Death in the Clouds. 1935.

The A.B.C. Murders: A New Poirot Mystery. 1936.

Cards on the Table. 1936.

Murder in Mesopotamia. 1936.

Murder in the Mews and Other Stories. 1937.

Death on the Nile. 1937.

Dumb Witness. 1937.

Appointment with Death. 1938.

Hercule Poirot's Christmas. 1938.

Murder Is Easy. 1939.
The Little Niggers. 1939.
The Regatta and Other Stories. 1939.
One, Two, Buckle My Shoe. 1940.
Sad Cypress. 1940.
Evil Under the Sun. 1941.
N or M? 1941.
The Body in the Library. 1942.
The Moving Finger. 1942.
Five Little Pigs. 1942.
The Mystery of the Baghdad Chest. 1943.
The Mystery of the Crime in Cabin 66. 1943.
Poirot and the Regatta Mystery. 1943.
Poirot on Holiday. 1943.
Problem at Pollensa Bay, and the Christmas Adventure. 1943.
The Veiled Lady, and the Mystery of the Baghdad Chest. 1944.
Death Comes as the End. 1944.
Towards Zero. 1944.
Absent in the Spring (as Mary Westmacott). 1944.
Ten Little Niggers. 1945.
Appointment with Death. 1945.
Sparkling Cyanide. 1945.
The Hollow. 1946.
Poirot Knows the Murderer. 1946.
Murder on the Nile. 1946.
Come, Tell Me How You Live. 1946.
The Labours of Hercules: Short Stories. 1947.
Witness for the Prosecution and Other Stories. 1948.
The Rose and the Yew Tree (as Mary Westmacott). 1948.
Taken at the Flood. 1948.
Crooked House. 1949.
The Mousetrap and Other Stories. 1949.
A Murder Is Announced. 1950.
They Came to Baghdad. 1951.
The Under Dog and Other Stories. 1951.
They Do It with Mirrors. 1952.
The Hollow. 1952.
Mrs. McGinty's Dead. 1952.
A Daughter's a Daughter (as Mary Westmacott). 1952.

After the Funeral. 1953.

A Pocket Full of Rye. 1953.

The Mousetrap. 1954.

Witness for the Prosecution. 1954.

Destination Unknown. 1954.

Hickory, Dickory, Dock. 1955.

The Burden (as Mary Westmacott). 1956.

Dead Man's Folly. 1956.

Spider's Web. 1957.

4:50 from Paddington. 1957.

Toward Zero (with Gerald Verner). 1957.

Ordeal by Innocence. 1958.

Verdict. 1958.

The Unexpected Guest. 1958.

Cat among the Pigeons. 1959.

Go Back for Murder. 1960.

The Adventures of the Christmas Pudding, and Selection of Entrees. 1960.

Double Sin and Other Stories. 1961.

1 3 4 for Luck! A Selection of Mystery Stories for Young Readers. 1961.

The Mirror Crack'd from Side to Side. 1962.

Rule of Three: Afternoon at the Seaside, The Patient, The Rats. 1963.

The Clocks. 1963.

A Caribbean Mystery. 1964.

Surprise! Surprise! 1965.

At Bertram's Hotel. 1965.

Star over Bethlehem and Other Stories. 1965.

Third Girl. 1966.

1 3 Clues for Miss Marple. 1966.

Endless Night. 1967.

By the Pricking of My Thumbs. 1968.

Hallowe'en Party. 1969.

Passenger to Frankfurt. 1970.

The Golden Ball and Other Stories. 1971.

Nemesis. 1971.

Fiddlers Three. 1972.

Elephants Can Remember. 1972.

Akhnaton. 1973.

Poems. 1973.

Postern of Fate. 1973.

Hercule Poirot's Early Cases. 1974.
Miss Marple's Final Cases. 1974.
Murder on Board. 1974.
Curtain: Hercule Poirot's Last Case. 1975.
Sleeping Murder. 1976.
An Autobiography. 1977.
The Mousetrap and Other Plays. 1978.

IVY COMPTON-BURNETT

1884–1969

IVY COMPTON-BURNETT was born on June 5, 1884, in Middlesex, England, to Katharine and James Compton-Burnett, a homeopathic physician. With her brothers Guy and Noll, she was educated at home, first by a governess and later by a private tutor. Eventually, she and her four younger sisters attended the Addiscombe College for the Daughters of Gentlemen. From 1902 to 1907, Ivy Compton-Burnett, by now a self-described classicist, attended the University of London's Royal Holloway College. While there, in 1906, she was awarded a Founder Scholarship in classics. The following year, she earned her bachelor's degree, with honors, and decided she wanted to be a writer.

Her first novel, *Dolores*, was published in 1911. Much of its plot and characters draw upon her family's relationships and her experiences at Royal Holloway. Stylistically, *Dolores* is unique in comparison to Compton-Burnett's later novels, and, although it was well received by critics of the time, she later dismissed it as juvenile. The same year, several family tragedies struck in quick succession: her father and both brothers died, and then two sisters committed suicide together. After suffering a long illness, her mother also died, and Ivy was charged with taking care of her younger siblings and the household. Emotionally weakened and lonely, she could no longer write and subsequently spent several recuperative years weaving tapestry chair seats.

A family friend introduced Compton-Burnett to Margaret Jourdain in 1921, starting a turning point in her recovery. Jourdain encouraged Compton-Burnett's return to writing, and the two women became lifelong friends and live-in companions. By 1925 Compton-Burnett produced *Pastors and Masters*, the first in a long series of oblique, witty novels written throughout her life. The follow-up novel, *Brothers and Sisters* (1929), sparked the critical and commercial success she enjoyed for the remainder of her career, culminating in 1957 with the James Tait Black Memorial Prize for *Mother and Son* (1955).

In 1951 Jourdain died, leaving Compton-Burnett desolate with a grief from which she never recovered. Though she continued to write and was awarded many honors—including an honorary doctorate from the University of Leeds in 1960 and being named a Dame Commander of the British Empire in 1967—she lived alone and traveled little until her death on August 27, 1969.

CRITICAL EXTRACTS

ELIZABETH BOWEN

As a title, *Elders and Betters* is ironical: everyone in this novel is the same age, and nobody is admirable. In a Victorian novel, the characters fail to impose upon the reader; here, they fail to impose upon each other. The revolution, foreseeable, long overdue, has arrived—without disturbing a single impalpable cup on the impalpable drawing-room mantelpiece. It has been succeeded by this timeless anarchy, in which meals are served and eaten, visits paid, engagements to marry contracted and broken off. Everything that was due to happen in the world the Victorians posited, and condoned, has happened—but, apparently, there is still more to come: such worlds are not easily finished with, and Miss Compton-Burnett may not see the finish herself. For one thing, that disrespect for all other people underlying Victorian manners (as Victorians showed them) has not yet come to the end of its free say, and fear has not yet revenged itself to the full. The passive characters, almost all young men, marvel at the others, but not much or for long; they return to marvelling at themselves. Only the callous or those who recuperate quickly can survive, but in *Elders and Betters* everyone does survive—except Aunt Jessica, who commits suicide after the scene with Anna. In this we are true to the masters; in the Victorian novel people successfully die of their own death-wishes (as Aunt Sukey dies in *Elders and Betters*), but nobody ever dies of an indignity.

Miss Compton-Burnett shows, in *Elders and Betters*, that she can carry weight without losing height. She has been becoming, with each novel, less abstract, more nearly possible to enclose in the human fold. *Elders and Betters* is, compared, for instance, with *Brothers and Sisters*, *terre à terre*; but with that I greet a solid gain in effect. The more she masters what I have called her logic, the more material she can use. Her technique for melodrama has been by degrees perfected, and is now quite superb: I know nothing to equal Chapter X of this book—the duel in Aunt Sukey's death-chamber, after Aunt Sukey's death. Only second to this is the lunch-party, at which two families voice their disgust at old Mr. Calderon's engagement to Florence, the governess's young niece. There is an advance, too (again, a logical one), in the articulateness of employed persons: nothing protects the Donnes against Cook and Ethel, with whom even Anna is placatory. The importance of money has not budged, but dependence is now felt by the monied side—also, there is, with regard to employed persons, either a weakening or a belated dawn of grace. In one of the earlier novels, it seemed consistent that a child of the house should laugh every time the governess eats; in *Elders and Betters*, a child suffers because he has left a governess out in the dusk and rain. And religion, the worship in the rock garden, for the first time enters the scene.

The post-Victorian novel, in Miss Compton-Burnett's hands, keeps its course parallel with our modern experience, on which it offers from time to time, a not irrelevant comment in its own language. To the authority of the old, relentless tradition, it has added an authority of its own.

—Elizabeth Bowen, "Ivy Compton-Burnett: II" (1944), *Collected Impressions* (1950), excerpted in *Twentieth-Century British Literature*, ed. Harold Bloom (New York: Chelsea House Publishers, 1985), 360

ROBERT LIDDELL

Miss Compton-Burnett has freed herself from all irrelevances in order to write the pure novel. And like Miss Austen she has a dislike for merely descriptive writing, which she uses with even greater economy. The village which is to be the scene of action is undescribed and, except for Moreton Edge in *Brothers and Sisters*, is not even named. Characters are often tersely but completely described, in terms which do not remain in the memory, and it is necessary to turn back if we wish to remind ourselves of their appearance. ⟨. . .⟩

Dialogue, to which in *Emma* Jane Austen had begun to give a far more important place, is the staple of this writer's work. It is a dialogue of a power and brilliance unmatched in English prose fiction. In her early and immature book, *Dolores*, the machine creaked audibly at times, but already functioned with precision. The style of that book is crude, bare and rather alarming. It is not like real English: it is like the language of translation. It reminds one of English translations of Russian novels and of Greek tragedy, and one may conjecture that both of them had formed an important part of her reading. Such a style is uneuphonious and harsh, but conscientiously renders a meaning— and that is what, like a translator, Miss Compton-Burnett already did, with a remarkable exactitude.

This ungainly, but precise language was later evolved into a dialogue, more dramatic than narrative, which, whether in longer speeches, or in the nearest equivalent in English to Greek tragic stichomythia, is an unrealistic but extraordinarily intense vehicle for the characters' thoughts and emotions, and enables their creator to differentiate them sharply, and, whenever she wishes, to condemn them out of their own mouths. Its nearness to or remoteness from ordinary spoken language will vary from place to place. There is no single formula that will cover it, and the author has indicated that no kind of 'figure in the carpet' is to be sought: 'it is simply the result of an effort to give the impression I want to give.'

'The key,' says one critic, 'is the realization that her characters speak precisely as they are thinking.' This key will not unlock more than a part of her work: part of the utterances of her good characters, and the utterances of exceptionally simple or straightforward characters.

For she excels particularly at the revelation of insincerity on all its levels: from that of characters who tell flat lies, to that of characters who have deceived themselves into believing what they say. In between are characters such as Dominic Spong, who are more than half-aware and are wholly tolerant of their own smarminess and their own insincere ways of talking: 'if I may approach so great a man upon a comparatively flimsy subject.'

Her idiom sometimes approximates to what one might actually say if one were in the character's skin and situation, but also to what one might think and conceal; to what one might think of saying and bite back; to what one might afterwards wish one had said; to what one would like other people to think; and to what one would like to think oneself. It is unlikely that these alternatives are exclusive.

—Robert Liddell, "The Novels of I. Compton-Burnett," *A Treatise on the Novel* (1947), excerpted in *Twentieth-Century British Literature*, ed. Harold Bloom (New York: Chelsea House Publishers, 1985), 357

BRENDAN GILL

Miss Compton-Burnett is ⟨. . .⟩ about as fastidious and detached as a writer can become and continue to set pen to paper—her dialogue, lively and witty as it is, gives the effect of having been delicately unwound, like a live nerve, from the lips of her troubled speakers, and I am assuming that it isn't rapped out on a typewriter—and it is probably no accident that the inhabitants of the big, cold houses and wet countryside of her novels are invariably more suspicious of praise than of blame.

⟨. . . Of⟩ all living writers Miss Compton-Burnett makes, I should think, the least concession to contemporary taste. She is neither obscure nor naturalistic. Her characters do not talk as real people talk, in starts and grunts and groans; they bubble up like never-failing springs. There are no streams of consciousness, only streams of conversation. Quietly, but ever so firmly, Miss Compton-Burnett hints that Joyce and Proust and Hemingway are all very well in their place but that there are hundreds of other ways to write a novel, and that the method of Jane Austen is, with certain remarkable modifications, good enough for her.

—Brendan Gill, "Ivy Compton-Burnett and the Gift of Gab," *The New Yorker* (19 June 1948), excerpted in *Twentieth-Century British Literature*, ed. Harold Bloom (New York: Chelsea House Publishers, 1985), 357–58

EDWARD SACKVILLE-WEST

Like a Picasso of 1913, a Compton-Burnett novel is not concerned with decoration or with observation of the merely contingent, nor is it ⟨concerned with⟩ exhibiting the author's personality or ⟨. . .⟩ exploiting a romantic dream. It is constructive, ascetic, low in tone, classical. It enquires into the meanings—the syntactical force—of the things we all say, as the Cubist enquired into the significance of shapes and planes divorced from the incidence of light and the accidents of natural or utilitarian construction. These novels contain very few descriptive passages, and none where description is indulged in for its own sake, or for Impressionistic ends; and in this connection it is significant that Miss Compton-Burnett seems to scorn the aid of images. This does not, I think, strike us at the time of reading; it is not until we take up some other book that we realise to what extent nearly all novelists rely on metaphor and simile to enliven their scene. ⟨. . .⟩

But it is her zeal for measuring the *temperature* of emotion—the graph described from moment to moment by the action of the plot on the alert sensibilities of her characters—which is responsible both for the continuously witty surface of her writing and the deeper truth of her picture. Like Henry James, Miss Compton-Burnett is much concerned to preserve an amusing surface, as well as a polite one; and this remains true of the tragic passages in her books. Indeed, in those which deal with the most frightful happenings (*Brothers and Sisters, Men and Wives, More Women than Men, A House and Its Head*) the comic relief is more pronounced and more evenly distributed than in the later novels, of which the plots are considerably less lurid. But it is her anxious attention to Truth which, more than anything else, gives to her books their quality of timeless relevance. Her wit has many sides, but it excludes absolutely the wise-crack, the smart epigram, the modish or private sally. "People don't feel as much as you want them to." This assumption is fundamental to all these novels: it is the arrow on the thermometer which marks 98.4°. And the movement of the book is the to-and-fro rhythm of a tug-of-war between those who do not wish to feel too much and those who are determined to make them feel more than they can bear—until the rope breaks.

I do not want to give the impression that I consider these novels faultless. In common with other important artists Miss Compton-Burnett has a number of failings which are perhaps inherent in her very personal idiom. They are easily described:

(1) She tends to fill her canvas too rapidly, and this mistake is aggravated by the perfunctory way in which she describes her characters, so that we are in constant danger of forgetting or confusing them. It must, however, be pointed out that in her later novels this fault is less apparent.

(2) She cannot manage masculine men. Her males are either overtly effete (e.g. Alfred Marcon in *Daughters and Sons*), or possessed by a feline power-mania (e.g. Duncan Edgeworth in *A House and Its Head*).

(3) Her plots are not easily remembered in detail, or distinguished one from another. This is not a serious charge, for her emphasis lies elsewhere; but it argues a certain rigidity of imagination ⟨. . .⟩

(4) Her subsidiary characters are often (but by no means always) too 'flat'. Even regarded as a chorus, they are too dim in outline and tend, moreover, to be always of the same type.

(5) Her chief characters do not develop in the course of the book, they only loom larger or dwindle, according as the author lengthens or shortens her opera-glass.

(6) When action supervenes, she skates over it as quickly as possible, in the manner of Jane Austen. At such moments a kind of deadly calm descends on the page; which is in a way effective, but tends to spoil what in music is called the balance of parts.

These faults, although they add up to something, do not seriously affect the brilliance and gravity of these amazing books, or the intense satisfaction that arises from submitting oneself to Miss Compton-Burnett's regime.

—Edward Sackville-West, "Ladies Whose Bright Pens . . .," *Inclinations* (1949), excerpted in *Twentieth-Century British Literature*, ed. Harold Bloom (New York: Chelsea House Publishers, 1985), 364

PAMELA HANSFORD JOHNSON

Miss Compton-Burnett expresses the wish that this early book ⟨*Dolores*⟩ should not be considered among her novels, as she regards it as *juvenilia* and outside the stream of her important work.

It would, however, be a pity if this novel were not eventually reprinted with a prefatory essay; for the relation which it bears to her later works is in about the same proportion as the relation of *Les Plaisirs et Les Jours* to *A la Recherche du Temps Perdu*. It is apart from the mainstream of her work in two important respects. Firstly, whereas the later novels have a preponderance of dialogue and singularly little commentary and narrative, *Dolores* has a preponderance of commentary and narrative and singularly little dialogue. What dialogue there is, however, strikes sharply on the ear and with all the familiar surprise; it is quite individual, standing out as if it were printed in phosphorus from a text that bears the marks of derivation from other works of fiction.

This leads us to the second point: that *Dolores* has several derivative sources—from *Middlemarch* (there is an echo of the Dorothea–Casaubon story), from *Scenes from Clerical Life*, and, more oddly, from *The Professor*, *Villette*, and even from *Jane Eyre*. At this time Miss Compton-Burnett *was* striving after visual effects; and when she attained them, they had something in common with Charlotte Brontë's emphatic chiaroscuro. With *Pastors and Masters* she deliberately reduced visual effect almost to nothing; but lately has begun to develop it once more.

The most interesting point of comparison between *Dolores* and the succeeding novels is the reversal of theme. *Dolores* concerns a plain, intellectual young woman who immolates her whole life upon the altars of other people— often, in a manner doing more credit to her staying-power than to her good sense. But the thesis is this: that to sacrifice oneself for the good of others is beautiful and ennobling. Fourteen years later, the thesis had altered—and this new thesis, either dominant or subsidiary in every novel Miss Compton-Burnett has written since, is as follows: that to sacrifice oneself for the good of others is splendid for others but horrible for oneself.

Though *Dolores*, like a good many first novels, is stamped with the influence of other books, to the student of Miss Compton-Burnett it is entirely fascinating, for her voice is in it, her wit glimmers sparse but bright where wit is least to be expected, and her force, her chill and her curious authority are clamped like hydraulic pressure upon the whole of it.

—Pamela Hansford Johnson, *I. Compton-Burnett* (1951), excerpted in *Twentieth-Century British Literature*, ed. Harold Bloom (New York: Chelsea House Publishers, 1985), 361

PAMELA HANSFORD JOHNSON

The peculiar charm of Miss Compton-Burnett's novels, the charm that has won her not merely admirers but addicts, lies in her speaking of home-truths. She achieves this by a certain fixed method. One character propounds some ordinary, homely hypocrisy, the kind of phrase from which mankind for centuries has had his comfort and his peace of mind. Immediately another character shows it up for the fraud it is, and does it in so plain and so frightful a fashion that one feels the sky is far more likely to fall upon the truth-teller than upon the hypocrite. In these books there is always someone to lie and someone to tell the truth; the power of light and the power of darkness speaking antiphonally, with a dispassionate mutual understanding. . . .

Do young people, like Daniel and Graham, adolescents like Isabel, children like Marcus, really speak in this measured and extraordinary fashion? Of course they do not. Miss Compton-Burnett's almost incessant dialogue has very little relation indeed to human speech; it is the speech of the secret understanding in all its rightness and all its crudity. Occasionally the Parents (or masters) speak in the convention of ordinary converse: the Children (or servants) speak only with their minds. What seems to be the recorded speech of the lips is really only the recording of that swift comprehension which can hardly find utterance in conscious thought. This is why Miss Compton-Burnett's writing appears so strange to the reader who comes upon it without warning, a gentle tea-cosy madness, a coil of vipers in a sewing-basket.

Yet readers who come to know her fascination will discern one startling fact; that this piercingly wise, discreet, mannered Victoriana conceals abysses of the human personality. There are monsters in her books, men and women a hundred times worse than the Murdstones, because they are indestructible— and incombustible also; they do not carry their own fire and brimstone about on their persons.

It is important to realize that the novels of Miss Compton-Burnett are *terrible*; though she uses the comic technique she is not a writer of comedies, and the reader who approaches her with Jane Austen in mind is either going to get a violent shock or to enjoy her in a happy state of total incomprehension. Her method is always a mask for her theme; indeed, if some of her themes were set out in a normal, unstylized manner, some of her books would find their way into the locked cages of sensitive librarians. Behind the veil of witty patter, question and response, the human horror stands up straight. If we do not always notice quite what a horror it is, this is because she allows her characters to beard her lions—even her worst monsters are always baited, always challenged. But in the end they devour the small and valiant prey, and no keeper ever comes in the last chapter to lock them up or shoot them down. In these books there is never a Fortinbras, never a Richmond, never a Malcolm. Evil is achieved, and the results of it are assimilated into the life from day-to-day, and the victims of it stand in the third and fourth generation.

—Pamela Hansford Johnson, *I. Compton-Burnett* (1951), excerpted in *Twentieth-Century British Literature*, ed. Harold Bloom (New York: Chelsea House Publishers, 1985), 365

WILLIAM GOYEN

⟨*Brothers and Sisters*⟩ is the infernal language of enclosed people who are talking each other to death, people inhabiting some dry hole of life which their good ancestors have hollowed out for them and furnished securely, all in high purpose. It is a language of a worn-out stock turned upon itself and upon its members within its narrow, hallowed trench: blood kin. Its career is relentless and unrelieved, turning up fresh losses and shocks and damning news as it chops on and on, and cutting under old layers of secrets and deceptions.

Miss Compton-Burnett's is a rhetoric created by prisoners of conversation where vocal self-explanation is the only action of the bound and the captive: the only freedom lies in a verbal attitude toward disaster, and the choice vocabulary is limited to concepts of irony, tragic wit, self-pity, condescension.

Her rarefied, elliptical, telescoped and bitten-off style is mannered beyond Gertrude Stein's anywhere or Virginia Woolf's in "The Waves" but recalls gentler overtones from the very different worlds of these two women.

How to describe this strange style and its grasp upon the reader? What is compressed as tightly as gunpowder to make a bullet must, because it is forced into a tight mixture of irreducible minimum, expand to its natural dimension and potency in some other place. This seems rather the natural and rightful demand of essences and concentrates. Where the inevitable diffusion and return to natural volume of her style occurs is in the mind of the reader where Miss Compton-Burnett fires her explosive compounds. This accounts for a reader's lagging behind her sentences or being snagged onto them for long lulled periods and for a feeling of suffocating closeness; but it is the very source of her striking power and explains the detonation of her savage wisdom into largeness and eventual fullness.

The author is observing her characters from a position deeply buried in the structure of their situation and so the writing appears directionless until one can find out what point of view is being taken. This obscures the reader's focus for a while for he has no help of time, of description, of narrative. But when a shape comes clear out of this stubbed thicket of conversation, it is constructed of perversely antic devices of Websterian melodrama in grand style— a key, a locked cabinet holding a terrible letter that divulges the doom of a household, the burning of a will, a photograph album revealing life-long secrets that taint forever. Her style and the breathless formal convention her novels take reproduce the very situation her characters are involved in: stratagem and high-toned cunning within family prison-life.

This novel is a picture of the devious, devilish and intricate results of the intermingling of brother and sister, illustrated by several sets of them living in an English village and especially in Moreton Edge, a manor house on the rim of the village inhabited by the Staces for generations. All these brothers and sisters are involved or on the point of getting involved with each other, treating their fathers, where there are any, like unfortunate pranks of nature and their mothers as something to win out over, which they do not.

When it turns out that mother and father Stace are themselves half-brother-and-sister, and this through the discovery of a dusty letter left long ago by Grandfather Stace, progenitor of all the woe that has followed, heretofore vaguely intoned ominous forecast materializes. Irony doubles back on itself and, twice strengthened, delivers that psychic blow which often turned Greek and Elizabethan tragedians' characters into madmen, but not Miss Compton-Burnett's. Commenting on their dreadful situation as brilliantly as ever, they harness their Sophoclean destiny with the bridle of cruel wit and trot on, conversing, into their future hells.

There seems little doubt that this extraordinary author binds one of the tightest knots in literary history; but the labored loosening of it is rewarding and its secrets at the core staggering.

—William Goyen, "Small Talk on the Way to Damnation," *The New York Times Book Review* (18 November 1956): 5, 36

BRIGID BROPHY

To my senses, Miss Compton-Burnett is not exactly an artist. She is something less valuable but rarer—the inventor of a wholly new species of puzzle. It is probably the first invention of the kind since the crossword, which it far outdoes in imaginative depth. Indeed, it is only a touch less profoundly suggestive than chess or formal logic. An extra attraction is that, though her novels are not themselves works of art, the rules of the puzzle are allusions to literary forms and conventions. Reading them is like playing some Monopoly for Intellectuals, in which you can buy, as well as houses and hotels, plaques to set up on them recording that a great writer once lived there.

The social nexus in which Miss Compton-Burnett assembles her speakers is such a memorial—to Jane Austen. The centre, the permanent set, in the new novel ⟨*A God and His Gifts*⟩ is a baronet's home in the country; the milieu consists of those grouped round the magic 'Sir'. At the start, the baronet's son Hereward is refused by a tenant, marries instead the daughter of the neighbouring house and brings her to live in the baronet's. Hereward is a popular novelist, which occasions a discussion in which the baronet and his butler gently disparage novels—a tacit allusion to the novels passage in *Northanger Abbey*. But the resemblance to Jane Austen is never more than allusion-deep. The composure of Jane Austen's prose is adaptable to expressing every nuance of social and individual idiom, whereas the sedateness of Miss Compton-Burnett's is wooden-featured. Where Jane Austen is concerned above all with her heroines' consciousness, Miss Compton-Burnett shuns—indeed positively and in panic flees from—the idea of entering anyone's consciousness. Only one paragraph in *A God and his Gifts* makes any attempt (and it is a sketchy one) to give the reader direct access to what someone feels.

In flight from the novelist's freedom to wander into minds, Miss Compton-Burnett is logically driven to embrace the restrictions of a dramatist. Her allusion now is to classical drama, whose conventions she abides by to the extent of having major events happen off-stage—though in her new book some curiously intimate ones, including a proposal, happen in public. Her text is as bare as Racine's of furniture or handkerchiefs, and you might say her speakers resemble his in all speaking alike; the trouble is that hers don't speak poetry. Their language is in fact a let-down. They exchange big, imprecise banalities, seeing paths plain before them, keeping a light touch, letting things loom large. Still, they toss these clumsinesses about with some grace, achieving the form if not the content of wit. It's like reading a Wilde comedy in algebra, the aphorisms reduced to 'All a's are really b's. Only y's ever think them z's.' Occasionally a speaker strikes off at least a common-sense-ism. When the baronet dies, his widow is offered the consolation of yet another banality. 'You will live in the past. That will always be your own': and she has the wits, if not quite wit, to reply 'I have lived in it. But then it was the present. And that was much better.'

The setting is not so much subject to the conventions as plain conventional—'book-lined'. Period is not indicated—you can't make much of the absence of cars and telephones when so few material objects are present anyway; the butler, however, has a presence which seems unmistakably Edwardian. (He is named, by the wittiest stroke in the book, Galleon.) The devices of the plot-making seem borrowed from the Edwardian theatre. Where except in a mustachio'd melodrama would a man betray, as Hereward does, that he is the real as well as the adoptive father of a child by letting himself be overheard exclaiming above the child's head 'blood of my blood, and so deeply deprived from me'?

Indeed, Miss Compton-Burnett creates a positively farcical pile-up of skeletons tumbling from the Edwardian cupboard. Piecemeal it is disclosed to his family (an allusion to the strip-technique of the *Oedipus Rex*) that Hereward is a man of unconfinable sexual appetite and charms. He, not the baronet (who is financially dependent on his son's royalties), is the head of the family, the boss stag in the herd who takes all the females as his right. This, since the herd is rather restricted and close-knit to begin with, involves him in the near-incest of taking his wife's sister and his sons' wives; when these have children by him, apparent cousins are really half-siblings (liable, of course, in the restricted milieu, to fall in love with one another) and the close-knit family has become inextricably inter-ravelled.

As a matter of fact, Hereward's unions always *are* fertile. I take it Miss Compton-Burnett is tacitly referring to the doctrine of pagan theology that gods never mate fruitlessly; for by the end Hereward's family have explicitly recognised him as the god of the title, identifying the paradox of their continuing respect for him with the paradox of the Greeks' basing their own restrictive sexual morality on a lecherous and incestuous pantheon. Presumably the particular god concerned is Zeus: the incest in Zeus's own ancestry is represented by the fact that Hereward's parents are distant cousins: Hereward is a Zeus with no need to usurp his father, having reduced him to financial impotence, but when, on the baronet's death, the butler greets the son as 'Sir Hereward' we understand that Zeus has come into his inheritance.

Inside this classical box, Miss Compton-Burnett's Chinese puzzle implicitly places another. The situation is an outline of Freud's theory of the primal horde. Indeed, I suspect Hereward's name of being compounded of 'herd' and 'horde'. The situation is, however, pointedly worked *out*, and not worked, in psychoanalytical jargon, *through*: and that the reader is not called on to involve his emotions is, I suppose, why the book remains an admirable and diverting puzzle rather than a work of art.

> —Brigid Brophy, "I. Compton-Burnett" (1963), *Don't Never Forget* (1966), excerpted in *Twentieth-Century British Literature*, ed. Harold Bloom (New York: Chelsea House Publishers, 1985), 363

MARY McCARTHY

There is something in her work that seems to encourage false generalizations about it. She has designed her books as curios, and the fate of a curio is to be ranged on a shelf. Though easy to read, she is a hard writer to grasp. Her books slip away from you, and the inclination, therefore, is to "place" them conveniently. Most criticism of her is replete with lists—of "good" characters and bad ones, flat characters and round ones, "likeable" persons and tyrants; her critics are prone to count, divide, and classify, not always accurately, to measure the ratio of dialogue to description on a page. This counting, these laborious measurements, as of an unknown object—a giant footprint or a flying saucer—denote critical bafflement. Doubtless by her own wish, she remains a phenomenon, an occurrence in the history of letters. It would appear to be hubris to try to guess her riddle.

Her work is strewn with big, amateurish-looking clues, like planted evidence to mislead professional pryers in search of meanings, wider applications, influences. She has a fondness for naming her people after the English Poets (no resemblance intended; that is the point), and one of her old women is named Regan—by mistake; her father had thought that Regan was one of Shakespeare's heroines. The English Novelists too, like a private joke, keep nudging each other in these texts, while the anxious reader asks himself what is the point of allusions to Smollett, Maria Edgeworth, Jane Austen, Miss Mitford, Mrs. Gaskell, George Eliot, Dickens. Is he missing something important? Where is the connection with the story? Many clues lead to Shakespeare (King Lear and his daughters, for instance, in *A Father and His Fate*), and the reader is early put on the scent of Oedipus, the Jane Austen trail having grown cold. The "incest theme," already prominent in *Brothers and Sisters*, reappeared in *Darkness and Day*, as though to confirm suspicion. Did the quirky author, hidden like one of her characters in the folds of her narrative, hope to overhear critics fondly talking about Greek tragedy in Victorian dress and the "stichomythia" of her dialogue?

The incest theme is surely a red herring. The coupling between blood relations (or between people who imagine they are blood relations) is never anything but a twist of the plot. The author is capable of the fullest realism in her treatment of the passions, including the sexual ones, but when she shows incest, it is not a passion but an accident. She is strong on presenting temptation, but we never see a character being *tempted* to commit incest, as we do in the case of murder. Anyone who thinks that incest is the "subject" of Compton-Burnett has failed to see her real interests and the real idiosyncrasy of her mind.

Her books are not like other books; they are, as she might say, books apart. They do not "relate" to their material in the ordinary literary way, but crab-wise. The subject of any given Compton-Burnett is simply a cluster of associations and word-plays, while the plot is usually made up of arithmetical puzzles and brain-twisters. ⟨. . .⟩

It is said (sometimes as a compliment) that Compton-Burnett has no interest in social problems. The world she has made, because there are no factories or slums in it, is mistaken for Jane Austen's "little bit of ivory." But the poor in Compton-Burnett are, precisely, made conspicuous by their absence—to be inferred by the reader, if he is paying the slightest attention, from the horrible scarves, shirts, and petticoats charitably knitted and sewn for them by the idle classes. The toiling, spinning masses are invisible and unheard, like the silent chorus of schoolboys whose marmalade is being watered. Remarks are made *about* them, and the worst are the "feeling" ones: "We should remember the less fortunate people when we are in want of nothing ourselves." Compton-Burnett has as much belief in philanthropy as Karl Marx himself. Whatever her voting habits, in her writing she is a strict economic realist with no partiality for the well-to-do. Her writing is extraordinary in its lack of social snobbery. Here she is far ahead of Jane Austen and of most of her own contemporaries. She does not even have an interest in social climbers, a sure sign of secret snobbery in an artist. That is probably why her books, despite the swarms of servants in them, have not found a larger public. They evoke "a vanished world" of privilege too unsparingly. Nor can a liberal reader flatter himself that the disappearance of a servant class has lent these novels a "documentary" interest; conditions have changed, but the condition has not.

What flashes out of her work is a spirited, unpardoning sense of injustice, which becomes even sharper in her later books. In her own eccentric way, Compton-Burnett is a radical thinker, one of the rare modern heretics. It is the eccentricity that has diverted attention from the fact that these small uniform volumes are subversive packets. If their contents had to be reduced still further, boiled down to a single word capable of yielding a diversity of meanings, the word might be "necessity." From strict to dire. From "constraint or compulsion having its basis in the natural constitution of things" to "the condition of being in difficulties or straits, esp. through lack of means; want; poverty." Not omitting its uses in phrases and proverbs or "a bond or tie *between* persons, *Obs. rare.*" It is a deep word, like her works.

—Mary McCarthy, "The Inventions of I. Compton-Burnett" (1966), *The Writing on the Wall and Other Essays* (1970), excerpted in *Twentieth-Century British Literature*, ed. Harold Bloom (New York: Chelsea House Publishers, 1985), 375

Bibliography

Dolores. 1911.
Pastors and Masters. 1925.
Brothers and Sisters. 1929.
Men and Wives. 1931.
More Women Than Men. 1933.
A House and Its Head. 1935.
Daughters and Sons. 1937.
A Family and a Fortune. 1939.
Parents and Children. 1941.
Elders and Betters. 1944.
Manservant and Maidservant. 1947.
Two Worlds and Their Ways. 1949.
Darkness and Day. 1951.
The Present and the Past. 1953.
Mother and Son. 1955.
A Father and His Fate. 1957.
A Heritage and Its History. 1959.
The Mighty and Their Fall. 1961.
A God and His Gifts. 1963.
The Last and the First. 1971.
Collected Works. 1972.

E. M. DELAFIELD

1890–1943

EDMÉE MONICA DE LA PASTURE was born on June 9, 1890, the
eldest child of popular novelist and playwright Elizabeth Lydia
Rosabelle and Count Henry Philip Ducarel de la Pasture, a descendant
of French nobility. Edmée grew up in a bilingual household with a
series of French governesses providing her early education. From the
ages of 10 to 18, she attended various convent schools throughout
Europe, nourishing a recurrent desire to become a Catholic nun.

Two years after her father's death in 1908, Edmée's mother married Sir Hugh Conrad, an author and literary critic. But despite the
family's literary milieu, Edmée's mother was reportedly not supportive
of her daughter's early writing efforts, so, following her desires, Edmée
joined a French religious order in Belgium in 1911. She lasted barely
a year in the cloistered life of a postulant, though, and would later
write about the experience as suffocating and unendurable. After leaving the convent, Edmée changed her name to Elizabeth and focused
her energy on the ensuing war effort and on her writing.

From 1914 to 1917, she worked as a volunteer at the Exeter
Voluntary Aid Hospital and at a supply depot in Bristol. During this
time, she completed her first novel, *Zella Sees Herself* (1917), under the
name E. M. Delafield, a nom-de-plume concocted by her sister, Yoé.
The novel was a success and introduced many of the themes and elements that would reappear in future novels: Catholicism and conversion; marriage, divorce, and broken engagements; childrearing; and
detailed descriptions of attire. Her second novel, *The War-Workers*
(1918), drew upon personal wartime experience to create a satire on
patriotism, volunteerism, and bureaucratic inefficiency that captured
the mood of the country.

By the age of 29, when she married Major Arthur Paul Dashwood,
Delafield had published two more novels, *The Pelicans* (1919) and
Consequences (1919). The couple lived for the first few years of their
marriage in Malaysia, while Dashwood worked as an engineer build-
ing the causeway from Singapore to the mainland. They returned to
England in 1922 with their infant son, Lionel Paul; their second child,
Rosamund, was born in January 1924.

While Rosamund was still a toddler, Delafield was recruited as a
justice of the peace at Collampton, at the time a natural outgrowth of
her well-known interest in criminology. This interest would be mani-
fest in her book *Messalina of the Suburbs* (1924), which was based on the

famous murder case of Edith Thompson (a subject also taken up by fellow novelist F. Tennyson Jesse). Delafield was also active in local women's causes, serving as President of the Women's Institute, an advocate organization geared toward helping rural women.

By the 1930s, Delafield was publishing at least a novel a year, writing for a variety of periodicals, and building a career in radio broadcasting, both straight reporting and comedy. Weekly installments of *Diary of a Provincial Lady* began appearing in *Time and Tide*. Published in book form in 1930, it was immediately chosen by the Book Society as a Book-of-the-Month selection. Delafield would later recast the mainly autobiographical characters of the popular novel in three future "Provincial Lady" books. Only a memoir based on an extended visit to Russia, urged by her publisher, tarnished her career: *I Visit Soviet Russia* (1937) drew almost unanimously harsh criticism for being ill conceived.

Delafield wrote her last novel, *Late and Soon*, while in almost constant pain. It appeared in print eight months before her death on December 2, 1943.

CRITICAL EXTRACTS

J. W. KRUTCH

"The Optimist" pokes away with the rapier of accomplished irony at a terribly benign old Canon who is ever ready, like Strachey's Dr. Arnold, to rise and explain "the general principles both of his own conduct and that of the Almighty." ⟨. . .⟩ The arguments ⟨. . .⟩ seem irrefutable, but direct satire upon the ideas of the eighteen-eighties, though no doubt still a pleasant sport, is but slaying the slain. The best novels are written from a point of view but they do not consist simply in a definition of it, and though it may be that the point of view altered so greatly during the past forty years that there was a period during which definition was the writer's first duty, that time has passed. The outlines of iconoclastic modernism have been laid and the future lies before the novelist who, assuming these as a background, will create character against them. ⟨. . .⟩

Though Miss Delafield is still struggling a little with the delusion that it is worth while to demonstrate her superiority to the Victorians, she has, in her latest novel, pretty nearly reached a real maturity, and this maturity lies not in the keenness of her dialectic but in the realization that such keenness is not enough. She is a clever writer but she has achieved what few clever writers achieve; she has created a character. One begins her book with admiration for her finesse but without great enthusiasm, for she seems bent upon a much simpler thing—the analysis of an outworn point of view embodied in a puppet. She lays upon the table her Optimist, the self-righteous old Canon, and begins to work upon him with a terribly keen scalpel of satire, laying bare the pomposity of his thoughts and the devastating character of his benign tyranny over his children. It is skilfully done but it has been done before, and the main thesis "that the normal evolution of self-sacrifice is self-advertisement" is almost banal.

Then gradually a surprising thing happens. The Canon gets up from the table, as it were, and begins to live in his own right. Miss Delafield forgets the superiority of herself and her readers, and the pasteboard embodiment of fatuity becomes a creature of flesh and blood. No less grotesquely wrong than he was before, he becomes understandable, and as he feels and suffers in his own right, as the children, victims of his own personality, drop here and there into their various fates, he takes on a pathetic dignity. The Optimist finishes as he had begun, and when, upon his deathbed even, he repeats in his wilful blindness his favorite phrase, "all things work together for the good of those who love God," even the most skeptical of the characters is compelled to agree with the daughter who has sacrificed her life to him. "He is magnificent." Without any weakening of her contempt and without yielding in her insistence that all was well to the Canon only because he was determined to see it so, Miss Delafield has given the devil his due. She has made her Optimist a real person and not a straw man made to be kicked by the clever, and as a result it becomes a matter of complete indifference that her thesis is not new.

Her book is a lesson to all young novelists, a proof that to be modern does not necessarily mean to leave the real business of fiction in order to argue, but it can be studied again by her with even more profit than by others. She can see how perilously she has stood upon the edge and how from time to time she has stepped over into the region of complacent superiority. Does anyone ever doubt that Flaubert was superior to the provincial ideals of Madam Bovary? Yet he correctly assumes that it is not necessary for him to say so and, similarly, no sophisticated reader needs to have it proved to him again that Victorian optimism was shallow. Yet character, Victorian or Babylonian, is still interesting.

—J. W. Krutch, "Slaying the Slain," *The Nation* (20 December 1922): 695

ROBERT T. HULL

When "Zella Sees Herself" appeared in 1917, Miss Delafield was immediately acclaimed for those powers of witty and devastating portraiture with which to-day she is extensively associated. It is a misfortune, perhaps, that critics have too often expected her to preserve a similar vein throughout the score of novels written since that date. As a satirist Miss Delafield has eminent gifts, but she may be credited, on the evidence of more recent volumes, with the increasing realisation that among aspects of life meriting discussion, some, at any rate, scarcely invite treatment in satirical terms. She is, for that matter, too fine an artist to acquiesce in infinite repetition of an early success. To dissuade admirers from their irrational clamour for an endless sequence of novels designed simply to reproduce, with slight variations, the entertainment of "Zella," must have been a delicate task; yet Miss Delafield, while submitting her style and subject-matter to stricter discipline, has contrived not only to retain but vastly to enlarge her public.

"Zella," "The War-Workers" and, to some extent, "The Pelicans" are all illustrative of experiences common to those whose instinct for self-dramatisation, or insincere conformity to type, outruns not only discretion but intellectual honesty. Selecting theses so various as conversion to Roman Catholicism and the exploitation of feminine tendencies to revere personalities above abstract values, Miss Delafield postulates "What is Truth?" as a question to be answered in the light of disasters and exposures inseparable from attempts to shirk this vital (if not always agreeable) issue. She never falsifies conclusions to secure the dubious advantage of a "happy ending," but neither are we vexed with those totally negative findings which can banish so successfully every vestige of interest from the problem discussed. Her most derided characters are, as a rule, less bad than sorely exercised in consistent preservation of their self-appointed pose. Miss Delafield knows them sufficiently to admit cool pity for such foolishness even while stripping, with consummate skill, the masks which they struggle so vainly to retain.

If the caustic ridicule enlivening many pages in these and other early novels seems on occasion too carefully underlined, the apposite nature of Miss Delafield's shrewd commentaries upon human frailties invites little dispute. Her characters, as we are constantly reminded, often represent types to be scarified but, with few exceptions, the author further persuades us to their existence as living people. The reality of Mrs. Lloyd-Evans in "Zella," of Chairman Vivian in "The War-Workers" and Nina Severing in "The Pelicans" remains with us long after the book is closed. There may be at times excessive anxiety to reinforce dialogue by emphasis upon satirical implications quite evident to the reader; yet Miss Delafield's insight can reach beyond scorn to accurately placed sympathy, and at the great moments her touch is unerring. ⟨. . .⟩

⟨. . .⟩ Throughout nearly a dozen novels Miss Delafield had wittily exploited, often with success and always with variety, the limitless manifestations of human nature governed by egotism and unheroic self-deception. "The Chip and the Block" portrays with refreshing irony an author whose uncommon power to misinterpret his innate selfishness and unjustified conceit as subscriptions to a lofty ideal of self-sacrificing parenthood are at first dimly realised, and at the last eminently unshared, by his clearer-sighted children. "The Way Things Are," more abundant in lighter moments, centres round a woman whose agonised incompetence as a housewife is equalled only by her distraught refusal of opportunity to escape from a husband in whose affections she has long been supplanted by the morning newspaper. Both novels are strong in characteristic touches; but one can sense the author's sharpened ambition for less charted seas; and the departure when it occurs comes suddenly.

"Turn Back the Leaves" suggests at first reading a complete metamorphosis. We find in these pages a new serenity of style; suppression of emphasis and incidental commentary; and qualities of permanent dignity enhancing portraiture memorable, in any event, for fine perspective and sympathetic vision. True it is that the crucial *motif*—the despair of an old Roman Catholic family at the marriage of their daughter to a Protestant—echoes to some extent the preoccupation of earlier novels; but beyond this point similarity cannot be pressed. The dominant tragedy of Miss Delafield's theme demands that humour, though allowable at moments of relief, shall be strictly disciplined. Here ridicule has no place. Such unaccustomed control has caused one or two critics, looking for wit where none is intended, to speak of this book as "disappointing." Yet to accept Miss Delafield on the terms she proposes—the only terms artistically tolerable for her subject—is to appreciate how immeasurably she has advanced upon her former standards by an achievement of exceptional notability.

—Robert T. Hull, "E. M. Delafield as a Novelist," *The Bookman* (August 1932): 240–41

HENRY SEIDEL CANBY

Readers of the first "Diary of a Provincial Lady" will not be disappointed in this sequel. These apparently random and artless notes upon the difficulties in being literary in Devonshire with a family on your back, and upon the trials of playing up to a literary reputation amidst the professional sophistry of London, are not so artless and so random as they seem, although their informality is an excellent medium for the witty charm of the book. Miss Delafield has made a self-portrait here ⟨in *Further Diary of a Provincial Lady*⟩, and a family portrait, and a portrait of that strange assemblage which buzzes about a new literary reputation, which are indeed more evidence that she is one of the really skilful novelists of manners in our day. Why has she not had the resounding critical success which so many English women writers less excellent than she have grown great upon? Because, I think, of her unpretentiousness, the unpretentiousness of one who, like Jane Austen, seems to write easily upon her lap, while others talk and clamor about her. She is somewhat too ironic, too unsentimental, to get the reputation (which she deserves) of humorist, too delicate, too unpointed in her satire, to arouse fear or indignation, too much concerned with the humors of everyday manners as the best index of society, to interest the heavy-handed advocates of social changes. She illustrates the difficulties of belonging to the Jane Austen school in the nineteen thirties. Not that she is antiquarian, in spite of her delightful "A Good Man's Love," which was a tragedy worked out in iced wedding cake, or imitative. She is of our age and no other; belongs to the genteel tradition of which she makes fun, while rather loving it; dips into the milieu of platinum blondes or Bloomsbury sexualists with a delight in new experience, not for an instant losing her head; is aware of all the new ideas and new moralities abroad without ceasing to love her own people who, by turns, make novelties incongruous, and are made incongruous by them. Indeed, if anyone writing fiction is better equipped for the business of comedy, I do not know her name.

I would not overstate the case of Miss Delafield. That would be to commit the precise error of which she is never guilty. She will never be a great novelist. She will never be a serious novelist in terms of that seriousness approved by those whose concern is with the class war, or the sex struggle, or the depicting of new and unlovely types thrown up by democracy. She is an aristocratic writer, which does not mean that she is in love with the aristocracy, but does imply a certain delight in the trials and errors of civilized living quite apart from concern as to its philosophy or sociology. I think that her circle of readers will widen and that those she gets she will keep.

—Henry Seidel Canby, "Charm with Irony," *The Saturday Review of Literature* (14 January 1933): 376

MARGARET LAWRENCE

In *The Diary of a Provincial Lady* ⟨E. M. Delafield⟩ set the reading English world smiling about the funny slant of an ordinary woman's existence. She has written other stories which in their way are good pieces of experimental portraiture of women, but none of them has the ingenuous sparkle of the provincial lady's record of her affairs. She has no affairs. She has a husband who hides behind his newspapers when she wants to talk to him, and reaches for his hat when the question of more money for household expenses comes up. He is a nice husband, and does take an interest in the things that go on in his home. He is nice, too, about allowing his wife to write in her spare time, but he is only a man, and a woman has to have some outlet for her thoughts other than a man. The book is significant for all its slightness because it is possibly the first time a woman ever set down the doings of her day-to-day life in all their simplicity, and attached to them her own tentatively philosophical conclusions.

The writing might appear at first glance to be the writing of a helpmeet. Certainly it is the writing of a woman painting the situation of a helpmeet woman. Living in honorable matrimony with a man, rearing his children, attending to his house. But the sophisticated element raises its signs in the fact that she thinks her own thoughts as she goes through her days, and also in the fact that these thoughts happen to be amusing thoughts. She is under no psychological strain about the unfair emotional relationship between men and women. She is under no need to worship her man. But she wants to be entertaining. She must be entertaining. So she in her limited circumstance makes a fine story out of the irritating visits of the rector's wife, and the daily struggle with inadequate help in her own house. It is all a great game to her. The husband is varyingly attentive to the entertainment she provides. He reads his papers. He gives a snort or a grunt as the case may be, and he sees fit to be amused or disgusted, but the show goes on whether he applauds or not. He sticks and that is the main thing. He pays the bills, which is another thing, and it is up, therefore, to any lady to make it all seem extraordinarily interesting. Which is exactly what she does, and while she does it, she draws a picture of the life of an average couple together after the tense emotion of romance has died down and the long business of pulling together in harness has engrossed them to the exclusion of almost every other consideration. It is more to the point that there is enough cream in the house for the tea than that a woman have power to rouse all manner of fine feeling around her. It is more important for a man to be able to pay the coal bills than to have power to drive a woman to distraction over the stray thoughts he may be thinking. The helpmeet woman would be concerned about the subsiding of the feeling. She would be digging and prodding into the reactions of the man—"Are you happy?" "Do I satisfy you?"—the sophisticate is practical. She takes it for granted that the man is happy, and she sees to it that she does her part to satisfy him. This is the example without par of the sophisticated lady handling the prevailing matrimonial situation in complete normality. It is a lady of the ingénue type, playing her simple part with all its funny nuances, easy on the emotions, easy on the mind, gentle yet lively, full of fun, yet full of technical appreciation of every least little movement there is to be taken with it.

—Margaret Lawrence, *The School of Femininity* (New York: Frederick A. Stokes Company, 1936), 301–3

MICHAEL T. FLORINSKY

It was in the incongruous setting of an expensive London restaurant, one of those strongholds of capitalism where caviar and champagne add greatly to the logical force and persuasiveness of any argument, that the suggestion of spending six months on a Soviet collective farm and of writing "a funny book about it" was first made to Miss Delafield. Her experience, demonstrating as it does the danger of meeting an enterprising American publisher in such a setting, should serve as a warning to her fellow-novelists. Little interested in Russia, knowing nothing about farming and with no desire to visit the land of the Soviet, she nevertheless gave in, reluctantly accepted the offer of her publisher, boarded a Soviet steamer and spent several months in Russia.

Her path was strewn with difficulties. Miss Delafield had no liking for communism and her hastily acquired knowledge of the Russian language was necessarily inadequate and of limited usefulness. She soon discovered that she was not wanted on a collective farm and was repeatedly told that her request to join one could not be granted. Fortunately for her, the Soviet Union is a country where the impossible sometimes happens. Contrary to the most authoritative opinions and just as her hope of becoming a Soviet worker seemed doomed to failure, Miss Delafield received through rather devious channels gracious permission to visit the Seattle Agricultural Commune and to stay there as long as she pleased. The experience proved highly instructive if not exactly enjoyable. ⟨. . .⟩

In spite of the obstacles, both external and psychological, Miss Delafield has produced a book that is not only informing and brilliantly written but also highly amusing. The "humorous slant" is provided by vivid sketches of the highly diversified types of people she came across during her visit to the Soviets. Her pen pictures, though seldom flattering, are never hostile and they give the impression of being remarkably true to type. It is difficult not to feel a certain sympathy for the conscientious and pathetic efforts of the youthful, carefully selected and carefully trained Intourist guides whose unenviable duty it is to persuade the miscellaneous collection of tourists from many lands that the Soviet Union is the only country worth living in; youths whose unshakable belief it is that not even sunshine, a blue sky or other beauties of nature are to be found outside the frontiers of the Communist State. The crudeness that is typical of Soviet policies is conspicuous in the manner in which the Intourist handles its voluntary victims, the motley crowds of international seekers after truth. Miss Delafield is at her best when she portrays the reactions of her bewildered fellow-travelers to Soviet conditions and to the orgy of Soviet propaganda. Some of her pages, with their underlying element of deep tragedy, are tinged with a delicate irony reminiscent of Chekhov.

Miss Delafield says that she had no intention to "emulate the Webbs," a decision on which she is to be warmly congratulated. If her impressions are frankly pessimistic, the fault is most certainly not entirely her own.

—Michael T. Florinsky, "E. M. Delafield's Visit to Russia," *The New York Times Book Review* (21 February 1937): 9

MARGARET B. MCDOWELL

In the preface to the crime novel *Messalina of the Suburbs*, Delafield explains that, because she believes "causes are more interesting than the most dramatic results," she has tried to "reconstruct the psychological developments that led, by inexorable degrees, to the catastrophe of murder." She addresses what she terms the "real issue" rather than the "sensational accessories." The real issue is to be found on that plane of thought where personalities are dissected, the only plane where true understanding of a murder case can emerge. Delafield calls the novel "my story about Elsie Palmer," and for this book the significance of the murder lies in its revelation of Elsie as an ordinary young woman with extraordinarily limited vision, hope, and imagination. The cause of the murder is not passion but complete lack of passion—a matter overlooked in newspaper coverage of the crime and trial. ⟨. . .⟩

The strength of this novel lies in Delafield's ability to counter sensational newspaper depictions of the accused murderess with a convincing portrayal of Elsie and her family as prosaic working-class people. Rather than showing what makes a murderess different from other people, Delafield concentrates on that which is common (and commonplace) in Elsie and in the other people in her life. The woman, dull in all respects, gradually intrigues the reader, because her ordinary characteristics suggest that murder can take place among people the reader might know.

Messalina of the Suburbs attests to the speed with which Delafield conceived and produced her novels: Percy Thompson (the model for Delafield's Williams) was killed on 5 October 1922, and Edith Thompson and her lover Frederick Bywaters were executed for complicity in his murder on 6 January 1923. Delafield had her book based on the case prepared for publication by August 1923.

Although the dry precision of much of Delafield's satire and her interest in the comedy of manners make many of her characters stylized rather than deeply developed psychologically, she presents the social conditions surrounding them and their institutions without evasion or hypocrisy. Delafield was an incisive interpreter of British life in the 1920s and 1930s and a shrewd and thoughtful analyst of the people she created in her fiction. One nearly always feels, as an anonymous reviewer for the *Times Literary Supplement* said of

Delafield's early books, that after reading a few pages "you are deep in realities, gripped by living people."

—Margaret B. McDowell, "E. M. Delafield," *Dictionary of Literary Biography*, vl. 34. *British Novelists, 1890–1929: Traditionalists*, ed. Thomas F. Staley (Detroit: Gale Research Company, 1985), 94–97

Nicola Beauman

"It dawned upon her dimly that only by envisaging and accepting her own limitations, could she endure the limitations of her surroundings." The last sentence of *The Way Things Are* (1927) is, like the title, pure E. M. Delafield. It is
weary, accepting, ironic, yet contains the undertone of tragedy that is the hall-
mark of all her books. It conveys the realism and detachment necessary to an
impassioned feminist statement (albeit one that few feminists would recognise). And it is perfectly judged in the way it mixes the lightly amusing read
demanded by the lending libraries with a statement about the female condition that is so crushing in its implications as to be almost unbearable. ⟨. . .⟩

This is E.M.D.'s funniest novel, its first few chapters bearing comparison
with the work of Jerome, the Grossmiths, E.F. Benson, Evelyn Waugh,
P.G. Wodehouse and Nancy Mitford. But because it has a darker side it has suffered the fate of any other novel that defies easy labelling: the reading public
likes to be told if a novel is funny/problem/social comedy and so on, and tends
to forget about those which lie outside an obvious category.

Hence the greater success of the book for which *The Way Things Are* was
the inspiration, and which remains its author's best known: *The Diary of a
Provincial Lady* (1930).

⟨. . . The⟩ diary form, for stylistic reasons, can (in the hands of E.M.D.) be
consistently funny. Consider the following passage:

> Robert startles me at breakfast by asking if my cold—which he has
> hitherto ignored—is better. I reply that it has gone. Then why, he
> asks, do I look like that? Refrain from asking like what, as I know
> only too well. Feel that life is wholly unendurable, and decide madly
> to get a new hat.

If this was transposed into the third person with the narrator "reading" the
provincial lady's thoughts, this would be a rather more ordinary, self-pitying
married exchange.

Even written from the narrator's point of view, however, *The Way Things Are*
is a very funny book, and many people prefer it to any of E.M.D.'s other works
because of the variety of themes underlying the humour; it has always been
my favourite out of the forty or so titles. "Unbrokenly hilarious" was the opin-

ion of the witty and perceptive reviewer in *The Times Literary Supplement*, who added, "we may feel that to laugh at Laura all through three hundred pages of what is torment for her is cruel; but there is no keeping a straight face". Then comes the nub. Is laughter compatible with realism, asks the reviewer, i.e., does the novel fit into a category?

> So rippled with enjoyment, in fact, is the surface of this sardonic narrative, that one cannot at times help feeling that despite the almost hallucinatory naturalism of the dialogue, this world is not—worse luck—the world we encounter.

But to thousands and thousands of middle-class married women with children this world is indeed the one we encounter. (Whether this novel is one that can be appreciated by readers outside this group is a question I cannot answer.) The details may have changed, but there are enough timeless qualities to make the insights quite as relevant as they were sixty years ago. Any woman who has found herself in a domestic situation from which, for reasons of love, loyalty, convention or finance, she cannot escape, will identify with the heroine; and most will sympathise with her acceptance of "the way things are".

—Nicola Beauman, "Introduction" to *The Way Things Are* by E. M. Delafield (New York: Penguin Books, 1988), v–viii

VIOLET POWELL

A Messalina of the Suburbs, the only novel of Elizabeth's to deal with an actual murder, was finished at Dawlish in 1923. The dedication to 'M.P.P.(Margaret)' is dated August 1923, so the move to Croyle, Elizabeth being five months' pregnant with Rosamund, must have followed immediately. The dedicatee was Doctor Margaret Posthuma, a psychiatrist, with whom Elizabeth enjoyed discussing all ideas that sprang from the perversity of the human mind. Doctor Posthuma was eventually responsible for bringing Elizabeth together with Cicely McCall, whose liveliness endeared her to the whole family and who became a cherished visitor to Croyle.

The plot of *A Messalina of the Suburbs* would have been familiar to every reader of newspapers, being undisguisably based on a famous murder case. The book's dénouement, the death by hanging of the heroine, had, in real life, been a matter of fierce debate among those for or against capital punishment. To recapitulate the foundation of the novel, Mr Thompson had been murdered by his wife Ethel's lover, a merchant seaman of the name of Bywaters. In the subsequent trial, which rocked the country, Mrs Thompson was tried as an accomplice of Bywaters, although when her lover attacked her husband she was certainly shocked and astonished. Her protests at the moment of the murder did not outweigh the letters she had written to Bywaters, describing the failure of attempts she had made to poison her husband. The jury did not believe that the letters were fantasies designed to keep Bywaters's interest in their affair from fading. Mrs Thompson and Bywaters were hanged in 1923, both declaring to the last that she was innocent of the crime.

Elizabeth was certainly not alone in finding the psychological aspects of the tragedy to be fascinating, but she was first in the field to use the tragedy as the foundation of a novel. Ten years later F. Tennyson Jesse, Elizabeth's earliest promoter at Heinemann, availed herself of the same tale of pity and terror with an increasing success. *A Pin to See a Peepshow* not only did well in dramatic form, but, nearly half a century later, became an admired television serial.

Although Elizabeth is never very clear as to which areas of London she considered to be suburban, her ingenuity makes *A Messalina of the Suburbs* a remarkable study of lower middle-class life at its most sordid. Elsie, the Messalina/Mrs Thompson, is seduced by the father of the family in which she works (to use today's idiom) as an au pair. The squalor of the seduction scene is illuminated by flashes of Gothic phosphorescence, and is as sexually explicit as the laws and reticences of the period would allow. Elsie's career then follows the pattern of a disagreeable marriage, and a lover over whom her hold is precarious. Unlike the climax of F. Tennyson Jesse's novel, Elizabeth did not, as it were, escort a woman convicted of murder to the scaffold. Elsie is last seen realizing that she is about to enter a tunnel at the end of which there is nothing but an inescapable drop.

—Violet Powell, *The Life of a Provincial Lady: A Study of E. M. Delafield and Her Works* (London: William Heinemann Ltd., 1988), 57–58

BIBLIOGRAPHY

Zella Sees Herself. 1917.
The War-Workers. 1918.
The Pelicans. 1919.
Consequences. 1919.
Tension. 1920.
The Heel of Achilles. 1921.
Humbug: A Study in Education. 1921.
The Optimist. 1922.
A Reversion to Type. 1923.

Messalina of the Suburbs. 1924.

Mrs. Harter. 1924.

The Chip and the Block. 1925.

Jill. 1926.

The Entertainment and Other Stories. 1927.

The Way Things Are. 1927.

The Suburban Young Man. 1928.

What Is Love? 1928.

Turn Back the Leaves. 1930.

Diary of a Provincial Lady. 1930.

Women Are Like That. 1930.

Challenge to Clarissa. 1931.

To See Ourselves: A Domestic Comedy in Three Acts. 1931.

Thank Heaven Fasting. 1932.

The Provincial Lady Goes Further. 1932.

The Time and Tide Album. 1932.

Gay Life. 1933.

General Impressions. 1933.

The Glass Wall. 1933.

The Provincial Lady in America. 1934.

The Bazalgettes (published anonymously). 1935.

The Brontës: Their Lives Recorded by Their Contemporaries (editor). 1935.

As Others Hear Us: A Miscellany. 1937.

Straw Without Bricks: I Visit Soviet Russia. 1937.

When Women Love. 1938.

Love Has No Resurrection, and Other Stories. 1939.

The Provincial Lady in Wartime. 1940.

No One Now Will Know. 1941.

Late and Soon. 1943.

DAPHNE DU MAURIER

1907–1989

DAPHNE DU MAURIER was born in London on May 13, 1907, to actress Muriel and actor/manager Gerald du Maurier. Her early education was handled by an unconventional governess, who was stolid but nurtured Daphne's love of literature. At 14, she wrote a book because it was "great fun." *The Seekers*, though juvenile, impressively recasts the young writer's teenage angst through the character of a male protagonist.

In 1925 Daphne was sent to study at a school in Camposena, a village outside Paris. By graduation, her family had moved to an estate in Cornwall, a region du Maurier drew inspiration from for many of her books. For the next several years she worked on numerous short stories and blank verse plays, starting work in 1929 on her first novel, *The Loving Spirit* (1931). Two more novels quickly followed. With their publication, she realized the legacy of her grandfather, the popular 19th-century novelist George du Maurier.

In 1931, Daphne du Maurier met Frederick A. M. Browning, a major in the Grenadier Guards. Their meeting was akin to a turn in one of the author's own romances. Browning, so entranced by Cornwall as du Maurier describes the region in *The Loving Spirit*, went there to visit and sought out the author a year later. The couple fell in love, married on July 19, 1932, and would have three children.

The 1936 publication of *Jamaica Inn*, about a hostelry in Cornwall, launched du Maurier's first commercial success: it sold more throughout England than her first three books combined. While stationed with her husband in Alexandria, Egypt, du Maurier became intrigued by the idea of writing a "psychological and rather macabre" novel. *Rebecca*, published in 1938, became a best-seller; Alfred Hitchcock's film version won an Academy Award for Best Picture. Hitchcock made two other films based on du Maurier stories, *Jamaica Inn* (1936) and "The Birds" (1952). The films greatly widened her readership both in England and the United States.

In 1943 du Maurier moved to an estate in Cornwall, Menabilly, where most of her other novels were written. Attracting legions of fans, she successfully integrated mystery, suspense, melodrama, and history in numerous best-selling novels. In addition to tales of intrigue and romance, du Maurier also documented her family history in two biographical works, *Gerald* (1934) and *The du Mauriers* (1937); completed several studies of Sir Francis Bacon; and wrote an autobiography.

Her husband's death in 1965 left du Maurier devastated. Four years later (when she was also named a Dame Commander of the British Empire), she moved to Par, a neighboring town in Cornwall. There she lived and wrote until her death on April 19, 1989.

CRITICAL   EXTRACTS

MARGARET LAWRENCE

When the women writers set out to portray men they also have to isolate them. Daphne du Maurier, who has drawn the most convincing portrait of a man as yet attempted by a woman, had to isolate her subject.

The Progress of Julius is her third book to be published.

She ⟨. . .⟩ has put aside the defiance of her generation. That is, her technical form shows a mind which is content to find freedom within conformity. Her prose is even and conventional. The subject of her first book, *The Loving Spirit*, was the traditional subject of feminine literary endeavor, the abiding love of women for their men. Her second book, *I'll Never Be Young Again*, was the study of the development of the temperament of the out-and-out *amoureuse* in a young girl. ⟨. . .⟩ She left the subject and passed on to something no woman had ever altogether accomplished, the portrait of a man. *The Progress of Julius* placed her in the ranks of the virile few.

She told the story simply. She threw off all the clouded experimentation of her contemporaries. She did no dallying with the stream of consciousness. She took Julius from the sternly objective view. He was a man who made himself a force in the commercial world with strict conservation of his emotions and by a strict concentration upon one idea. She began with his childhood and his background. He was a blend of peasant French and Algerian Jew. He was a small child during the siege of Paris by the Germans. His French peasant grandparents taught him to bargain. He witnessed his mother's infidelity and his father's anguish. It gave him a low opinion of women. He saw his father murder his mother. He saw it unmoved, believing that she deserved it, as did every unfaithful woman. He was an Oriental. But he decided that no woman would ever rouse him to such a pitch of emotion. All his ardor went into building himself a fortune. He got to England. He built the fortune. He played with women; he bullied them; his treatment of them paid off the consistent subconscious desire for revenge upon the mother image in himself. He loved no woman until he came to love his own daughter. His love of her paid off all the stored-up accounts of his own emotional starvation. When she told him she was going to marry a man, unreasoningly he considered it infidelity to him, and murdered her. Thus was the line of his fate fulfilled.

It is the work of a mind which courageously has brought itself to realize the impossibility of dealing with emotion. It is a sincere and serious admission. It defies all the nonchalance of the rebellious generation which naïvely believed that the only damage came from repression, and proceeded to toss over all the repressions. It defies also the doctrine of the diversion of emotion into the profitable economy of personal career. It carefully avoids the inconsequential though tantalizing foibles of emotion differentiating between the male and female expression of it. The mind of this young Du Maurier accepts emotion as a great implacable mystery taking possession of men and women in one way or another, at some time or another, as something that comes down upon them and throws them from experience to experience. A power like wind and rain and the heat of the sun. Not to be placated. But maybe to be worshiped. Certainly to be endured with fatalistic submission. What she says with clear young courage the psychiatrists are also saying. And wondering if worship in religion or in romance is the key to the answer. If emotion comes down upon the life with religion, the spirit is steadied by contact with the vast body of faith before it and around it. This is the blessing of religion. If emotion comes down upon the life with romance, the spirit is steadied by its own heroism. It sees itself as part of the great story. It pursues its story bravely and beautifully, literally drinking the cup to its dregs. Religion and romance give their own peace, and the votaries of both know ease with themselves. They have not said to emotion, "Do this," or, "Do that"; they have said, "I follow."

The Progress of Julius is technically magnificent.

It rises from its beginning to its culmination with simplicity that is Greek in its austerity and modern in its power.

—Margaret Lawrence, *The School of Femininity* (New York: Frederick A. Stokes Company, 1936), 179–82

J. D. BERESFORD

Rebecca is a book temptingly easy to criticise or to praise. It will unquestionably be popular, a book to be read on holiday or at any other time. After the rather too highly coloured first chapter, which with the beginning of the second might more fitly have come at the end instead of the beginning, the story is one that will abstract the attention from the most insistent surroundings, a crowded beach or an hotel lounge. I am not ashamed to say that it held me so powerfully that I grudged all interruptions until it was finished.

Nevertheless, if I am to be honest in criticism, I must not let my enthusiasm forbid any reference to the faults of which I was actually conscious in reading. Of the other faults I recognise now, nearly a week later, I will say nothing. They represent the chilly business of purely literary criticism. But even at the moments of deepest absorption I was a little irritated by my consciousness that two of the characters were overdrawn. The first of them is Mrs. Danvers, the housekeeper of the lovely house in the West Country, known tout court as Manderley, in which the greater part of the action is played out. All I have to say of Mrs. Danvers is that she is like a character of one of Le Fanu's most bizarre novels, a creature of the novelist's imagination. The other is Jack Favell, who is consistently more caddish than any man ought to be, even in fiction. These two people momentarily disturbed my sense of reality in reading, as did also the "cold dank fog" that came up from the sea on the wrong kind of day at the wrong time of year and endured just long enough to serve the author's rather too evident purpose.

But, having entered a note of these reactions, I can now praise *Rebecca* without stint. ⟨. . .⟩

I have no intention of spoiling the reader's pleasure in the book by revealing the plot. It is sufficient to suggest that our girlish heroine, so deeply in love with her middle-aged husband, so painfully conscious of her own gaucherie and ignorance in that world still overpoweringly redolent of the beauty and efficiency of the dead Rebecca, emerges at a stroke from her oppression by that powerful ghost not by any forcing of the circumstances or action but by a sudden revelation of what is, in effect, the inevitable truth, which explains, as truth must, without any distortion of the facts. And, as a last word, I must add that the actual writing of the book has the compelling quality that holds the attention in thrall, keeping our interest unintermittently rapt in the story.

—J. D. Beresford, "Two Novels for the Holiday," *Manchester Guardian* (5 August 1938): 5

JOHN RAYMOND

In the 'thirties Miss du Maurier was a kind of poor woman's Charlotte Brontë. Her *Rebecca*, whatever one's opinions of its ultimate merits, was a *tour de force*. In its own way and century, it has achieved a position in English Literature comparable to "Monk" Lewis's *The Bleeding Nun* or Mrs. Radcliffe's *Mysteries of Udolpho*. To-day Miss du Maurier the novelist is Miss Blurb's favourite Old Girl whose published appearances are heralded with the brouhaha of a privileged ex-hockey captain come down to give the home team a few hints about attack. This, one imagines her telling newcomers to St. Gollancz's, is how it should be done. Frankly, I cannot help feeling that Miss du Maurier's books have been successfully filmed so often that by now she may be said not so much to write a novel as shoot it. The present scenario ⟨*My Cousin Rachel*⟩ is a honey for any Hollywood or Wardour Street tycoon. Slick, effective, utterly mechanical, the book is a triumphant and uncanny example of the way in which a piece of writing can be emasculated by unconsciously "having it arranged" for another medium. Close-ups, fade-ins, sequences by candlelight or long shots from the terrace—it has all been taken care of in the script and there is little call for anything in the way of imagination on the part of the director. One can hear the Technicolor cameras turning happily on page 59:

> The waggonettes were silhouetted on the further hill, and the waiting horses and the moving figures black dots on the skyline. The shocks of corn were golden in the last rays of the sun. The sea was very blue, almost purple where it covered the rocks, and had that deep full look about it that always comes with the flood tide. The fishing fleet had put out and were standing eastward to catch the shore breeze. Back at home the house was in shadow now, only the weather-vane on the top of the clock-tower catching a loose shaft of light.

The recipe is a simple but golden one. Time (vaguely Regency), place (Cornish Riviera) and Theme (the Wicked Lady) have all been unerringly chosen. The cast—Siren, Siren's lover, Hero-narrator, Hero-narrator's cousin, Nice Girl, Nice Girl's Father, Family Butler, Family Butler's Stooge—loom up appealingly at us out of *Spotlight*. Producers, admiring the general effect, will forgive such occasional anachronisms, as "forget it," "slapped my bottom with a hair-brush," and "Why not tell these gossips I'm a recluse and spend all my spare time scribbling Latin verses? That might shake them." Boyish sulks, mares in a lather, and a lot of old lace at the throat and wrist, eked out with constant cups of poisoned tisane, complete the formula. A rare and irresistible bit of *kitsch*, whose clichés will soon be jostling and clashing in merry carillons up and down the premier cinema circuits of the English-speaking world.
—John Raymond, "New Novels," *New Statesman and Nation* (11 August 1951): 163

Sylvia Berkman

Daphne du Maurier is a specialist in horror. Her creative intelligence is resourceful, her command of eerie atmosphere persuasive and precise, her sense of shock-timing exceptionally skilled. In this collection of eight stories ⟨*Kiss Me Again, Stranger*⟩ (of which all but two are very long) she explores horror in a variety of forms; in the macabre, in the psychologically deranged, in the supernatural, in the fantastic, most painfully of all, in the sheer cruelty of human beings in interrelationship. Yet on the whole the volume offers absorbing rather than oppressive reading because chiefly one's intellect is engaged: the emotional content remains subordinate. Broadly speaking, for the most part these are stories of detection as well, with the contributing elements of excitation, suspense, and climax manipulated with a seasoned hand.

Miss du Maurier is most successful, I believe (as most of us are), when her intentions are unmixed. "Kiss Me Again, Stranger," the title story, adeptly marshals the ingredients best suited to her abilities. Here in a trim, fluently moving narrative she developed an incident in war-torn London, with no purpose beyond the immediate recounting of a sad and grisly tale. A young mechanic, a simple, sensitive, likable good chap, attracted by a pretty usherette at a cinema palace, joins her on her bus ride home, to be led, bewildered, into a cemetery, where her conduct baffles him, to say the least. The girl, so gentle, wistful, languorous, and sleepy, turns out to be psychopathically obsessed, with a vindictive animus against members of the R.A.F. The summary is unjust, for Miss du Maurier forcibly anchors her story in a strange lonely graveyard atmosphere, with night rain falling cold and dreary on the flat tombs, which both reflects and reinforces the mortal impairment of the young girl's nature and the destruction of the young man's hopes, in a charnel world dislocated by the larger horror of war.

In "Kiss Me Again, Stranger," all separate aspects of the narrative fuse. "The Birds," however, essentially a far more powerful story, is marred by unresolved duality of intent. Slowly, with intensifying accurate detail, Miss du Maurier builds up her account of the massed attack of the starving winter birds on humankind, the familiar little land birds, the battalions of gulls bearing in rank upon rank from the sea, the murderous predatory birds of prey descending with ferocious beaks and talons to rip, rend, batter, and kill. The struggle involved is the ancient struggle of man against the forces of nature, Robinson Crusoe's struggle to overcome an elemental diversity through cunning, logic, and wit. The turning of this material also into a political fable, with overt references to control from Russia and aid from America, to my mind dissipates the full impact of a stark and terrifying tale. ⟨. . .⟩

Miss du Maurier is not primarily concerned with character. Her figures are presented with swift unhesitating strokes; through them a fairly complicated history unfolds. Yet every account of human action contains its residue of human experience; and Miss du Maurier's main themes, if seriously regarded, are neither haphazard nor trivial: again and again she returns to the consideration of our human predicament, to frustration, destruction, loss, betrayal, and needless suffering, Joyce's themes of the *Dubliners*, conveyed through the obverse method of a decided emphasis on plot. In general in this volume complexities of plot disinfect horror to a pungent and provocative spice.

—Sylvia Berkman, "A Skilled Hand Weaves a Net of Horror," *New York Herald Tribune Book Review* (15 March 1953): 4

LaTourette Stockwell

Daphne Du Maurier is one of the most widely read of contemporary novelists, but rarely, and then only in reviews, have her writings been responsibly considered by serious critics.

How does it happen that an author who labors so diligently and well as to be irresistible to millions of readers in at least seven countries is ignored by the literary critics? What do her readers find so satisfying? Why do the critics turn away? If these questions are explored and answered it may be possible not only to assess fairly Miss Du Maurier's considerable literary effort but also to arrive at some conclusions about contemporary taste and the difference between a popular novel and an important one. 〈. . .〉

E. M. Forster, some years ago, characterized one type of novel reader (*not* the kind he admires) as saying, "What does a novel do? Why tell a story of course, and I've no use for it if it didn't. Very bad taste on my part no doubt, but I like a story. You can take your art, you can take your literature, you can take your music, but give me a good story. And I like the story to be a story, mind, and my wife's the same."

Liking a good story has been a characteristic of the human race for some time, and Mr. Forster's man epitomizes the attitude of the "common reader," of whom there are many more today than there have ever been. Miss Du Maurier is a masterly teller of stories, and, in all fairness, it must be said that it is unlikely that her main purpose has been anything more than to entertain. At her best, she entertains superbly. Her facility as a raconteuse, her skill in building up dramatic suspense, the fertility of her invention in creating characters who live adventurously and love unconventionally (but never with shoddy eroticism), all these appeal overwhelmingly to the average reader looking for a temporary escape from the perils of this mortal life.

But art goes beyond the immediate interest and satisfaction of the uncritical reader. Virtuosity and literary technique alone cannot produce a work of art. If a novel is to possess even the intimations of immortality, there must be a relationship between literature and ideas, between literature and society. Convictions must be shaken, emotions disturbed. It is here that Miss Du Maurier fails, and the critics walk out. In indulging her predilection for creating an escape world for her readers, she has set a serious limitation upon her talents, and it is positively exasperating to have to conclude that an author who writes as well as Miss Du Maurier does has yet to produce an important novel.

—LaTourette Stockwell, "Best Sellers and the Critics: A Case History," *College English* 16, no. 4 (January 1955): 214, 221

ROGER BROMLEY

First published in 1938, at a time ⟨. . .⟩ when capitalist society was experiencing one of the deepest crises in its history, Daphne du Maurier's *Rebecca* at first sight seems remarkable for its total lack of reference to anything that might even hint of the existence of that crisis. The simplest way of accounting for this lack of reference would be to consign the text to the category of 'escapist fiction', a means of relief for people whose everyday experience was dominated by the reality of the depression. Another response would be to describe the text as likely to be read by those upon whom the realities of unemployment and deprivation would be likely to have had little impact. It is very difficult, at this distance in time, to reconstruct a map of the possible readership of the novel, but that it was an immediate bestseller indicates that it is improbable that a simple pattern of readership along class lines could be produced. This would certainly be even more improbable for an analysis of the cinema audiences that saw the film version in 1941. ⟨. . .⟩

As surface explanations these accounts might seem adequate, but a cultural analysis of *Rebecca* ⟨. . .⟩ argues for a reading of the text that sees its apparent absences as determining presences at the level of its deep structures. In other words, *Rebecca* can be read as a response to the crisis of the 1930s, if it is seen in the broader context of the various means sought to resolve what was not only an economic crisis but also a crisis in hegemony. ⟨. . .⟩

In bourgeois ideology, woman's sexuality and reproduction have to be incorporated in the sphere of the family which, in turn, becomes the repository of emotions, of sexuality, physical well-being, and the space for situating the free choice of a unique beloved. ⟨. . .⟩ In *Rebecca's* extensive crisis of self and family, Maxim's emotional distress, physical ill-health, absence of affection, and his 'possession' by Rebecca all thwart the fulfilment of the bourgeois ideals. The terror and neurosis experienced by the heroine at Manderley reproduce his experience crisis, which can only be resolved in mutuality and exile from Manderley. Their original return to Manderley could be structurally related to a desire in the thirties for a return along the road back to 1913, the gold standard, free trade, laissez-faire, etc. This was an economically nostalgic solution to 1931 and the crisis, as was their attempt to return to a pre-bourgeois Manderley in which the heroine sought to reproduce the image and style of Rebecca. Both actions were doomed, and could only persist at a distance and in retrospect as a cultural memory and image of an *idea* of a golden age: socially marked by grace, beauty, and an edenic landscape; economically, by free trade, a non-interventionist stage, the gold standard, etc.

The heroine grows as Rebecca recedes, as she expels her shadow self, the image within. The text ritually sheds the 'perverted' woman, Eve incarnate, the spoiler of the paradisal estate, to which there is no going back. It is important that Rebecca's body is recovered from the sea, because until that time her spirit cannot be laid. Her significantly decomposed *body* (vessel of life for woman and, in this instance, the agency of carnality) is buried in the family vault. This burial marks not just her displacement by the heroine (the truly spiritual woman, though materially poor and of 'humble' origin) but it denotes the burying of a model of family also. The seemingly spiritual woman is revealed as grossly carnal, and the recovery of her body prefigures the guarantee of the real aristocratic legacy, its persistence as an *idea*, or a codification of a set of ideas, which have no practical function but serve the ruling bloc as a series of fundamental principles, general truths, and rules of conduct (maxims, in other words!) manifested above all in style—'gestures which reveal quintessences'— and, at a local level, in the private co-existence of an exclusive, bourgeois-styled relationship enjoyed in exile by Mr. and Mrs. de Winter, sustained by a cultural memory. ⟨. . .⟩

Maxim loses his country house (a reference to a specific historical reality recognised by the text) and gives up many of the functions, political and social, consequent upon its ownership, for a personal life relatively confined and austere, and in some ways rootless. What he recovers and retains, through the fusion and assimilation of his 'lowly' second wife, is a transfusion of ideals and values, and a *style* with an important ideological function, that of the gentleman, signed by a morality of fair play, selflessness, courage, moderation and self-control, independence and responsibility. All of which can be summed up by the word *authority*, commanding deference. This authority is something which, incidentally, is bestowed upon the narrative by the nature of its being a personal testament (the ultimate reference in a liberal ideology): an 'I' for the truth, commanding acquiescence in its veracity. The text, therefore, has an authoritative structure as well as being about authority.

—Roger Bromley, "The Gentry, Bourgeois Hegemony and Popular Fiction," *Literature and History* 7, no. 2 (Autumn 1981): 166, 172–73, 176

RICHARD MICHAEL KELLY

The Loving Spirit is based upon du Maurier's obsession with the various generations of the Slade family she came to know and study in Cornwall. The novel combines her interest in the past, in Cornwall, in the sea, and in the theme that the power of love transcends one's mortality. The story is set in Plyn, Cornwall. The heroine, Janet Coombe, the source of the loving spirit, is depicted as a female Byronic hero. We first see her standing alone, observing the small world beneath her feet: "Janet Coombe stood on the hill above Plyn, looking down upon the harbour." Du Maurier quickly establishes Janet's romantic, aloof, contemplative, melancholy, and restless nature. "There was a freedom here belonging not to Plyn" (3), she writes.

The novel's central theme is that love must be free to grow despite the shackles that society, with its conventions and codes, threatens to impose upon the individual. The threat to Janet's sense of freedom in this instance is her forthcoming marriage to her cousin Thomas. The duality within du Maurier herself—her desire for adventure and freedom on the one hand, and her longing for love and security on the other—is reflected in her young heroine: "it seemed that there were two sides of her; one that wanted to be the wife of a man, and to care for him and to love him tenderly, and one that asked only to be part of a ship, part of the seas and the sky above, with the glad free ways of a gull" (8). It is as if du Maurier embodies two conflicting characters: her mother's and her father's, the former calling for conventional domesticity and the latter seeking some indefinable idea. This theme of the double appears many times throughout du Maurier's subsequent novels and becomes a central feature of her romantic fantasies. ⟨. . .⟩

The psychology of this novel is interesting and paradoxical. On the one hand, it seems to assert that a woman should be free from the encumbrances of domestic life and that she must become like a man in order to realize her potential for adventure. The inner debate over this issue is never clearly resolved in the person of Janet Coombe. She rebels at the notion of becoming a conventional wife, but, at the same time, when her son Joseph is born, she focuses all of her maternal and erotic energies upon him. She acquires a certain kind of freedom after she dies and becomes the spirit within the figurehead that directs the lives of later generations, but this is a far fetched and unconvincing solution to one woman's problems.

Jennifer Coombe, on the other hand, although somewhat unconventional as a child, grows up to be a stereotypical mother. Unlike her ancestors who were possessed by the restless Byronic spirit of Janet, she becomes a happy housewife who insists that the most important thing in life is that she and her husband love one another and share the delightful presence of their baby. This hardly sounds like Janet Coombe, a woman possessed by the mystery and adventure of the sea, who longed always to be by herself with her dreams, who possessed her son and ignored her husband.

The novel is thematically flawed in its confused treatment of the idea of freedom and rebellion. By the end of the book the powerful figure of Janet Coombe is reduced to that of a fire alarm that sends John on a rescue mission. The key to Janet Coombe lies in du Maurier's own chameleonlike personality. Like Janet she harbors the overwhelming need of a teenager to rebel against her parents, to assert her independence, to be alone with her dreams of Cornwall, her dreams of writing books, and her visions of the perfect lover—a composite of paternal, sexual, and filial love.

—Richard Michael Kelly, *Daphne du Maurier* (Boston: Twayne Publishers, 1987), 28–29, 32–33

MARGARET FORSTER

⟨Daphne du Maurier's⟩ writing career, properly beginning in 1931 with the publication of *The Loving Spirit*, and effectively ending in 1977, spanned a time of great change in literary fashions and tastes and in the growth and importance of women's fiction. For a while, Daphne was flowing with the tide, but after the publication of *The Scapegoat* in 1957 her kind of novel, as she herself realized, was no longer in sympathy with the trend towards the realistic fiction she hated. She had it in her to change and produce something different but not the desire: she wanted to stay true to an older tradition. Her writing self, that 'No. 2' which caused her so much trouble, demanded escapism, not reality, and it was only obliquely, and especially in her short stories, that she was able to give expression to it. This distinction—between her living self and her writing self, between the person she was on the outside and the quite different person she knew herself to be on the inside—was one she herself made repeatedly. When she was able to balance the two selves, she was happy, as she was in the thirties, but when the two separated, as they began to do towards the end of the fifties, she was miserable, and the strain of juggling these two different personae brought her near to breakdown. In the mid-seventies, when her writing ability left her, it became tragically clear that her 'living' self could not be content, or even survive, on its own. Never was there a clearer case of a writer who 'lived to write', or of a writer for whom life came to have no meaning and little joy without writing.

Daphne du Maurier, Dame of the British Empire, a world-wide and enduring bestselling author for nearly fifty years, had a loving family, devoted friends, and everything, it would seem, a woman could possibly have wanted, but if she could not write all this seemed worthless. Her novels and stories gave pleasure to millions, and among them were at least three worthy of a place in any literary canon—*Rebecca*, *The Scapegoat* and *The House on the Strand*—but what they gave to *her* was more important. Through writing she lived more truly than she did in her daily life—it gave her satisfaction, release and a curious sense of elation. Norman Collins so astutely said, 'No one ever imagined more than Daphne.' And it was the fire of her imagination which warmed and excited her millions of readers, and still does.

—Margaret Forster, *Daphne du Maurier* (London: Chatto & Windus, 1993), 415–16

SALLY BEAUMAN

The question of how we name and identify—and the ironies and inexactitudes inherent in that process—is central to "Rebecca." Both female characters—one dead, one alive—derive their name, as they do their status, from their husband. The first wife, Rebecca, is vivid and vengeful and, though dead, indestructible: her name lives on in the book's title. The second wife, the drab, shadowy creature who narrates the story, remains nameless. We learn that she has a "lovely and unusual" name, and that it was bestowed upon her by her father; the only other identity she has was also bestowed by a man—she is a *wife*, she is Mrs. de Winter.

That a narrator perceived as a heroine could be nameless was a source of consuming fascination to du Maurier's readers. It also fascinated other writers—Agatha Christie corresponded with du Maurier on the subject—and throughout her life du Maurier was plagued with fan letters seeking an explanation. Her stock reply was that she found the device technically interesting. The question is not a trivial one, for it takes us straight to the core of "Rebecca"—and that may well be the reason du Maurier, a secretive woman and a secretive artist, avoided answering it. ⟨. . .⟩

One way of reading "Rebecca" is as a love story, in which the good woman triumphs over the bad by winning a man's love: this version, which confirms cherished conventions rather than challenges them, is the one that the nameless narrator would like us to accept, and it is a reading that undoubtedly helped make "Rebecca" a best-seller. Another approach is to see the novel's imaginative links not just with earlier work by female authors ("Jane Eyre" being, indeed, the most obvious antecedent) but also with later work, and in particular with Sylvia Plath's late poems. "Rebecca" is narrated by a woman masochistic and desperate to be loved—a woman seeking an authoritarian father surrogate, or, as Plath expressed it, a "man in black with a Meinkampf look." Her search involves both effacement and abnegation, as it does for any woman who "adores a Fascist." She duly finds such a man in de Winter, whose last name indicates sterility, coldness, an unfruitful season, and whose Christian name—Maxim, as she always abbreviates it—is a synonym for a rule of conduct and is also the name of a weapon (a machine gun).

This woman, not surprisingly, views Rebecca as a rival; what she cannot perceive is that Rebecca is also her twin, and ultimately her alter ego. The two wives have actually suffered similar fates. Both were taken as brides to Manderley—a male preserve, as the first syllable of its name (like Menabilly's) suggests. Both were marginalized within the confines of the house—Rebecca in the west wing, with its view of her symbol, the sea, and the second wife in the east wing, overlooking a rose garden, that symbol of husbandry. The difference between them is in their reactions: the second wife submits, allowing her identity to be dictated by her husband, and by the class, attitudes, and value systems he embraces; the first wife has rebelled. Rebecca has dared to be an unchaste wife, to break the "rules of conduct" that Maxim lives by; her ultimate transgression is to threaten the system of primogeniture. That sin, undermining the entire patriarchal edifice that is Manderley, cannot be forgiven, and Rebecca dies for it.

The response of the narrator to Rebecca's rebellion is deeply ambivalent, and it is this ambivalence which fuels the novel. Her apparent reaction is that of a conventional woman of her time: abhorrence. Yet there are indications throughout the text that the second Mrs. de Winter would like to emulate Rebecca, even to be her. Although Rebecca is never seen, is dead, and has in theory been forever silenced, Mrs. de Winter's obsession with her insures that Rebecca will triumph over anonymity and effacement: even a bullet through the heart and burial at sea cannot quench her vampiric power. Again, one is reminded of Plath's embodiment of amoral, anarchic female force—"I rise with my red hair/And I eat men like air." Within the convention of a story, Rebecca's pallid successor is able to do what she dare not risk in everyday life: celebrate her predecessor.

The final twist of "Rebecca" is a covert one. De Winter kills not one wife but two. He kills the first with a gun; he kills the second by a slower, more insidious method. The second Mrs. de Winter's fate, for which she prepares herself throughout the novel, is to be subsumed by her husband. Following him into that hellish exile glimpsed at the beginning, she becomes again what she was when she met him—a paid companion to a tyrant. For humoring his whims and obeying his dictates, her recompense this time is love, not money, and the cost is her identity. This is the final irony of the novel, and the last of its many reversals. A story that attempts to bury Rebecca, the "unwomanly" woman, in fact resurrects her, while the voice that narrates this story is that of a ghost, a true dead woman.

—Sally Beauman, "Rereading Rebecca," *The New Yorker* (8 November 1993): 130–31, 133–34

B I B L I O G R A P H Y

The Loving Spirit. 1931.
I'll Never Be Young Again. 1932.
The Progress of Julius. 1933.
Gerald: A Portrait. 1934.
Jamaica Inn. 1936.
The du Mauriers. 1937.
Rebecca. 1938.
Come Wind, Come Weather. 1940.
Happy Christmas. 1940.
Frenchman's Creek. 1941.
Escort. 1943.

Consider the Lilies. 1943.

Hungry Hill. 1943.

Nothing Hurts for Long and Escort. 1943.

Spring Picture. 1944.

Leading Lady. 1945.

The Years Between. 1945.

London and Paris. 1945.

The King's General. 1946.

September Tide. 1949.

The Parasites. 1949.

The Young George du Maurier: A Selection of his Letters, 1860–67 (editor). 1951.

My Cousin Rachel. 1951.

The Apple Tree: A Short Novel and Some Stories. 1952.

Happy Christmas. 1953.

Mary Anne. 1954.

The Scapegoat. 1957.

The Breaking Point: Eight Stories. 1959.

Early Stories. 1959.

The Internal World of Branwell Brontë. 1960.

The Treasury of du Maurier Short Stories. 1960.

Castle Dor (with Sir Arthur Quiller-Couch). 1962.

The Glass-Blowers. 1963.

The Flight of the Falcon. 1965.

Vanishing Cornwall. 1967.

The House on the Strand. 1969.

Not After Midnight and Other Stories. 1971.

Rule Britannia. 1972.

The Birds. 1972.

Golden Lads: Sir Francis Bacon, Anthony Bacon, and their Friends. 1975.

The Winding Stair: Francis Bacon, His Rise and Fall. 1976.

Echoes from the Macabre: Selected Stories. 1976.

Growing Pains: The Shaping of a Writer. 1977.

The Rendezvous and Other Stories. 1980.

The Birds and Other Stories. 1980.

The Rebecca Notebook and Other Memories. 1980.

Daphne du Maurier's Classics of the Macabre. 1987.

Selections from Menabilly: Portrait of a Friendship. 1992.

RUMER GODDEN

B. 1907

MARGARET RUMER GODDEN was born December 10, 1907, in
Eastbourne, Sussex, England. The following year, her parents, Arthur
Leigh Godden and Katherine Norah Hingley, took her to India,
where her father worked in the Indian shipping industry. She would
travel back and forth many times: Godden lived in London with her
grandmother until the outbreak of World War I, when she was sent
back to India. She again returned to England in 1920 to attend school
and study ballet, but at the age of 18 she rejoined her parents in
Calcutta where, despite their objections, she opened a successful
dance school for children. Growing up in two such disparate cultures
had a profound influence on Godden's later literary work and became
the subject of *Two Under the Indian Sun* (1966), a fictionalized account
of her early childhood written with her older sister, the novelist Jan
Godden.

In 1934 Godden married Laurence Sinclair Foster, a stockbroker.
A year later, she gave birth to their first daughter and completed her
first novel, *Chinese Puzzle* (1936). The couple had a second daughter in
1938, and, soon after the publication of her second novel the same
year, *The Lady and the Unicorn*, Godden sold the dance school to devote
herself fully to writing. While these first two books were considered
charming, it wasn't until the publication of *Black Narcissus* (1939) that
her distinctive style emerged. Though many of her early novels were
dismissed by critics as light and whimsical, they prove a subtle study in
contrasts, particularly when comparing Eastern and Western cultures.

Godden was somewhat secretive about various aspects of her personal life. She was married twice, though the reason for and timing of
her first husband's departure is unclear. During World War II, she lived
in peaceful seclusion with her two daughters in Nepal, first at the
Namring Tea Estate under the Himalayas and later in a small farm-
house high in the mountains of Kashmir. She documented the early
part of this period in a reflective autobiographical work, *Rungli-
Rungliot Means in Paharia, Thus Far and No Further*. These years of retreat
also provided the inspiration for several other books: *Breakfast with the
Nikolides* (1942), *Kingfishers Catch Fire* (1953), and the nonfiction mono-
graph *Bengal Journey* (1945).

In 1949, Godden married James L. Haynes-Dixon, a civil servant.
Although they settled in England, Godden revisited India several
times, most notably in 1964 for the filming of Jean Renoir's version of

her novel *The River* (1946)—considered one of Godden's finest works, for both its compact narrative and its effective expression of such timeless themes as love, death, and loss of innocence.

Since her return to England in 1945, Godden's focus has shifted to writing for children. In all, she has written 15 children's books, several entirely in verse. A prolific author, she also completed verse translations of two books by Carmen Bernos de Gasztold, a biography of Hans Christian Andersen, and numerous articles for such popular periodicals as *Saturday Review*, *House and Garden*, and *Vogue*.

CRITICAL EXTRACTS

EDWIN BERRY BURGUM

This altogether ingratiating novel of English family life ⟨*Take Three Tenses*⟩ will appeal to two quite different groups of readers. Those who like stories of old comfortable ways of living will find it an unusually fresh version of familiar material; and restless readers who feel they cannot face another story about retired generals with beautiful nieces will succumb both to the success with which Miss Godden has individualized her characters and her method of narration, described in the title as "a fugue in time."

Old General Rolls Dane is a Victorian type. The last of nine children of a well-to-do family, living alone with a manservant in the ancestral house on a not too fashionable square, his thoughts are with the past. But the author handles her stream of consciousness freely and readably. When Rolls' thoughts drift back to events in the early married life of his parents (which he could have known only through hearsay) there is no blurring of images. On the contrary, Miss Godden's method reconstructs this past life of the house so vividly that it takes on the sense of the present and can be offered as independent narrative.

The picture thus invoked of the Victorian family is as graphic as a sensitive print, undistorted by either satire or sentimentality. Old Eye, the father, dominates the household without being aware of it, subjecting the mother to mounting domestic burdens, until both have died, and the focus changes to three grown children—Selina, who manages the house with the prerogative of a spinster; Pelham, who soon escapes to America, and Rolls himself, who leaves for India. The disintegration of the family is further promoted by an orphan girl named Lark, whose parents were friends of the Eye and who arouses Selina's jealousy, mild Pelham's chivalry, and the love of the young blade Rolls.

Into these recollections the present obtrudes—the nephew of Lark (who had married an Italian Marquesa) falling in love with the granddaughter of Pelham. In the new tone of Rolls' revery is a philosophical meaning, for he feels in this love affair the beneficent functioning of time. The incompleted action of the past, which had torn him away from Lark, is completed in the present.

Such a philosophy would seem solidly based unless one believes in the general degeneration of the human society. And it is unfortunate, I think, that this quite tenable conception of the constructive function of time should have been so definitely associated with the survival of houses. When bombs are destroying those down the street, even though this house survives it can hardly be used as an adequate symbol of continuity, of the permanence of the family. The old man's imagination, that had been so lucid about the past, here becomes sentimental about the future, and the author shares his changes of mood. For to make the house the symbol, is to believe that the future completes the past without essential change—to suggest that the past must dominate the future.

When the narrative turns objective, however, it gives us two young people of a different generation, the one from America, the other from Italy. It suggests that the completion of the love of Rolls for Lark—in this new love of Grizel and Pax—cannot possibly be in the terms of Victorian insularity. It cannot be, symbolically, in the same house. If the story had not sunk into the vague wish-fulfillment of the old general, "Take Three Tenses," instead of being merely one of the most readable novels of the season, would have refuted the pessimism of Virginia Woolf on her own level of distinction.

—Edwin Berry Burgum, "Love Skips a Century," *The New York Times Book Review* (11 March 1945): 7

ANNE FREMANTLE

"Take Three Tenses" ⟨. . .⟩ opens with the statement: "the house, it seems, is more important than the characters. 'In me you exist' says the house." And with these words also ⟨Rumer Godden⟩ ends her story, which she subtitles, "A fugue in time." Actually, even more than the 99-year-leased house, it is the stream of consciousness that is her novel's hero, as she emphasizes in her repetition, no less than three times, of the same lines from Mr. T. S. Eliot's "Four Quartets." This gives the reader, by the time he meets the same chunk of verse from East Coker, a slight sense of being shouted at. "Yes, yes," he exclaims, "I read it on the first page. I know we must be still and still moving, but let's get to the story, since that too must move." ⟨. . .⟩

"Take Three Tenses" ends with Pelham's American granddaughter, Grizel, a WAC officer in this war, and married to Pax, Lark's nephew, whom she meets in "the" house, living there with their baby daughter, Verity. So the wheel has come full circle, the serpent's tail is securely in its mouth, and, as Mary Stuart said before Mr. Eliot plagiarized her, "in my end is my beginning." Miss Godden is a pointilliste, a perfectionist, building up her effects with the lightest of touch, without shock; she uses the simplest things, food, servants, scrubbing brushes, children's clothes, linoleum, smells, sounds, as materials for her magic. And her reader believes, in the hat and in the rabbit, in conjuror and conjured, and in every conversation. There is nothing to stretch either the faith or the imagination: the instant reaction, is, of course it must have been like that, *is* like that. Evocation, invocation, can do no more; here, in perspective as solid as Piranesi's, is a conversation piece executed in the subtlest of monochrome wash.

But, as Swinburne once remarked, a primrose by the rivers brim, dicotyledon was to him, and it was nothing more. There is in this novel no conflict, except in Griselda (who had poor George Eliot's dislike for "the Slavery of being a girl" without the "man's force of genius" that the latter felt in her). And even for Griselda, the conflict is external, between herself and her circumstances, nothing more, nothing deeper. ⟨. . .⟩ Miss Godden's characters are etiolated, unreal, sprouting damply in basements, or in the rarified air of attics—anyway, indoors: they are never exposed to sun, and therefore not to shadow. She gives herself away by prefacing her book with a sentence by Lawrence Abbott describing a Bach fugue. And her characters are indeed notes, chords, sounds; for her, human relationships are simplified by the family, are reduced by a sort of unitary method to phrases in the Book of Common Prayer, children are arrows in the hand, man is cut down like a flower.

—Anne Fremantle, "Whose Fountains Are Within," *The Commonweal* (4 May 1945): 73–74

ELIZABETH JANEWAY

Reading a novel by Rumer Godden is always an interesting experience. She is so good at what she does, and what she does is so unimportant, that one is left openmouthed as one sometimes is at the circus, contemplating the infinite care and skill with which a performer balances himself on one finger atop a teetering pile of furniture. An astonishing feat! And even more astonishing is the realization that someone has gone to all that trouble to learn how to do it.

In "China Court" Miss Godden is telling the story of a Cornish family, resident for five generations in a Cornish house of that name. And, with the greatest deftness, she is telling it all at once. This is no clumsy, labored exercise in "and then this happened, and then that happened." Miss Godden has grandly done away with the ordinary passing of time, and allowed the generations to mingle in the rooms of China Court, so that we see the house through a flashing shimmer of images nodding to each other across a century

and more. One confrontation echoes another fifty years before, ghosts of conversations interweave, and all manner of great and small events—births,
deaths, love affairs, drives and dinners—reflect and enlarge each other. Several
stories, thus, go on at once, cleverly corresponding, contradicting and contributing to each other in a real triumph of plotsmanship. It must have been
great fun to write.

Is it great fun to read? The answer depends on whether or not you like
romantic fantasy, for all Miss Godden's artful and intricate apparatus is
employed to set forth a sentimental story in which five generations of stock figures step through one hundred and twenty years of predictable episodes. ⟨. . .⟩

It is a tough and long-lived genre, which must obviously give considerable
pleasure to many readers: the sentimental romance. These romances have
their own conventions and create their own world in which the flux and chaos
of life are replaced by order, the terrors by turnip-ghosts, and the range of the
unexpected narrowed.

How such conventions differ from those of art—why melodrama, for
instance, is not drama—has been and will be argued for centuries. The
romances go on. Indeed, they have been written and read for so long that one
must really be dogged and determined to quarrel with them; to maintain in
humorless irritation that novels should not be cheapened so, or formal talent
as superior as Miss Godden's wasted; that fiction is serious, is a way of understanding to the full. Let us drop such out-size and irrelevant arguments and
agree that fantasy and daydreams have their place today as much as they did
when Jane Austen laughed at them in "Northanger Abbey," and they and Jane
both survived. Then it's simply a matter of whether or not Miss Godden's daydreams suit you.

—Elizabeth Janeway, "Five Generations and How They Grew," *The New York Times Book Review*
(5 March 1961): 4

NEWSWEEK

The novel ⟨*The Battle of Villa Fiorita*⟩ is the thirteenth which Rumer Godden has
written, and she has worked her writing down to a fine, sure style. One knows
it at once—it jumps from every page—"skips," she might say. Women eat it
up—American women, too, even though Miss Godden, of course, is British.
There are lovely words, swaying together, and glimpses of truth. There are
interesting characters, only a little wispy. And beyond that, the plot, always in
motion. That part of it has to do with two children moving into the villa of
their mother, Fanny, and their stepfather-to-be, determined to prevent their
parents' divorce—an astonishing divorce, because they had been married
about twenty years. The plot is beautiful. But most of all there is the style.

It is a style, one finds straight off, that spreads even to the characters who "finish the author's sentences," suggests a voice, and "occasionally each other's," says another. "And tense-jump," a third might have added, "to express what they might have said." There are marvelous listings by way of scene-setting; tear bottles, *prie-dieux*, gilt-and-brocade beds, and "glimpses of tumbling flowers, of honeysuckle and wisteria," writes Miss Godden. And, she adds, later, "the hedges of forbidding prickly whitethorn." There are flashbacks, too, lots of them, all over, even little flashbacks inside big flashbacks.

Still it all seems somehow skimpy. Contrived, too, "made up," a ruder voice might have said. And there is no getting around the tripe which washes up every few pages in the form of coincidence or coyness, just as there is no getting around the fact that it is clever, a difficult piece of juggling, or the fact that it has little sharp strokes which rouse one, briefly, just when one has about given up on the whole shebang. What one is left with, really, is the queer sense of a fine intelligence at play—but not, one adds, "at work." Because no matter how deft, or clever, or sensitive, or intelligent one may be, still, when all is said and done, it is a cheat to write for one sex only.

—N.A., "For Women Only," *Newsweek* (30 September 1963): 88–88B

RUMER GODDEN

⟨Every⟩ piece of writing, book or short story, play or poem, starts from what I call a "grit," something large or small, usually small, a sight or sound, a sentence or a happening that does not pass away leaving only a faint memory— if it leaves anything at all—but quite inexplicably lodges in the mind; imagination gets to work and secretes a deposit round this grit—"secretes" because this is usually an intensely secretive process—until it grows larger and larger and rounds into a whole. The result, of course, is seldom a pearl, but an author at work is like an oyster, clam-quiet and busy.

A name, a few words, can become a grit—perhaps end as the title of a book; a grit could be a glimpse, such as I had of the chef at the Pierrefonds beckoning that little lady. Sometimes a happening makes a story of itself, as with "To Uncle, with Love"; but even then it has to be given substance and shape: the smallest dust of anything can set it off, and there is no knowing how far or to what depth it will take you; the two words "Black Narcissus" grew into a novel and set me off on a lifetime of thought and reading.

Nor can one say why a particular "something" stays when thousands upon thousands simply pass by; why does "this" stay and not "that"? Wanting seems to have little to do with it. Often one tries to ignore the something or dislodge it, but a real writer knows there is only one way to do this—let the thing grow and then write it. Mysteriously, with most of us, once a thing is written, for the writer it ceases to have any interest at all.

—Rumer Godden, "Preface" to *Gone: A Thread of Stories* (New York: Viking Press, 1968), vii–viii

HASSELL A. SIMPSON

Rumer Godden's prose style is made of many things, not only the contrasts both obvious and subtle which she finds in experience, but also the sensitive modulation among degrees of contrast; not only the diction both crude and delicate which she employs as narrator or gives to her characters, but also the fusion of two or more levels of language into an ordered and consistent whole. More is involved than these characteristics, however; and perhaps most important of all is her skillful poetic marshaling of images and symbols to extend the effects that she seeks to create beyond the mind and within the heart. Rarely are her figures obtrusive, drawing attention to themselves. As William York Tindall observed some years ago, "Whereas the 'black narcissus' of Rumer Godden's novel of that name seems no more than the perfume ignominiously used by an oriental dandy, it acquires connotations that justify the emphasis placed upon it. Sister Phillippa wants jonquils and daffodils for the convent garden. Like that perfume, these flowers of the narcissus family call to mind the original Narcissus, who, suggesting both Sister Clodagh's vanity and her rebirth, summarizes in one allusive image the principal theme of the novel. The blackness of this flower implies not only a nun's habit and the unworldliness that threatens rebirth but also the period of trial and deprivation that must precede it."

It has been suggested ⟨. . .⟩ that the symbols involved in *The River* are entirely natural and that they sink into the consciousness before a reader is aware of them as symbols. The river itself is one of the great streams of India, an immutable geographical feature; on its banks live Harriet's family, for whom the river is a hard fact that must be acknowledged in the daily movements of everyone. Beside it live other families as well, both Indian and European; and beside it, too, live hundreds of other beings, including the cobra that causes the chief crisis. But the river is also a figurative presence, not merely a literal one. Its unceasing flow, its perpetual flux in constancy, is perceived by characters and readers alike as a sort of whispered *memento mutare* that precedes and prefigures a bitter lesson Harriet learns: *memento mori*.

Still other frames of symbolic reference inform the story. Harriet's house is situated in a garden, not an extraordinary circumstance surely; but the Garden also suggests the innocence of Harriet and little Bogey who, partly because she fails to shield him, falls victim to the cobra. That snake, too, is symbolical—the Serpent in Eden, the type of Knowledge, of Evil, and of Death; and in Harriet's garden it is associated with the peepul tree—not only implying in the sound of its name the Fall of Man but also representing the Tree, in her case and Bogey's, of the Knowledge of Good and Evil. Bogey's name (though not the child himself) suggests in its similarity to "bogey-man" some Satanic influence like that in Paradise. Bogey's funeral procession, with flower-laden launches moving upstream on the River, marks the end of Harriet's childhood; it is their expulsion from Eden, and she longs to preserve both the happy past and the bitter Fall: "The river can't close over this, thought Harriet; then she seemed to see again, in the water, the handful of ashes that had been Ram Prasad's wife, and she remembered how they had been washed, round and round, gently, on the water, before the current took them away."

—Hassell A. Simpson, *Rumer Godden* (New York: Twayne Publishers, Inc., 1973), 124–25

JEAN PICKERING

The stories in Rumer Godden's *Swans and Turtles*, most of which were originally published in such magazines as *Ladies' Home Journal*, *Harper's*, and *Collier's*, are prefaced by descriptions of the incidents they are based on and arranged to form a record of the events and ideas important in her life and thought. Her awareness of the appropriate detail makes her particularly successful in evoking psychological states through setting. The house in "Time Is a Stream," with the ha-ha and the green light filtered through the elms, makes real the despair of the aging woman who, unable to look after herself, no longer cares where she lives or if she lives at all; and the cinder path in "You Need to Go Upstairs," suggested through the senses of touch and smell, clearly renders a blind child's determination to be independent.

The most successful stories had their genesis in childhood trauma: Godden and her sister suffered when they were sent to England to learn the manners and accent proper to middle-class girls. The solidity of a prosperous Edwardian household so reassuring to the proprietors is a source of terror to the smaller inhabitants; five-year-old Alice in "Down under the Thames" clutches "her frilled drawers, . . . her knees and fingers desperately clinging" to the mahogany seat that stretches from wall to wall, while the willow pattern china pan looks big enough to drown in. The adults seem as unaccommodating to the children as is the furniture: Aunt Gwenda rips all the stitches out of Alice's embroidery with the injuction "*That* will teach you!" Alice, angry at last in a house where her typical response has been fear, flushes away her rejected traycloth.

A similar reversal occurs at the end of "The Little Fishes." Two sisters find the English boarding school run by Anglican nuns totally foreign; the climate, the bare building without privacy, the emphasis on competition and sports-manship make no sense to the girls from India, "where people are not in a hurry." The headmistress, whose puffy cheeks swell when she grows angry, calls them "the scum of the school" in front of a visiting priest, who, when the elder sister raises her hand to protest the insult, silently pressures Sister Gertrude to apologize. The contrast between the lush Indian garden the children left behind and the cold, dark school parallels the difference between the loving treatment accorded by family and servants and the bullying of the girls and nuns.

—Jean Pickering, "The English Short Story in the Sixties," *The English Short Story 1945–1980*, ed. Dennis P. Vannatta (Boston: Twayne Publishers, 1985), 104–5

RUMER GODDEN

A Fugue in Time had been written in those long solitary evenings in Dove House in winter, under an oil lamp—we had had no electricity. It had been bitterly cold; I had a 'kangri,' the Kashmiri firepot, filled with hot coals, a wicker shield round it to keep me warm; I wrote again in the dawn hours when I got up at half past four to write before the children were awake. Trying to weave the three generations of characters together, telling of them not consecutively but interwoven, I wrote the book over and over again and thought I should never succeed. It was not until I tried putting the past into the present tense, the present into the past that I had found the key. This sounds improbable but worked so smoothly that most readers—even editors—never noticed.

A Fugue in Time though had been written a long time ago. I had shown nothing to anyone since. There is a saying of Chekhov's, written to a young writer he had tried to help:

> What is needed is constant work day and night, constant reading,
> study, will. Every hour is precious for it . . . it is time.

I had, I had to get to work, my work.

—Rumer Godden, *A House with Four Rooms* (New York: William Morrow and Company, Inc., 1989), 33

BIBLIOGRAPHY

Chinese Puzzle. 1936.
The Lady and the Unicorn. 1938.
Black Narcissus. 1939.

Gypsy, Gypsy. 1940.

Breakfast with the Nikolides. 1942.

Take Three Tenses: A Fugue in Time. 1945.

Bengal Journey: A Story of the Part Played by Women in the Province, 1939–1945. 1945.

Rungli-Rungliot Means in Paharia, Thus Far and No Further. 1946.

The River. 1946.

A Candle for St. Jude. 1948.

In Noah's Ark. 1949.

A Breath of Air. 1950.

Kingfishers Catch Fire. 1953.

Hans Christian Andersen. 1955.

An Episode of Sparrows. 1956.

Mooltiki: Stories and Poems from India. 1957.

The Greengage Summer. 1958.

China Court: The Hours of a Country House. 1961.

The Battle of Villa Fiorita. 1963.

Two Under the Indian Sun (with Jon Godden). 1966.

Gone: A Thread of Stories. 1968.

In This House of Brede. 1969.

The Raphael Bible. 1970.

Shiva's Pigeons: An Experience of India (with Jon Godden). 1972.

RADCLYFFE HALL
1886–1943

MARGUERITE RADCLYFFE-HALL was born in 1886 in Bournemouth, Hampshire, England. She was raised by her mother and her Italian stepfather, who were by turns indifferent and emotionally and physically abusive. From her maternal grandmother, who was affectionate and encouraging, she developed lifelong interests in nature, animals, music, and fine arts.

When she was 17, Hall inherited a considerable fortune from her natural father, whom she had met only twice. She purchased a house for herself and her grandmother and traveled extensively throughout Europe, eventually arriving in London, where she attended King's College for a short time; she later studied briefly in Germany.

An accomplished pianist, Hall was encouraged by her grandmother to publish the poetry she had written as lyrics to her piano compositions. *'Twixt Earth and Stars*, her first book of poetry, appeared in 1903. Over the next 12 years, Hall would publish several more volumes of poetry, all notable for their free expression of passion between women.

Around this time, Hall met Lady Mabel Batten, who became her lover and adviser. In an effort to further Hall's career, Batten introduced her to members of London's literary circles and urged her to write fiction as a further outlet for her increasingly autobiographical and erotically explicit poetry. In 1915, Hall met Lady Una Troubridge, Batten's cousin; Troubridge would become her lifelong companion and eventual biographer.

Hall published two novels in 1924, *The Forge* and *The Unlit Lamp*. The latter addresses same-sex relationships with such restraint that most reviewers did not mention it, yet scholars now consider it a precursor to *The Well of Loneliness*, Hall's 1928 novel that openly took lesbianism as its subject. In 1925 she published *A Saturday Life*, but not until the 1926 appearance of *Adam's Breed*, an autobiographical novel with a male protagonist, was her literary reputation secured. The novel won a James Tait Black Memorial Prize, a Femina-Vie Heureuse Prize, and an Eichelberger Humane gold medal.

Hall consulted Una Troubridge before beginning her most famous and most heavily autobiographical work, *The Well of Loneliness*. The only novel in which Hall dealt explicitly with lesbianism, *The Well* was banned as obscene in England and in the United States. Among the members of the literary community who supported her during the obscenity trial were Leonard and Virginia Woolf, Bernard Shaw, H. G. Wells, Aldous Huxley, and Hugh Walpole; others feared being associated with such a controversial subject. The novel was eventually cleared by a United States court and has since become a classic of lesbian fiction.

Hall, who frequently dressed in men's clothing and referred to herself as "John," continued to write with compassion about nonconforming individuals. Her devout Catholicism and her belief in psychic phenomena are reflected in such novels as *The Master of the House* (1932), *The Sixth Beatitude* (1936), and *The Well of Loneliness*. After years of illness and repeated surgery, Hall died of cancer on October 7, 1943. She was buried according to her wishes in a plot between Batten and Troubridge, believing they would all be reunited after death.

CRITICAL   EXTRACTS

HAVELOCK ELLIS

I have read *The Well of Loneliness* with great interest because—apart from its fine qualities as a novel by a writer of accomplished art—it possesses a notable psychological and sociological significance. So far as I know, it is the first English novel which presents, in a completely faithful and uncompromising form, one particular aspect of sexual life as it exists among us to-day. The relation of certain people—who, while different from their fellow human beings are sometimes of the highest character and the finest aptitudes—to the often hostile society in which they move, presents difficult and still unsolved problems. The poignant situations which thus arise are here set forth so vividly, and yet with such complete absence of offence, that we must place Radclyffe Hall's book on a high level of distinction.

    —Havelock Ellis, "Commentary," *The Well of Loneliness* (New York: Anchor Books Doubleday, 1956, orig. pub. 1928), 6

CYRIL CONNOLLY

The Well of Loneliness is a serious novel on the theme of homosexuality in women. It is a long, tedious and absolutely humourless book. There is a very simple literary rule in dealing with this kind of subject. What the author takes for granted, the reader will take for granted, what the author makes a fuss about the reader will fuss about too. A very easy instance of this is the fact that no reader of Sherlock Holmes questions his right to inject himself freely with cocaine—a slight twist in the author's sense of values would have altered this into a terrible weakness which would in its turn have shocked and grieved the reader. Similarly one of the most successful novels of the last few years described an episode as typical as any in *The Well of Loneliness*, but because it was described without flourish or comment it was quite quietly received. It is just this rule which Miss Hall failed to keep. *The Well of Loneliness* is a melodramatic description of a subject which has nothing melodramatic about it. What literary interest it has, and it might have a great deal, is obscured by the constant stream of propaganda of every kind, and the author's perpetual insistence that the invert is a great tragic figure, branded with the mark of Cain, set apart from her kind as the victim of the injustice of God and the persecution of the world. The book is really a chronicle of the misfortunes of the invert, but since it assumes the invert to be born an invert and condemned beyond all hope of cure to remain one, it can hardly be said to point a moral of any kind. It is presumably a plea for greater tolerance, but the world is perfectly prepared to tolerate the invert, if the invert will only make concessions to the world. Most of us are resigned to the doctrine of homosexuals, that they alone possess all the greatest heroes and all the finer feelings, but it is surely preposterous that they should claim a right, not only to the mark of Cain, but to the martyr's crown. The tragedy of Stephen Gordon, the heroine of this book, is not really that of inversion but of genius; but if of genius, it is that of any sensitive, artistic, religious and uncompromising human being who refuses to adapt herself to the conditions of life. ⟨. . .⟩

The Well of Loneliness may be a brave book to have written, but let us hope it will pave the way for someone to write a better. Homosexuality is, after all, as rich in comedy as in tragedy, and it is time it was emancipated from the aura of distinguished damnation and religious martyrdom which surrounds its so fiercely aggressive apologists. Stephen Gordon is a Victorian character, an *âme damnée;* once we are reconciled to her position, we are distressed by her lack of spirit, her failure to revenge herself on her tormentors. Sappho had never heard of the mark of Cain, she was also well able to look after herself, but never did she possess a disciple so conscious of her inferiority as Stephen Gordon, or so lacking—for 15s.!—in the rudiments of charm.

—Cyril Connolly, "New Novels," *New Statesman* (25 Aug. 1928), excerpted in *Twentieth-Century British Literature*, ed. Harold Bloom (New York: Chelsea House Publishers, 1986), 1032–33

UNA, LADY TROUBRIDGE

It was after the success of *Adam's Breed* that John came to me one day with unusual gravity and asked for my decision in a serious matter: she had long wanted to write a book on sexual inversion, a novel that would be accessible to the general public who did not have access to technical treatises. At one time she had thought of making it a 'period' book, built round an actual personality of the early nineteenth century. But her instinct had told her that in any case she must postpone such a book until her name was made; until her unusual theme would get a hearing as being the work of an established writer.

It was her absolute conviction that such a book could only be written by a sexual invert, who alone could be qualified by personal knowledge and experience to speak on behalf of a misunderstood and misjudged minority.

It was with this conviction that she came to me, telling me that in her view the time was ripe, and that although the publication of such a book might mean the shipwreck of her whole career, she was fully prepared to make any sacrifice except—the sacrifice of my peace of mind.

She pointed out that in view of our union and of all the years that we had shared a home, what affected her must also affect me and that I would be included in any condemnation. Therefore she placed the decision in my hands and would write or refrain as I should decide.

I am glad to remember that my reply was made without so much as an instant's hesitation: I told her to write what was in her heart, that so far as any effect upon myself was concerned, I was sick to death of ambiguities, and only wished to be known for what I was and to dwell with her in the palace of truth.

Then and there she set to work on *The Well of Loneliness*.

—Una, Lady Troubridge, *The Life and Death of Radclyffe Hall* (1961), excerpted in *Twentieth-Century British Literature*, ed. Harold Bloom (New York: Chelsea House Publishers, 1986), 1031

MARGARET LAWRENCE

Radclyffe Hall suggests without actually declaring it that the women of the Lesbian group with which she deals in one section of the book are women of out-and-out muscularity of brain. It leaves the reader with still another question in mind, and that is the possibility of mental muscularity presupposing a definite amount of masculine content in a woman; and the corollary that the woman who uses her brain in the struggle of accomplishment becomes more and more masculine with time. And that question also has to be left unanswered inasmuch as the history of feminism is still too young to indicate any reliable answer.

Apart altogether from its psychiatric implications, *The Well of Loneliness* produces an artistic impression which is somewhat similar to the artistic impression of the Greek tragedies. The Greeks accepted inversion in all its variations as being of excellent dramatic substance. The Greeks were able to separate their intellectual curiosity from their instinctive regard for the preservation of the normal, which fact alone makes them stand out in history a superior peo-

ple. Radclyffe Hall set herself the mission of portraying to the normal the sufferings of the invert in society. She pleads for pity and for understanding. She
says that mankind, having only just begun to find the laws relating to sex, may
in a relatively short time discover that there are biological accidents producing inversion. Her heroine she presents as a victim for our sympathy. The pity
note in the book is pity that goes out to all creatures who are not able, through
her theory of biological accident, or through the psychiatric theory of trauma,
to partake of normal experience.

There is pity also for the race which, through its terror of the abnormal,
punishes the victims, and may thereby lose valuable services in the fields that
are other than racial. She believes that these people, because of their pecu-
liarity, have something else to do for the race than to continue it. She stresses
their acutely sensitized nerves—the nerves that always go with beings of high
capacity. She dwells upon the invert's susceptibility to sound. Radclyffe Hall
herself writes with mystical sensitivity to tone. Her phrasing shows it. Her
words are put down in relation to their sounds set against other sounds. She
produces by this means a disturbing emotional effect.

The importance of her fictional comment upon the situation of the invert
lies in this—that inasmuch as inversion, by reason of its distortion of nerves,
can at least be tentatively held to be a nervous disorder, the invert should not
be treated as a pariah, but rather as a person who through no fault of his or her
own is suffering from nervous excitement coming from the kinetic response of
the whole human fabric to change. It can be drawn from her story that only
the highly sensitized members of society take shock acutely enough to be disorganized away from the normal, and that in the long run it is only the highly
sensitized members of society who are in the spiritual sense valuable. The race
goes on. The normal people see to that. But art and religion and thought and
science have always been maintained in the race by the variously abnormal,
and meanwhile they suffer tortures through being unable to adjust themselves
to normality.

—Margaret Lawrence, "Priestesses," *The School of Femininity* (1936), excerpted in *Twentieth-
Century British Literature*, ed. Harold Bloom (New York: Chelsea House Publishers, 1986), 1033

JANE RULE

The Well of Loneliness by Radclyffe Hall, published in 1928, remains *the* lesbian
novel, a title familiar to most readers of fiction, either a bible or a horror story
for any lesbian who reads at all. There have been other books published since,
better written, more accurate according to recent moral and psychological
speculation, but none of them has seriously challenged the position of *The Well
of Loneliness*. Often a book finds momentary identity only by negative comparison with that "noble, tragic tract about the love that cannot speak its name."

Along with the teachings of the church and the moral translations of those teachings by psychologists, *The Well of Loneliness* has influenced millions of readers in their attitudes toward lesbians.

Radclyffe Hall's intention was to write a sympathetic and accurate book about inversion. She was already a novelist and poet of some reputation, and, if she had neither the craft nor the power of insight of her contemporary D. H. Lawrence, she shared his zeal for educating the public. Scientific books were not at that time generally available. Krafft-Ebing's famous *Psychopathia Sexualis* was directed at the medical profession, and details of case studies, like the title, were written in Latin lest the book fall into the wrong hands and corrupt the naive reader. Radclyffe Hall had read Krafft-Ebing, as well as the less well-known studies of Karl Heinrich Ulrichs, himself a homosexual trying to prove that inversion was as natural an orientation as left-handedness. She obviously read not only with a scholar's interest but with a desire to understand herself, a congenital invert in her own eyes whose sexual appetites were satisfied exclusively by women. *The Well of Loneliness* was, therefore, not only a novel intended to give insight into the experience of inverts but also to justify Radclyffe Hall's own life. She must have been the more pressed to defend the innocence of her nature because she was a Catholic, apparently thoughtfully and deeply committed to most of the doctrines of the Church. She died, after a long struggle with cancer, serene in her belief that she would be only temporarily separated from Una, Lady Troubridge, the woman with whom she had lived for some years. She did not expect that reunion to take place in the appropriate circle of Dante's hell, for, if there was anyone responsible for her nature, it was God, Who "in a thoughtless moment had created in His turn, those pitiful thousands who must stand forever outside His blessing." Outside His blessing on earth, she must have rationalized. Or in some way she singled herself out, redeemed by the book she had written in which her last plea is "Acknowledge us, o God, before the whole world. Give us also the right to our existence." There is no final evidence for how she reconciled her sexual life with her faith. There is only the testimony of those closest to her that she had resolved the conflict for herself. ⟨. . .⟩

Though *The Well of Loneliness* was viciously attacked for its sympathetic idealizing of the invert, giving it greater importance at the time than it deserved, its survival as the single authoritative novel on lesbian love depends on its misconceptions. It supports the view that men are naturally superior, that, given a choice, any woman would prefer a real man unless she herself is a congenital freak. Though inept and feminine men are criticized, though some are seen to abuse the power they have, their right to that power is never questioned. Stephen does not defy the social structure she was born into. Male domination is intolerable to her only when she can't assert it for herself.

Women are inferior. Loving relationships must be between superior and inferior persons. Stephen's sexual rejection of Martin, though it is offered as conclusive proof of her irreversible inversion, is basically a rejection of being the inferior partner in a relationship. Her reaction is one of "repulsion—terror and repulsion . . . a look of outrage." In her relationship with Mary, Stephen is "all things to Mary; father, mother, friend and lover, all things, and Mary is all things to her—the child, the friend, the beloved, all things." The repetition of "all things" is not persuasive enough to cover the inequality of the categories. When Stephen decides not to fight for Mary, she gives her to Martin much as one would give any other thing one owns. And though her altruism is sometimes associated with her female gender, it is more often likened to the virtues of Christ. It is courageous or foolhardy for a woman to behave like a man, but, since she accepts herself as a freak, since in fiction if not in life she is made to give up the ultimate prize, she is no political threat to anyone. The natural order of things is reasserted, and she is left on the outside, calling to God and to society for recognition. ⟨. . .⟩

Radclyffe Hall was a courageous woman, and *The Well of Loneliness* is an important book because it does so carefully reveal the honest misconceptions about women's nature and experience which have limited and crippled so many people. Radclyffe Hall did think of herself as a freak, but emotionally and intellectually she was far more a "womanly woman" than many of her literary contemporaries. She worshiped the very institutions which oppressed her, the Church and the patriarchy, which have taught women there are only two choices, inferiority or perversion. Inside that framework, she made and tried to redefine the only proud choice she had. The "bible" she offered is really no better for women than the Bible she would not reject.

—Jane Rule, *Lesbian Images* (1975), excerpted in *Twentieth-Century British Literature*, ed. Harold Bloom (New York: Chelsea House Publishers, 1986), 1035, 1038

LOUISE BERNIKOW

The Well of Loneliness is about exile. Its mood is apologetic; it is meant as a plea for tolerance (of "inversion") and it is dense with self-hate . . .

Shadow and sunlight, clouded and free, victimized and defiant, these are the terms that come to mind as *The Well of Loneliness* is placed beside *Orlando* and both placed in historical context. Shadow, clouds, victimization, emanating from self-hate, which itself emanates from the contagion of homophobia in the surrounding culture. This characterizes not only Radclyffe Hall's novel, but the diary that Vita Sackville-West kept about her affair with Violet Trefusis. This is "monster" literature—the lesbian as deviant, deformed, sick—in which ethics require her defeat. Most masculine literature about love is in this vein. The woman must be vanquished; the man in the story triumphs.

The context is homophobia. Opposition comes from all quarters. Definitions are made—heterosexuality is the norm in language and culture—applied and, often, internalized. Whatever the core of the love experience, its encounter with the world ends in devastation. Shakespeare showed this in Romeo and Juliet, and those lovers remain in readers' minds with benign grace and the youthful aura of tragedy. Not so lesbian lovers, who, like Radclyffe Hall's protagonist, must parade their pain, express anger at heterosexual tyranny by passivity: look what you have done to me.

Opposition comes from all quarters, even in the period under considera-tion, the only time in history, except, perhaps, for Sappho's, when a culture to support the literature thrived. E. M. Forster, for example, indignant as he became at the suppression of *The Well of Loneliness*, told Virginia Woolf that he did not, in fact, approve of lesbians because he "disliked the idea of women being independent of men." . . .

Opposition comes also, and perhaps more painfully, from women. In *The Well of Loneliness*, it is Stephen's mother who reviles her and sends her into exile. In their confrontation, the mother begins with her own physical revulsion—"a desire not to touch or be touched by you—a terrible thing for a mother to feel"—and moves, as tyrants always do, from the personal to the universal with no thought or feeling in between. The mother, enforcer, in this novel of patri-archal values, says easily that Stephen is "unnatural" a "sin against creation," but especially "a sin against the father who bred you." Stephen defends herself against her mother and against the world by accepting their terms and trying to put herself into the existing scheme of things. "As a man loves a woman," she says, "that was how I loved."

—Louise Bernikow, "Lovers," *Among Women* (1980), excerpted in *Twentieth-Century British Literature*, ed. Harold Bloom (New York: Chelsea House Publishers, 1986), 1034–35

CLAUDIA STILLMAN FRANKS

I have called this study 'Beyond *The Well of Loneliness*' because I have wanted to dispel the misconception that Radclyffe Hall was a one-book thesis novelist, and because I believe that she should finally be acknowledged as a writer who successfully employed a variety of fictional themes, personality types, and nar-rative tones in her work. Indeed, one of the most striking features of her fic-tion, when it is viewed in its entirety, is the large panorama of characters who inhabit her world. They come from all walks of life, all social classes, and all age groups; they also vary widely in intellectual capability, creative capacity, and sexual inclination. Many are conventional, and many are unconventional; some melt into the crowd, and others are loners or eccentrics. Once it is rec-ognized, however, that *The Well of Loneliness* represents merely one part of

Radclyffe Hall's total achievement, it is worth asking to what extent the book is representative of all her writing; in other words, to what extent is Stephen Gordon a kind of paradigm of the alienated individual within the context of Radclyffe Hall's universe? And how does Radclyffe Hall characteristically order her fictional world?

At the centre of each of Radclyffe Hall's seven novels and five short stories stands a character who is marked by unusual sensitivity, by vague or concrete longings or ambitions, and by a tendency to reject the limitations of his or her environment. Joan Ogden of *The Unlit Lamp*, Susan Brent of *The Forge*, Sidonia Shore of *A Saturday Life*, and Stephen Gordon of *The Well of Loneliness*, all temporarily or permanently refuse to accept a woman's traditional role: Gian-Luca of *Adam's Breed*, Christophe Bénédit of *The Master of the House*, and Hannah Bullen of *The Sixth Beatitude* reject the purely materialistic orientation of their milieu and perish in the attempt to incorporate spiritual reality into the context of mundane experience; and the protagonists of *Miss Ogilvy Finds Herself* are isolated by self-deception, by contingencies of time and place, or by a value system which is incomprehensible to other people. Stephen Gordon, then, is far from an unusual character in the Radclyffe Hall canon, and, although the problems she faces as a lesbian in society are painfully real, I do not think that it is an exaggeration to say that her lesbianism also serves as a type of metaphor for the alienation that Radclyffe Hall saw at the root of human existence, just as racial and ethnic characteristics have been used partially as metaphors for alienation in modern literature.

Despite the sense of personal alienation which dominates her fiction, however, Radclyffe Hall's world is not a uniformly bleak one, for it does contain sources of joy. Among these are human love, community feeling, apprehension of divinity, and receptivity to natural beauty. Except in her two comedies, though, none of these sources of fulfilment proves permanently sustaining for the central characters, at least not within the context of their ordinary lives. ⟨. . .⟩

The basic theme of the individual's ultimate isolation, whether it is socially-imposed, self-imposed, or the result of impersonal natural laws, dominates Radclyffe Hall's writing. There is no development of this concept throughout her fiction; rather, it is a given condition of the world she creates. Only in her comedies does she make exceptions, but even there, the feeling of isolation is evoked by important secondary characters—Venetia Ford in *The Forge*, and Frances Reide in *A Saturday Life*. In view of the most crucial episodes in Radclyffe Hall's life, her fictional emphasis is hardly surprising. When one considers her major biographical events and circumstances up to 1916—her lonely childhood, her unsympathetic mother and step-father, her longing for her real father, her subservient devotion to Agnes Nichols, her frustrating

affairs with women, her almost unavoidable sense of inferiority in her relationship with Mabel Batten, then finally Ladye's tragic death—one sees that
the underlying tone of Radclyffe Hall's life quite naturally manifested itself in
her fiction. Her happiness with Una Troubridge may have freed her to realize
her creative potential, but it could hardly have been expected to wipe out the
effects of her first thirty-five years.

And so all of Radclyffe Hall's writing is partially autobiographical in that
it reflects a vision of the world in which the individual is necessarily thwarted—
if not by sexual nature, then by some other condition of life. It is in this wider
context that *The Well of Loneliness* should be seen; Stephen Gordon is not merely
the somewhat masochistic outcast who cries to an unlistening god for the
right to existence; instead, in her sensitivity, her struggle for happiness, and
her inevitable failure, she is typical of Radclyffe Hall's major protagonists, like
them embodying aspects of her creator, and like them reflecting parts of her
rich and complex personality.

—Claudia Stillman Franks, "Conclusion," *Beyond* The Well of Loneliness (1982), excerpted
in *Twentieth-Century British Literature*, ed. Harold Bloom (New York: Chelsea House Publishers,
1986), 1038–40

INEZ MARTINEZ

I believe that Hall's rendering of the psyche in her two lesbian novels has little to do with what she read or what she had her characters read, and I believe
the power of her portrait of the lesbian hero in love with the beautiful woman
accounts for the continued meaningfulness of the novels, even to "hip" readers. Modern readers persist through her prose (written appropriately enough
in the mode of heroic elaboration rather than, say, ironic or elliptical terse-
ness) because Hall wrote of the failure of hero-beauty eros, and because she
grounded this failure in the hero's worship of a consuming mother.

Eros based on opposition involves an attempt to unite with what one is
not. The hero-beauty opposition poses strength or feats at one pole and beauty
or being at the other. Historically, of course, strength and doing have been
associated with the male hero, and beauty and being with the adored female.
The terms in which Hall rendered the basic emotional dynamic between these
two poles are conventional enough: her heroes have to struggle against fear,
draw upon personal resources, and be endlessly protective in order to offer
feats to the worshiped woman; the female is charged with so valuing her beautiful being that she is willing to be worshiped, gratefully accept protection
from her hero, and bestow on her hero approval, admiration, and her self. The
hero does not consciously identify as the beautiful flower who needs protection and whose life purpose is fulfilled simply through being—even if to be so

serves her. In turn, the worshiped female—even if controlling events herself—does not identify with the competitor triumphing through personal strength and gaining life's purpose by winning a flower to protect.

Hall departed from convention by simply removing the sex-linking from these two poles. In Joan Ogden, hero of *The Unlit Lamp*, and in Stephen Gordon, hero of *The Well of Loneliness*, but particularly in Stephen, Hall created female protagonists who naturally and utterly identify with the heroic position. These characterizations imply that the hero-beauty dynamic is archetypal, i.e., a way of manifesting a human potential (in this case erotic attraction) inherent in the human psyche.

Although Hall created lovers for her heroes, lovers who identify with the worshiped female, the women who possess the power of approval for Joan and Stephen are their mothers. In most respects no two women could be more different than Mrs. Ogden and Anna Gordon, but the two of them are identical in refusing to affirm the maturation of their daughters and in assuming that absolute service from them is their due. Ultimately, it is in the struggle against the values of their mothers that Joan and Stephen must choose between self-affirmation and self-sacrifice.

This dilemma led Hall to an uncharacteristic critique of self-sacrifice. In her other novels Hall idealized characters capable of total self-abnegation in the service of others. In Madalena of *Adam's Breed*, in Hannah of *The Sixth Beatitude*, and in Christophe of *Master of the House* Hall seemed to think the Christian cross, the nailing together of love and death, a vindication of human suffering. Because Hall's attitude in these novels is passionately orthodox, her description of the destructiveness of self-sacrifice in her lesbian heroes is particularly arresting. As she has plotted their lives, maturation demands self-affirmation at the cost of pain to the beloved.

At this point a wary reader might think I am writing in support of the commonplace idea that lesbian love is a substitute mother-daughter relationship. ⟨. . .⟩

The pattern in Hall's novels at once resembles the commonplace idea about lesbian love and differs essentially from it. In Hall's rendering, both heroes have mothers who are intensely selfish and do not want their daughters to be themselves. But the solution for the daughters does not lie in a substitute mother-daughter relationship; rather, Joan and Stephen are tasked to wrest the affirming power from their mothers and assume it themselves. In Hall's novels, such self-affirmation is a condition for successful lesbian love; unfortunately, it is by definition inaccessible to the heroic attitude.

—Inez Martinez, "The Lesbian Hero Bound: Radclyffe Hall's Portrait of Sapphic Daughters and Their Mothers," *Literary Visions of Homosexuality* (1983), excerpted in *Twentieth-Century British Literature*, ed. Harold Bloom (New York: Chelsea House Publishers, 1986), 1040–41

CATHARINE R. STIMPSON

Lesbian novels in English have responded judgementally to the perversion that has made homosexuality perverse by developing two repetitive patterns: the dying fall, a narrative of damnation, of the lesbian's suffering as a lonely outcast attracted to a psychological lower caste; and the enabling escape, a narrative of the reversal of such descending trajectories, of the lesbian's rebellion against social stigma and self-contempt. Because the first has been dominant during the twentieth century, the second has had to flee from the imaginative grip of that tradition as well. ⟨. . .⟩

If the lesbian writer wished to name her experience but still feared plain speech, she could encrypt her text in another sense and use codes. ⟨. . .⟩ In some lesbian fiction, the encoding is allegorical, a straightforward shift from one set of terms to another, from a clitoris to a cow. Other acts are more resistant to any reading that might wholly reveal, or wholly deny, lesbian eroticism. ⟨. . .⟩

⟨. . .⟩ As if making an implicit, perhaps unconscious pact with her culture, the lesbian writer who rejects both silence and excessive coding can claim the right to write for the public in exchange for adopting the narrative of damnation. The paradigm of this narrative is Radclyffe Hall's *The Well of Loneliness*— published, banned in England, and quickly issued elsewhere in 1928, by which time scorn for lesbianism had hardened into orthodoxy. Novelist as well as novel have entered minor mythology. Hall represents the lesbian as scandal and the lesbian as woman-who-is-man, who proves "her" masculinity through taking a feminine woman-who-is-woman as "her" lover. In a baroque and savage satire published after *The Well of Loneliness*, Wyndham Lewis excoriates a den of dykes in which a woman artist in "a stiff Radcliffe-Hall collar, of antique masculine cut" torments a heterosexual fellow and dabbles with a voluptuous mate. He is too jealous and enraged to recognize either the sadness of costume and role reversal (the stigmatized seeking to erase the mark through aping the stigmatizers) or the courage of the masquerade (the emblazoning of defiance and jaunty play). Be it mimicry or bravery, the woman who would be man reaches for status and for freedom. The man who would be woman, because of the devaluation of the female and feminine, participates, in part, in a ritual of degradation.

Comparing *The Well of Loneliness* to Hall's life reveals a discrepancy between the pleasures she seems to have found with her lover, Una Taylor, Lady Troubridge, and the sorrows of her hero, Stephen Gordon. Hall offers a parallel to the phenomenon of the woman novelist who creates women characters less accomplished and successful than she. In addition, the novel is more pessimistic about the threat of homosexuality as such to happiness than Hall's earlier novel, *The Unlit Lamp* (1924). ⟨. . .⟩

⟨. . .⟩ In brief, *The Well of Loneliness* tends to ignore the more benign possibilities of lesbianism. Hall projects homosexuality as a sickness. To deepen the horror, the abnormal illness is inescapable, preordained; an ascribed, not an achieved, status. For Stephen is a "congenital invert," the term John Addington Symonds probably coined around 1883. ⟨. . .⟩

The congenital female invert has male physical traits—narrow hips, wide shoulders—as "part of an organic instinct." Stephen also has a livid scar on her cheek. Literally, it is a war wound; socially, a mark of the stigmatized individual who may blame the self for a lack of acceptability; mythically, the mark of Cain. *The Well of Loneliness* stresses the morbidity of a stigma that the politics of heaven, not of earth, must first relieve.

Yet Hall planned an explicit protest against that morbidity. Indeed, having Stephen Gordon be a congenital invert who has no choice about her condition strengthens Hall's argument about the unfairness of equating homosexuality with punishable deviancy. The novel claims that God created homosexuals. If they are good enough for Him, they ought to be good enough for us. Hall cries out for sacred and social toleration, for an end to the cruelties of alienation. In the novel's famous last paragraph, Stephen gasps, "God . . . we believe; we have told You we believe. . . . We have not denied You, then rise up and defend us. Acknowledge us, oh God, before the whole world. Give us the right to our existence." Ironically, the very explicitness of that cry in a climate increasingly harsh for lesbians, combined with the vividness of Hall's description of homosexual subworlds, propelled *The Well of Loneliness* into scandal while the far more subversive, if subtle *Unlit Lamp* was a success. To double the irony, Hall's strategies of protest against damnation so entangle her in damnation that they intensify the sense of its inevitability and power. The novel's attack on homophobia becomes particularly self-defeating. The text is, then, like a Janus with one face looming larger than the other. It gives the heterosexual a voyeuristic tour and the vicarious comfort of reading about an enforced stigma—in greater measure than it provokes guilt. It gives the homosexual, particularly the lesbian, riddling images of pity, self-pity, and terror— in greater measure than it consoles.

—Catharine R. Stimpson, "Zero Degree Deviancy: The Lesbian Novel in English," in *Feminisms: An Anthology of Literary Theory and Criticism*, ed. Robyn R. Warhol and Diane Price Herndl (New Brunswick: Rutgers University Press, 1992), 301–5

LILLIAN FADERMAN

Hall believed that her novel would provide lesbians with a moral and medical defense against a society which viewed same-sex love as immoral or curable. If a female argued that she chose to center her life on another female, she laid herself open to accusations of immorality, she willfully flew in the face of the conventions of her day. If she accepted the psychoanalytical theory that something had happened to her in childhood to cause her aberration, she had no excuse not to seek a cure which would undo the trauma and set her straight. But if she maintained that she was born with her "condition," although some might consider her a freak she could insist, as Hall actually did, that God created her that way, that she had a purpose in God's scheme of things even if she was a freak. Unless a lesbian accepted the congenitalists' theories, her grounds for not changing were indefensible if she did not live in a society totally committed to the principle of free choice—and Hall knew that her barely post-Victorian society had no such commitment. ⟨. . .⟩

There was probably no lesbian in the four decades between 1928 and the late 1960's capable of reading English or any of the eleven languages into which the book was translated who was unfamiliar with *The Well of Loneliness*. Del Martin, co-author of *Lesbian/Woman*, has called it a "Lesbian Bible." It was widely used in college abnormal psychology classes, and was the only lesbian novel known to the masses. But many lesbians who read the book during Hall's day and after felt angered and betrayed by it. An American sociological study of lesbians in the 1920's and 1930's indicated that "almost to a woman, they decried its publication." They believed that if the novel did not actually do harm to their cause, at the least it "put homosexuality in the wrong light." The responses of individual lesbians were similar. The artist Romaine Brooks, for example, called *The Well* "a ridiculous book, trite, superficial" and Hall "a digger up of worms with the pretention of a distinguished archaeologist." Violet Trefusis in a letter to her lover, Vita Sackville-West, declared the book a "loathesome example," and said she longed herself to write a story of same-sex love in response that would be very different.

Nor has the novel brought much satisfaction or joy to women in more recent times. It has often served to label for a woman what her love for another female has meant to society in the twentieth century, and it plays a sad, prominent part in many an individual lesbian history. ⟨. . .⟩

The Well has had generally such a devastating effect on female same-sex love not only because its central character ends in loneliness but—and much more significantly—because its writer fell into the congenitalist trap. She believed that if she argued that some women were born different, society would free them to pursue their independence; instead, her popular rendition of "congenital inversion" further morbidified the most natural impulses and healthy views. It reinforced the notion that some women would not marry not because the institution was often unjust, that they sought independence not because they believed it would make them whole people, that they loved other women not because such love was natural—but instead because they were born into the wrong body. To be born into the wrong body was freakish. Many a woman must have decided to tolerate even the worst heterosexual inequities rather than to view herself in such a way.

   —Lillian Faderman, *Surpassing the Love of Men: Romantic Friendship and Love Between Women from the Renaissance to the Present* (New York: Quality Paperback Book Club, 1994), 317–18, 322–23

BIBLIOGRAPHY

'Twixt Earth and Stars. 1903.
A Sheaf of Verses. 1908.
Poems of the Past and Present. 1910.
Songs of Three Counties, and Other Poems. 1913.
The Forgotten Island. 1915.
The Forge. 1924.
The Unlit Lamp. 1924.
A Saturday Life. 1925.
Adam's Breed. 1926.
The Well of Loneliness. 1928.
The Master of the House. 1932.
Miss Ogilvy Finds Herself. 1934.
The Sixth Beatitude. 1936.

WINIFRED HOLTBY

1898–1935

WINIFRED HOLTBY was born in Rudston, Yorkshire, on June 23, 1898. Her parents farmed 940 acres on the Wolds in East Yorkshire; although her father retired early to live a quiet life, her mother was active in local affairs. Winifred grew up among cousins and school friends and with a sense of social commitment inherited from her parents. Her childhood was happy in spite of constant illness, including a serious case of scarlet fever. She possessed a strong imagination and enthusiasm for the natural world, which formed the subject of her first collection of poems—published surreptitiously by her mother when Winifred was just 13. She published again during high school, this time a journalistic account of the Germans' attack of Scarborough in a Cumberland newspaper.

In World War I, Holtby served in France as a member of the Women's Auxiliary Army Corps. After the war, she attended Somerville College, Oxford, where she met Vera Brittain. Champions of each other's literary career, the two shared a flat in London, a practical arrangement that marked the beginning of a strong, lifelong friendship. While a lecturer at the university, Holtby campaigned for feminist causes, sat on various political committees, and found time to become a prolific journalist, writing for the *Manchester Guardian*, the *News Chronicle*, and the *Time and Tide*. She became director of the last in 1926.

Vera Brittain's marriage signaled a change in Holtby's literary path; she began talking about writing novels and soon did, publishing *Anderby Wold* in 1923. An early indication of her eye for creating scenes inhabited with unique characters, *Anderby Wold* echoed the village life she knew so well from her childhood. The book was not well received, however, and Holtby herself came to share critics' impressions of it. Over the next 10 years, she would publish four more novels; volumes of poetry; short stories; and two nonfiction studies. A fifth novel (published posthumously in 1936), *South Riding*, won the James Tait Black Prize in 1936. Generally considered Holtby's masterpiece and most famous novel, *South Riding* was translated into numerous languages and made into a film by producer Victor Saville.

Winifred Holtby died at age 37 from kidney disease, likely complicated by the scarlet fever she had suffered as a child.

CRITICAL EXTRACTS

MABEL S. ULRICH

Every now and then there appears a book—usually it arrives unheralded—which makes so personal an appeal to one's own brand of humor and philosophy, that even a hardened reviewer reads it with his critical sense held in abeyance to his pleasure, and for a cool, objective criticism a second reading is essential. Rarely in my experience has this happened with an "important" book—never a Spengler nor a Whitehead. No, usually it is a "South Wind," a "Mr. Fortune's Maggot," a "Monkey Wife," a "High Wind in Jamaica." Today it is "Mandoa, Mandoa!" Not that Winifred Holtby's story is like any of these,—very likely it is not technically so good as the best—but it shares with them a richness of imagination and a biting, ironic humor which makes of each a sheer delight to the lover of true satire.

Mandoa, "founded as a Catholic colony of Abyssinia" in the heart of Africa, is inhabited by "a brown-skinned, straight-haired, swarthy, handsome race"—and by slaves. Forgotten by the Mother Church, its religion has become a pragmatic mixture of Christianity and paganism, which sees nothing incongruous in a hierarchy of six hundred and seventy-nine archbishops headed by an Arch-archbishop who combines the offices of pope and medicine-man; a dignitary who has gained his ascendency and his additional *arch* by praying so successively for God's blessing on his sovereign, that the Virgin Princess is delivered at the end of nine months of a Royal Princess. (Should the child prove to be a male the archbishop "simply disappeared.") Sovereigns were invariably female since women were "easier to manage. They must be respected but they need not be obeyed." For the dispensing of culture there was Hollywood Hall 〈. . . .〉

We shuttle from the heart of Africa with its color, its smells, its slave-trains, its feasting, its blood-curdling cruelties, to present-day London and back again. We are in on a General Election, and watch for the returns with London's social elect; we see the dole at work, meet the sophisticates and Lord Lufton's little group of serious thinkers; we watch the clear-eyed Jean Stanbury go down to her defeat in the office of the radical editor; we dine with politicians, and get a glimpse of the ways of Westminster. In short we have a very good time indeed while the futility of our present-day civilization unrolls against the background of a country eager to emerge from its barbarism by way of bath-tubs, cosmetics, and safety razors.

Miss Holtby seems not to have missed a single opportunity, and she presents her pictures with so much vigor and wit, that one is tempted to quote from almost every page. ⟨. . .⟩

Miss Holtby's characters, so deftly and wittily presented to us, display a rather curious lack of interest in love-making. To those who have felt for years that possibly love-making does not, as so many novelists would have us believe, consume three-fourths of life's activities, this is of encouraging portent. Nevertheless I should have liked to have "listened in" on Jean's surrender of her freedom. Jean herself is so shyly treated—because she is autobiographic?—that she rarely emerges completely. And when she does it is to utter matter-of-fact, if seldom uttered, truths about women and their jobs, about marriage and love, which will, I fear, arouse antagonism rather than sympathy in the average novel reader.

—Mabel S. Ulrich, "Salvaging the Savages," *The Saturday Review of Literature* (16 September 1933): 107

THE NEW YORK TIMES BOOK REVIEW

Miss Holtby's many-bladed satire cuts a wide swath. Her view of the vainglory of the world is that all people have their full and disarmingly vulnerable share of it, and so when she has laughed at her people for a time she has the skill and imaginativeness to turn and explore their serious sensibilities. In this way she has managed to give her "comedy of irrelevance" a core of sound characterization that few of these tales of foolish white people in mythical alien kingdoms possess.

The savage and spectacular Mandoa that she has invented in the perennially lacerated heart of Africa with the help of a guidebook and many memories of Abyssinia has its legion of predecessors in fiction. They must go back at least to Prester John's time. Evelyn Waugh's "Black Mischief" comes inescapably to mind in reading "Mandoa, Mandoa!" as one of its more recent and distinguished predecessors in this sort of thing. That book also drew much of its bloom from the stimulating accounts of Ras Tafari's fabulous coronation and his kingdom. Miss Holtby's Mandoa is ruled, by way of a change, through the unbroken succession of a dynasty of miraculously unmarried queens. ⟨. . .⟩

It is Miss Holtby's most rewarding ability to keep all ⟨the⟩ spectacles and alarums and excursions in constant, fluid motion that gives the story its vitality. There is, in fact, a satiating quality about its abundance. One has the feeling that she is wasting her ammunition in taking the familiar pot-shots at the vulgarities of the talkies, at Members of Parliament, at London's Chelsea smarties, at tourists, and so on. But in the main pattern of her story she has shown some of the people of her day with Amazonian wit and vigor.

—N. A., "An Exploited People," *The New York Times Book Review* (17 September 1933): 7

KENNETH YOUNG

What manner of book is *South Riding*? Why, when ⟨Winifred Holtby's⟩ earlier
works were somewhat tepidly received, did this have so grand a success? In the
first place, it is a finely organised novel on a grand scale; there are 167 characters listed at the front of the book (though some are listed humorously—
such as Ellen Wilkinson, M.P., and Elsie and Doris Waters, the famous wireless
entertainers), and their stories are made to interlock in the most skilful way;
moreover they are brought together not merely because they live in the same
small area but also because they are linked in one way or other by local gov-
ernment. This, indeed, is perhaps the greatest novel of English local govern-
ment ever written; and Winifred Holtby named the eight books into which
her novel is divided after such aspects of Council work as "Education", "Public
Health", and "Mental Deficiency".

Only to those who have never read *South Riding* will this sound dreary. In
fact it was a means of control which Winifred Holtby brought to bear upon
her imagination that burgeoned and could have run riot when she sat down to
write her masterpiece. For the larger characters she created here would break
the bonds of any artificial scheme and would live their lives—and keep on living them in the imaginations of readers—even were they to have first
appeared in weekly parts in pulp magazines.

There is Robert Carne, the "big, handsome and unhappy looking" sport-
ing farmer, whose wife is in a mental home and who is on the verge of bank-
ruptcy. For him—and for his small daughter, the neurotic Midge—there is
love of two distinct kinds: from Alderman Mrs. Beddows, tough but wise old
woman, and from Sarah Burton, daughter of a Yorkshire artisan who becomes
headmistress of Kiplington High School. Sarah, red-haired, snip-snap, small
and fortyish, is one of the most original creations in 20th-century fiction (she
was over-glamourised in the film); but she is matched for originality by the
odd Alderman Snaith who can be a good public servant while at the same time
lining his own pocket (a commoner type in real life than in fiction). Some of
the smaller characters, too, are originals—Tom Sawdon, the landlord of the
Nag's Head for example; only one or two seem to be cast in a mould already
familiar in fiction, such as Huggins, the local preacher who has got a girl into
trouble.

With infinite skill, Winifred Holtby brings her people together and
towards a grand and tragic moment. But on the way there are constant smaller
crises; character is revealed in depth and with all its twists and turns; it is a novel
full of tiny surprises but scarcely one of them will not be recognised as credible. We find ourselves saying: "Yes, that is how he *would* have felt or acted, surprising though it is."

But *South Riding* is not merely an eminently satisfying novel of narrative; it is also written with great lucidity and startlingly apt observation whether it be of a country cottage, Maythorpe Manor, a music-hall or a near-derelict hutment. It is not merely about "real" people; it bodies forth a whole region of England that has had few to celebrate it, before or since.

—Kenneth Young, "Introduction" (1966) to *South Riding* by Winifred Holtby (London: Collins, 1986), xiii–xv

MARY CADOGAN

Almost everything in *Anderby Wold*, from the mundane to the aspirational, is expressed in country or farming terms. For example, Mary considers her elderly relatives (now retired from farming) 'lifeless as . . . uprooted trees', and their conversation 'meaningless as the rustle of dry leaves on brittle twigs'. Her own youth and childhood are occasionally recollected in rushes of vibrant images arising from country sights or scents, as in the moment when the sweetness of a paddock rich with hawthorn becomes a symbol of Mary's personal and secret 'garden of romance'.

Seasonal landscapes reflect the intensity of Winifred Holtby's pictorial imagination. She is at her best with wintry scenes of the clear, curving wolds and blackened twigs against stark skies; but whether lush or low-key, her physical settings frequently illuminate the psychological moods of her main characters.

One part of the book's appeal lies in its sense of place and scene, and another is in the ebullience of its female characterisations. There is no doubt that generally women emerge from the pages of *Anderby Wold* more compellingly than the men, who are less three-dimensional and even, ocasionally, cyphers. ⟨. . .⟩

Away from the farm and village, in the Cranfordian cluster of Robson relatives who live in the town of Market Burton, it is very much what the women think that matters. However ineffectual they might *seem*, it is they who damn with faint praise or caustic reproach; who shred reputations and relationships; who decide when their husbands or brothers are ready for retirement; or whether Mary is beginning to overstep the mark in ruling her village roost. ⟨. . .⟩

Winifred Holtby, through Mary Robson, expressed her own capacity to recognise truth, even when this came in unpalatable forms like rejection or antagonism. Though always identifying herself with progressive ideas, Holtby could still acknowledge their occasional crudity and ruthlessness. She challenged the new as well as the old in her exploration of the levels at which social reforms or political achievements could operate. In *Anderby Wold* there are instances of idealistic progressiveness and individual aspirations that quickly turn sour. Her later novels voiced the conviction that ultimately we are all a part of each other, and that only in the recognition of this can failure and success be reconciled. Mary fumblingly moves towards this understanding in *Anderby Wold*, though she is hardly able to articulate it: 'The broad view . . . If one could only take the broad view . . . David's courage and service not wantonly wasted, his desire for progress not frustrated, but fulfilled at last because of him—even remotely because of her . . .'. There are moments, however, when she is able to transmute her personal and restricted experience into something universal. The lambent quality of Holtby's life and work glows occasionally through the heroine of her first novel, and especially in situations that offer her little expectation of happiness. It is sometimes expressed through spontaneous physical exhilaration: 'Really John's stupidity mattered very little on a morning like this. She wanted to race with the wind, to jump, to shout, to sing.' There is an intimation here of the transforming experience in *South Riding*, triggered off by the observation of some frisking lambs, which momentarily lifts the tired and anguished Miss Sigglesthwaite out of her sense of failure.

A theme that crops up in several of Holtby's books (notably of course in *The Land of Green Ginger*) is the uncovering of the magic that the author believed lay just below the commonplace surface of life. In *Anderby Wold* Mary Robson senses this magic in the early days of her love for David, and in her strong response to natural beauty.

There are indications that Winifred Holtby, like several other women writers, looked to nature as a refuge from the world of demanding relationships. Her aspirations as a creative artist not only conflicted at times with the needs of friends and family, but with her own ambitions as a social reformer. (She campaigned throughout her life for the causes of feminism, racial equality, world unity and pacifism.) The only way in which she could reconcile all these conflicting elements was by occasional withdrawals that she described as entering 'the nunnery of the mind'. But, in fact, the convent of her imagination seems to have been the sweeping vastness of the Yorkshire countryside that she frequently visited in order to find renewal, even when she was deeply involved in London life and work. In *Anderby Wold* there is a conscious looking back to the settings of her childhood, and an unconscious forward projection towards '*South Riding*', her last and most significant novel which also had a Yorkshire background.

—Mary Cadogan, "Introduction" to *Anderby Wold* by Winifred Holtby (London: Virago Press, 1981), xi–xiii, xvii–xix

MARION SHAW

Like other such works—*Gulliver's Travels* and *Animal Farm* come to mind—*Mandoa, Mandoa!* is less interested in psychological and social realism than in the creation of characters who typify human attributes and of situations which show those attributes in action. With schematic thoroughness it assembles a large cast of cultural and class types and draws them into a complex situation by means of a narrative which is simple—a wedding to which many guests come—but a brilliant focus for the interaction of the economic, racial and personal forces involved. Much of the humour and satirical thrust of the novel depends on the incongruities which arise from such interaction, for example, those caused by the impact of technology on a primitive people. Winifred Holtby's comic penetration is well illustrated in the instance of Talal's infatuation with motor cars, cocktail shakers, telephones and steamboats, which is not only amusing, and even absurd, given the absence of technology in his country, but sharply questions the benefits civilisation bestows. Do such commodities represent the summary of Western achievement, and is Talal's susceptibility to them an avenue to his and his country's exploitation? To Winifred Holtby's contemporary readers, themselves precariously embarking on an era of the mass production of consumer goods as well as of colonial contraction, such questions must have seemed doubly relevant.

But *Mandoa, Mandoa!* is more of a hybrid work than, say, *Animal Farm*; it has ambitions other than single-minded political satire, and, as contemporary critics noted, occasionally shifts gear from caricature and near-fantasy into realism. This is particularly true of the two main English characters, Jean Stanbury and Bill Durrant. Jean Stanbury is brought into the novel not for her usefulness to the plot but as a foil to the extravagant characters around her. Admirable, hard-working Jean, who is so much a projection of Winifred Holtby herself, provides a standard of common sense, practical dedication, and liberal tolerance, what is good, in fact, in Western society, against which the excesses and idiosyncracies of other characters, both European and African, can be measured. She is a figure of enlightened English ordinariness: "We have to work for the world as we know it as best we can . . . we have to go on," she says at the end of the novel, and this is the belief *Mandoa, Mandoa!* adheres to and which underlies its political satire and also its racial and cultural assumptions. The "world as we know it" is one in which the values of Jean Stanbury are considered if not superior then certainly the standpoint from which those of other cultures are viewed. Inevitably, therefore, the African characters are portrayed as comic or barbaric and Mandoa itself as a fantasy country in which types, even stereotypes, can flourish without too much regard for cultural accuracy or neutrality. As Winifred Holtby said, her concern was not with "tribal experience" but with "the human story" of her imaginary place. *Mandoa, Mandoa!* is only superficially an African story; its main purpose is with the variousness of political and social behaviour defined in Western terms. Although it would be too crude to say that *Mandoa, Mandoa!* is peopled with English eccentrics, some of whom have blackened faces, there is a sense in which, like Swift's Lilliput, it is less the people and conditions of Mandoa that are of interest than what they tell us about English society. ⟨. . .⟩

⟨. . . Her⟩ purpose in *Mandoa, Mandoa!* was largely an intellectual one: "I want to do something hard, muscular, compact, very little emotional, and with the emotion hammered into the style. Metalwork, not water-colour."

In this respect *Mandoa, Mandoa!* is different from Winifred Holtby's other novels. Whilst not "water-colour", they follow conventional patterns of the nineteenth-century realist novel in their concern with the details of parochial, domestic and personal issues. This is the mode she returned to in her final novel, *South Riding*, which is in the tradition of George Eliot's *Middlemarch*. But *Mandoa, Mandoa!* is an expression of the political acumen and acerbity of mind which made her so good a journalist. ⟨. . .⟩

It is also an unusual novel for a woman to have written. Several of its reviewers remarked on this: she showed "an almost masculine appreciation of practical issues", L.P. Hartley wrote, and, with some surprise, Graham Greene likened the strength of her writing in *Mandoa, Mandoa!* to that of Waugh and Conrad. Indeed, the novel can be seen as the antiphonal voice to that of a work which was being written alongside it, Vera Brittain's highly personal and "feminine" *Testament of Youth*. There is a certain irony in that the only book Winifred dedicated to Vera, the Very Small Very Dear Love of the inscription, should be so different from anything Vera wrote herself. "Hard, muscular, compact" are the last adjectives one could apply to *Testament of Youth* but they are, for the most part, true of *Mandoa, Mandoa!*, as is Winifred's later description of it as "vital and gay". The endeavour and achievement of *Mandoa, Mandoa!* was for Winifred Holtby a form of control over her illness, her fear of death, and her grief at the failure of love; it is as much a Testament as Vera Brittain's book. But with an interesting defiance of traditional modes of female writing about such subjects, Winifred Holtby chose an escape into what is generally regarded as a masculine form, the novel of political comedy.

—Marion Shaw, "Introduction" to *Mandoa, Mandoa!* by Winifred Holtby (London: Virago Press, 1981), xiv–xv, xviii–xix

GEORGE DAVIDSON

Poor Caroline is about the divergent tendencies of philanthropy and exploitation, and the humour, tinged with sadness, arising from their clash in an oddly constituted Company, bringing together incompatible people. The Jewish merchant, Isenbaum, and the dilettante, St Basil, scratch each other's backs. Johnson and Macafee are out solely for themselves. Roger and Eleanor have more palatable ulterior motives, but they too use Caroline. Eleanor is no impressionable altruist, but entertains self-professed business ambitions and involves herself in her relative's project for the sake of being associated with an apparently good cause. Even Caroline, the only true believer in her brain-child for the actual spiritual benefits she intends it to bring, is perhaps merely trying to justify herself when society has no real further need of her. Although Vera Brittain accurately described her as 'a self-deceived optimist with an unbalanced devotion to hopeless projects', Caroline is so observed as to be likeable despite her absurdity. Her world of 'uplift, good works and propaganda' was very much her creator's sphere as a fervent believer in education and the benefits of religion. Winifred, however, was no unrealistic idealist like Caroline. Her optimistic canvassing on behalf of the League of Nations or South African Trades Unions was not so earnestly self-important as to be above self-mockery—there could be an element of self-parody in her Caroline, despite Winifred assuring Lady Rhondda: 'Caroline is not a symbol of me, but an expression of herself . . . I meant to leave the impression of someone silly but vital, directly futile but indirectly triumphant.'

Caroline's demise is not treated tragically, because it leads to the prospect of future benefit. Parallel with this undefeated attitude lies a positive view of progress, both moral and technical. *Poor Caroline* may not be most memorable as a discussion of the ethics of scientific progress, but the issue is not raised lightly, and admonitions concerning society's future are deliberately made. ⟨. . .⟩

A fine writer's themes and obsessions continually engage important issues with a perspicacity which remains modern and pertinent over and beyond the particular fictional and historical context. Winifred Holtby was a flash of brilliant dynamism, who threw herself with a combined sense of duty and conviction into the burning issues of her day, hoping to help improve society. Her texts and speeches were persuasive in the twenties and thirties and, fortunately, she left an artistic testament which enriches posterity. For despite her dichotomy she was able to combine her dual instincts as writer and reformer without making Caroline's alleged sacrifice of one for the other: 'If I'd had more time I could have been a poet . . . only between the claims of art and science I had to choose, being by nature a pioneer and fighter.'

—George Davidson, "Introduction" to *Poor Caroline* by Winifred Holtby (New York: Penguin, 1985), xv–xvii

JEAN E. KENNARD

Despite the fact the *South Riding* shows more respect for connection than her earlier novels, Holtby still stresses the value of independence, particularly female independence. There is no happiness for her characters without achievement and self-respect. The successful people of *South Riding* are two strong and independent women, Sarah Burton and Mrs. Beddows. They form the mother-daughter pair of this novel and illustrate the conflict Holtby claimed was the core of *South Riding*, "between the people who want to plan and change things by deliberate will, and the people who just want to 'let things happen.' "

Sarah Burton, high school principal, feminist, and advocate for social change, is the David Rossitur of this novel. Since *Anderby Wold* Holtby has in some ways tempered her political views, become reformer rather than radical, but she makes their spokesperson a woman rather than a man. The portrait of Sarah draws on the experiences of Holtby's friend Jean McWilliam, a high school principal in South Africa, but it is most obviously a portrait of Holtby herself. "Winifred thought of Sarah Burton as herself," Brittain writes, "though she made her heroine small and red-haired, with the appearance of Ellen Wilkinson, M.P., whom she had always liked and admired." ⟨. . .⟩

Sarah is a sexually passionate person. Against her better judgment she falls in love with a local conservative landowner, Robert Carne, although she knows "I oppose everything he stands for . . . feudalism, patronage, chivalry, exploitation" (193). This is, of course, Holtby's characteristic heterosexual love relationship, perhaps based on her own with Harry Pearson, in which attraction reaches across wide differences in personality and views. She has reversed the situation of *Anderby Wold* in which conservative Mary Robson loves socialist David Rossitur, but the pattern is the same. Sarah's desire for Carne is convincingly portrayed in the hotel scene, where they meet by chance and she invites him to her room, but Holtby does not romanticize sexual desire. The romanticism of Mary Robson has no place in Sarah Burton's life. Holtby replays the scene from *Anderby Wold* when "heroine" suddenly meets "hero," "a big dark man on a big dark horse" (137). This time, however, the "heroine" herself comments ironically on the echoes of *Jane Eyre*: "into Sarah's well-educated mind flashed the memory of Jane Eyre and Mr. Rochester" (138). Sexuality is a powerful but not central part of Sarah Burton's life, and because society now allows her to express her feelings much more freely, it has far less control over her than it might have had in an earlier era. Holtby's world has come a long way from the prewar one of Mary Robson and even further, of course, from that of Maggie Tulliver.

Nowhere in *South Riding* does Holtby suggest that women can successfully combine marriage and a career. Indeed, Holtby continues what seems to have been an ongoing debate with Brittain over the necessity of marriage for fulfillment. As she had in *Women and a Changing Civilisation*, Holtby challenges Brittain's suggestions in *Testament of Youth* that the single life is somehow psychologically undesirable by ridiculing those women who want marriage at any cost and by dignifying those who have made other choices. 〈. . .〉

Holtby's sympathy is most in evidence in her portrayal of Agnes Sigglesthwaite, the unmarried science teacher who cannot control the students and is treated by them as a figure of fun. Through Sarah Burton Holtby creates respect for her scholarship and understanding for her need to teach to support her elderly mother. Holtby even attributes to Agnes Sigglesthwaite a particularly significant spiritual experience of her own that had occurred just after she learned she had only two years to live and that she did not describe to Brittain until three months before she died. Walking in despair close to a hillside farm, Holtby broke the ice for some lambs who needed water. "Suddenly, in a flash, the grief, the bitterness, the sense of frustration disappeared; all desire to possess power and glory for herself vanished away, and never came back."

— Jean E. Kennard, *Vera Brittain and Winifred Holtby* (Hanover: University Press of New England, 1989), 166–69

BIBLIOGRAPHY

My Garden. 1911.
Anderby Wold. 1923.
The Crowded Street. 1924.
The Land of Green Ginger. 1927.
Poor Caroline. 1931.
Virginia Woolf. 1932.
Mandoa! Mandoa! 1933.
The Astonishing Island. 1933.
Women and a Changing Civilisation. 1934.
Truth is Not Sober. 1934.
The Frozen Earth. 1935.
South Riding. 1936.
Pavements of Anderby. 1937.
Take Back Your Freedom. 1939.

VIOLET HUNT

1866–1942

ISOBEL VIOLET HUNT was born in 1866 in Durham, England. As the daughter of landscape painter Alfred William Hunt and novelist Margaret Raine Hunt, she grew up among the pivotal artists and poets of the Pre-Raphaelite movement, including Robert Browning, Edward Burne-Jones, Ford Madox Brown, John Ruskin, and Christina and Dante Gabriel Rossetti, who would later be the subject of her highly acclaimed biography, *The Wife of Rossetti* (1932).

While in her early teens, Hunt studied painting at the South Kensington Art School and wrote poetry and fiction, mentored by Christina Rossetti. At 17, she met Oscar Wilde, shortly after he arrived in London. They developed a special friendship rumored to have culminated in Wilde's proposal of marriage. Although Hunt even as a young girl possessed what her mother called the "savoir vivre of a woman of 50," the association with Wilde marked her true coming of age, a 10-year relationship recorded in Hunt's unpublished essay "My Oscar."

In her early 20s, Hunt wrote a column for the *Pall Mall Gazette* and regularly contributed to other popular Victorian periodicals. A feminist who resisted conventional social mores and sexual repressiveness, Hunt created protagonists who were largely autobiographical— although the heroine of her first novel, *The Maiden's Progress* (1894), does eventually yield to convention and marry. Later novels, such as *Unkist, Unkind!* (1897) and *The White Rose of Weary Leaf* (1908), would delve into the female psyche and the complexities of sexual politics.

Hunt's artistic and sexual lives coalesced in her numerous love affairs with literary men, including W. H. Hudson, W. Somerset Maugham, and Oswald Crawford. She met Ford Madox Ford at *The English Review* in 1908, and the two began a long affair that produced several collaborative accomplishments, including the short story collection *Zeppelin Nights* (1916) and the discovery of young novelist D. H. Lawrence. Ford left Hunt in 1918, however, when he became involved with her friend Stella Bowen. The majority of Hunt's novels were written during this 10-year period, including *The Governess* (1913), which was begun by her mother and finished by Hunt.

In writing her later novels, *Their Lives* (1916) and *Their Hearts* (1921), Hunt drew much of the conflict from the difficult relationships she had with her two sisters, who opposed her sexually free lifestyle. In *The Flurried Years* (1926), an intimate memoir, Hunt used her novelistic abilities to portray vividly her insider's perspective on English literary society and her friendships with contemporaries like W. Somerset Maugham, Henry James, May Sinclair, Rebecca West, and H. G. Wells.

Until her death from syphilis on January 16, 1942, Hunt continued to live at the center of England's cultural elite, writing and remaining an active feminist.

CRITICAL EXTRACTS

FREDERIC TABER COOPER

The White Rose of Weary Leaf, by Violet Hunt, is best defined as a sort of modern *Jane Eyre* story, possessing all the defects of the Charlotte Brontë school and few of its merits. It is sensational, melodramatic, often crude in construction and in character drawing—and nevertheless there is a certain relentless sincerity in the story of the central character, a certain poignant tragedy in her fate that make it a book difficult to lay aside, in spite of one's frequent sense of exasperation, and equally difficult to forget after finishing it. The Jane Eyre of this story is not an inexperienced young girl, but a sad, disillusioned woman, who has long looked the world in the face and expects nothing from it but injustice. The Mr. Rochester has been married, not once, but twice; the surviving wife is not crazed, but simply a self-satisfied little fool. The spectacular tragedy is not a fire, but a railroad wreck, and even here the wife, though badly hurt, insists upon recovering, in spite of the doctor's assurances that she will die. The man, however, allows the other woman to believe that the wife is dead; and from this initial wrong the story moves strongly on to a double expiation, told in a spirit of grim fatalism. It is astonishing that a book so faulty should here and there show streaks of such undeniable merit.

—Frederic Taber Cooper, [Review of *White Rose of Weary Leaf*], *The Bookman* (August 1908): 578–80

MAY SINCLAIR

⟨Among Violet Hunt's novels⟩ there are five outstanding ones. These compel you to remember them: *White Rose of Weary Leaf*, *Their Lives*, *Their Hearts*, *Tales of the Uneasy*, and *Sooner or Later*. This last I should place a little lower than the other four. *White Rose*, even while remembered, can be read again and again with pleasure.

The others must be slightly forgotten to renew their appeal. They should be read separately with a stretch of time between. Taken as the critic must take them, one on the top of the other, their effect is a little stifling. There is a want of perspective and relief. It is like listening to a person with a fixed idea; like looking at repeated portraits of the same figure. There never was such a gallery of English *demi-vierges*.

To be sure, their demi-virginity is purely mental. They are betrayed first by their own minds. There is a *naïveté* about them, an innocent uncertainty. Rosette and Christina offer themselves to their lovers, but they only half know what they are doing; it is partly because they desire to know that they do it. Their passions are too exalted, too pathetic, too foredoomed to count as sensual. Their senses are dumb, unawakened, or superseded. It is their hearts that clamour, unsatisfying and unsatisfied. That is the trouble with them all. One burst of honest sensuality would have settled their business for them and left them calm. But no; they are too subtle for their own or their lovers' satisfaction. They are born to torture and be tortured. ⟨. . .⟩

Scenes repeat themselves. Passion, foreboding, reproach, recrimination, repudiation, despair, and more passion. A vicious circle. These figures have no background that counts. Wherever they are, the effect is always the same, of naked passions played out on bare boards before a dark curtain. They may be walking on the Yorkshire moors, or by the bracing north-eastern sea, in woods smelling of damp moss and earth, in gardens by the Solent, and instantly the air is changed; it becomes sultry with passion; it is the air of a stuffy bedroom with the windows tight shut; there is a smell of hair-brushes, cigarette smoke, and warm sachet.

We are least aware of it in *White Rose of Weary Leaf*, because the dominant character, Amy Stephens, is a higher and healthier type. The atmosphere is cleared by conflict, by the beating of her wings as her will resists her lover.

White Rose is perhaps the best book Violet Hunt has written yet; the finest in conception, in form and technique. It is a surprising piece of psychology, male and female. There is no important character in it that does not live, from the amazing and complex Amy Stephens to the too simple and degenerate Dulce Dand, who will go mad if she is not married. Jeremy Dand, Amy's middle-aged married lover, is the one entirely successful male figure that Violet Hunt has created. It is more than a portrait; a portrait is painted in the flat, as are the figures of Robert Assheton and Euphan Balfame, in the two dimensions of brutality and sensual passion. Jeremy Dand is a three-dimensional form that we can walk round; he is not drawn, but hewn, chiselled faithfully in his many-sided detail. He is the average sensual man, but he is never brutal like Assheton and Balfame; Violet Hunt has abandoned the fallacy of the ruling passion and presented him as he is, with all his inconsistencies; selfish and unselfish, generous and mean, faithful and faithless, a human battlefield, till in the end his passion for Amy masters him. Whatever he is at the moment, he is given with an unfaltering rightness. All his mental processes are inevitable.

And the drawing of Amy is as masterly. Nothing she does and feels and says could have been done or felt or said differently. This intricate, utterly feminine soul is laid bare to its last throbbing nerve, its ultimate secret thought. We have the whole of it, all the wonderful detail, its courage, its reck-lessness, its pity, its scrupulousness, its essential decency, its all but indestruc-tible loyalty, its strength and the infinite pathos of its weakness.

The tragedy is worked out to its end with unrelieved, unrelenting gloom. Every line has the effect of rightness, of a flawless finality. It is so far beyond anything that mere cleverness can do. *White Rose of Weary Leaf* alone should have placed Violet Hunt high in the ranks of the tragic realists.

—May Sinclair, "The Novels of Violet Hunt," *The English Review* 34 (January to June 1922): 108–11

LADY DOROTHY MILLS

Miss Violet Hunt's flurried years, 1908–1914, included the women's suffrage movement, the founding of the *English Review*, of which Mr. Ford Madox Hueffer was the first editor, her personal relations with him, and much family trouble concerning these relations, and also concerning her administration of the affairs of her mother. The object of the book is not to give a detailed account of the facts. As Miss Hunt writes, "There are some things no one tells, some things that no woman tells, some things I cannot tell, but people know them"; and those who do not know them will not learn them very clearly from this book. It is not easy, indeed, to say what is the object of the book. It is not an *apologia*; but just in so far as it is obviously an outlet for the author's feelings, this, like any other intimately personal book, makes the reader feel uncom-fortable. Its claims upon attention will be found, perhaps, to be two: first, that the story brings in several great figures in English literature who were Miss Hunt's friends; and secondly, that the story and the characters have laid hold upon the novelist in her. What she has written is the material for a very inter-esting novel of the literary life. It seems a pity that she has been content with the material and did not write the novel. The additional labour would have refined away a good deal of the soreness and the fretfulness that were inevitable in a book of this nature. We should have seen the heroine under the influence of other things than persecution. And there would still have been enough memories of Henry James, of Conrad, of Hudson, to be worth putting in an autobiographical work of a tone other than this.

Still, it is worth while reading through a distressing book because amid these materials *pour servir* there are many very good things.

⟨. . .⟩ And Miss Hunt can tell brilliantly a delightful story of how James read to her his article for Mme. Duclaux's Book of France, how she accused him of being "passionate," how he glared, searched for the *mot juste*, and found it:—

> He turned on me an eye, *narquois*, reflective, stork-like, a little dev-
> ilish, calmly wise—the Henry James eye, in fact—and, with a little
> pompous laugh . . . the male warding off any attack that the persever-
> ing female might possibly be contemplating against his supreme
> bachelordom:
> "Ah madam, you must not forget that in this article I am address-
> ing—not a Woman, but a Nation!"

Of that kind of reminiscence—sharp, irreverent, but not unkind or belit-
tling—there is plenty; and this novelist-daughter of a painter and a novelist
has known many men and women worth recording. There are flashes, too, of
shrewd and sensible criticism of popular idols and others. The book's other
claim upon attention cannot be illustrated by quotation. It is in its very spirit,
as well as in its material, that it exhibits—sometimes more clearly than its
author knew—the incompatibility between ordinary life and what Miss Hunt
calls genius, but is perhaps more safely called the temperament possessed by
some novelists, dramatists, and poets, whose reality is not the reality of the
world in general.

—Lady Dorothy Mills, [Review of *The Flurried Years*], *The Times Literary Supplement* (18 February
1926): 111

GEOFFREY ROSSETTI

That there are but few examples of good biography proves how extremely difficult it is to tell the story of a person's life so as to be faithful at once to art
and to truth. ⟨. . .⟩ In Miss Violet Hunt's life of Elizabeth Siddall her novelist's
imaginative talent comes first and her sense of fact follows very half-heartedly
in the rear. The documentation for many hitherto unpublished details in the
lives of the well known figures who occur in her book is meagre. The story of
the piece of paper which Ford Madox Brown found on the nightdress of Mrs.
Rossetti when she was dead surely should receive some documentation. There
is probably little doubt that Miss Hunt was told this very interesting detail by
someone else. But why is the source not referred to in a foot-note?

Miss Hunt's obvious sympathy with her heroine hardly allows for the fact
that Miss Siddall was playing with fire the whole time. From the experience
she had had before she married Rossetti, Miss Siddall must have known that
he was an odd creature. Indeed she seems to have been no less odd herself, and
certainly far more fractious and disagreeable. ⟨. . .⟩

But this biography undoubtedly reveals that Miss Hunt has a very strong sense of melodrama. In Sir Hall Caine's biography of Rossetti, and now in Miss Hunt's biography of his wife, there is a strong tendency to exaggerate the melodramatic and the sensational. Nevertheless, we must confess we are becoming a little tired of those "great flares by night in the cemetery" when the coffin was being exhumed, and the anguish of the poet before the dead body of his beautiful young wife. Miss Hunt's story will touch those who are touched by this sort of thing, but to those who are most anxious to know exactly what did occur, and have no wish that any true fact should be concealed, this book will be somewhat disappointing.

Yet it must not be thought that Miss Hunt has produced a worthless or uninteresting piece of work. Her accounts of the Bohemian life led by the various members of the Pre-Raphaelite group are most entertaining.

—Geoffrey Rossetti, [Review of *The Wife of Rossetti*], *The Bookman* (October 1932): 56

THE NEW YORK TIMES BOOK REVIEW

The Blessed Damozel, as all persons who are acquainted with the story of the Pre-Raphaelite Brotherhood know, was Elizabeth Eleanor Siddall, long the model of Dante Gabriel Rossetti and for a briefly tragic period his wife. Like that other Dante's Beatrice, of whom the world knows little, she was the inspiration of one of the great sonnet-sequences of the world, the "House of Life" series, and her story is indelibly set forth in "The Wife of Rossetti," by Violet Hunt. ⟨. . .⟩

Let us start the picture as Violet Hunt starts it. "Models! Models! and more models!" This, she tells us, was the constant cry of the painters in the early '50s, especially the younger painters, among whom was one Walter Howell Deverell ⟨. . . who⟩ found The Sid and carried the news of her wondrous beauty to his brother artists, who were already calling themselves Pre-Raphaelites. Elizabeth Eleanor Siddall, that being her full name, was in the employ of a millinery establishment whence had come more than one model. But she, with her chaste and stand-offish air—how was she to be approached? Young Deverell (there was no impecuniousness there) induced his mother to go to the shop, buy herself several bonnets and tactfully approach the girl on the question of posing. This she did, with the result that The Stunner (later she was The Sid) gave her consent. Rossetti singled her out for his own, and although she posed, as time went on, for several of the brotherhood, under the code she was the especial property of Rossetti. With the moment of their meeting began one of the most unusual and the most poignant of stories, a story not unlike, yet vastly dissimilar to, the story of Robert Browning and Elizabeth Barrett; alike, because it is a story of the love of artist for artist, and dissimilar because on the man's side there was nothing of gallantry, and on the woman's the artist was negligible. Moreover, it was the man who postponed marriage, not the woman.

And here we touch on what underlies the volume by Violet Hunt. The author everywhere adumbrates rather than specifies, and the reader is not always certain that her implications are what they appear on the surface. But it would seem, without the mention of Freud, that it is Miss Hunt's thesis that any study of Dante Gabriel and Elizabeth Siddall should be made from the Freudian approach if any satisfactory conclusion is to be arrived at. If the reviewer is right, then, in this book, extensively and intensively complete, and documented at every point, but never pedestrian in its narrative, is all the material for that study, the key to which would be that Rossetti demanded of Miss Siddall, although most of the time housed with her, a rigid observation of chastity, not from any ethical motive, but in order that he might preserve toward her a rigidly esthetic attitude. A strange tale indeed, if we read the biographer aright in it, and one offering not merely startling conclusions, but conclusions from which one instinctively shrinks. For if Rossetti commanded of The Sid this cloistral existence, he himself led anything else but; and it would appear to be the thesis that it was this self-repression, while at the same time she was forced to suffer the humiliation of Rossetti's disaffection—had the two been married one would call it infidelity—which gradually wore her down. When Rossetti eventually married her, ten years after their first meeting, she was wan and emaciated, far gone in a hopeless malady which may have been tuberculosis, incapable of bearing living children. She used laudanum daily. When she died from an overdose of the drug the coroner's jury, after an examination of witnesses, cleared her of the stigma of suicide, although with many the thought will not down that she willed her death; though she may not deliberately have brought it about. ⟨. . .⟩

⟨. . .⟩ But her pathetic story is brilliantly told by Violet Hunt. Indeed, so brilliantly told is her story, with such an assimilation of fact and rehabilitation of fact as few biographers attain, that "The Wife of Rossetti" is one of the most expertly executed biographies of recent years. Miss Hunt has done for Elizabeth Eleanor Siddall what "The Barretts of Wimpole Street" did for Elizabeth Barrett, or "Ariel" did for Shelley.

—N. A., "That Tragic Figure, Rossetti's 'Blessed Damozel,'" *The New York Times Book Review* (30 October 1932): 3

EDA LOU WALTON

The experience of reading this biography is very much like spending a week end with a houseful of famous artists and writers, most of whom are strangers to you. You find yourself in a large roomful of people who know each other intimately. You hear first one bit of gossip, then another. Women and men address each other by first names and nicknames. You cannot quite fix any of them at first. All seem to have lived very complicated lives. There are hints of scandal and frequent gossip about a certain tragic suicide—Gabriel's wife— yes. Motives are suggested, then dropped.

You strain your ears trying to determine something about this story. After a few hours of desperate listening you come to the conclusion that every one in the room is just a little mad, after the manner of artists, and that you, your- self a very commonplace person, may turn mad too if you linger long in this fascinating and exotic company. You soon realize that you cannot quite believe all you hear, that tales are contradictory. These people are given to ghosts, too, and hallucinations. How to piece it all together! Truly this is a brilliant gathering. The women in their rich, full, clinging gowns are beautiful in the golden light of the late afternoon. The men, perhaps a little given to eccentricities of manner and egomania, are men of genius. ⟨. . .⟩

⟨. . . It⟩ is from memory and from the gossipy notebooks and letters of these people, that Miss Hunt reconstructs the innumerable amazing scenes in the lives of the Rossettis and of their many famous friends. The result is a biog- raphy which is really a kind of moving picture with sound in which expert photography has caught every gesture, every expression—expert recording, every quality of the voice, even every half-spoken phrase or whisper. The book is tremendously alive, much more dramatic than most more convention- ally written biographies. And if the reader is sometimes a little sceptical, a lit- tle suspicious of the author's exaggerated sensibility to all that she saw or heard or read about the P. R. B., it is nevertheless this very heightened imagination that makes possible the recapturing of the words, the feelings, the dramatic attitudes of every actor in this most un-Victorian group. ⟨. . .⟩

"The Wife of Rossetti" is an absorbing memoir devastatingly analytical at times, richly embroidered in all kinds of carefully searched out details, now and then a little sensational because of its author's superstitious and morbid interest in her heroine. One feels that Violet Hunt might well have been one of these Pre-Raphaelite women herself, she interprets them with such roman- tic and yet satirical accuracy. They are not pictures to her, they are living women capable of creating glamour, frustration, and bitterness. She under- stands them even better than she does their more famous husbands. She can follow them into their bedrooms where they giggle and chatter while their husbands argue academically in the studio. Here they all are, tall, full- throated, with heavy-lidded eyes, dressed much alike in the "unstayed" fash- ion their painter husbands thought medieval and therefore beautiful.

And here, too, presented with a little less penetration, perhaps, are their husbands and lovers, all men obsessed by Art and by themselves, the sensual and yet sensitive Rossetti, the impotent and business-like Ruskin, the strong and slightly inhuman Browning; the weakling Swinburne; the gentle Hunt; the reticent, and wise Allingham, the clumsy Morris. And all these men, being artists, are from a woman's point of view, inept as husbands, and, for the most part, incapable as business men. And so when the week end—on the reading of this memoir—is over, one feels as if one knew every character in this famous Brotherhood and Sisterhood, for it was that, too, almost too intimately, as if one would choose to get off alone for a while and think them over, these people who are bound to haunt one's dreams.

 —Eda Lou Walton, "Pre-Raphaelite House Party," *New York Herald Tribune* (30 October 1932): 1, 6

Robert and Marie Secor

⟨As⟩ an historian of the social implications of the Pre-Raphaelite period, Violet Hunt may have left her mark not in her biographical books and essays, but in her fiction. Perhaps nowhere can we find what it meant to be a young woman born into Pre-Raphaelite society as convincingly depicted as it is in her autobiographical novels, *Their Lives* (1918) and *Their Hearts* (1921). Important early readers recognized the value of these novels. May Sinclair praised them for "the naked thoughts, the naked lives of people we have known" ⟨*English Review*, February 1922⟩. Ford Madox Ford claimed that *Their Lives* had "the character of the work of history. It *is* history—and it makes it plain" ⟨"Preface" to *Their Lives*, 1918⟩. Rebecca West said *Their Lives* gave "a cold white vision of reality that recalls Maupassant; it is a valuable historical document . . . It is a study of girlhood which is worth the entire two volumes compiled by Professor Stanley Hall on 'Adolescence,' and which is worthy to stand beside Dostoevsky's 'A Raw Youth.'" Over sixty years later, Rebecca West still remembers the novel fondly, saying "there is nothing quite like it" ⟨*Daily News*, 7 March 1916⟩.

 Their Lives tells the story of Christina, Virgilia, and Orinthia Radmall, daughters of a respected if not properly honored Pre-Raphaelite painter. Like other Pre-Raphaelite women and children, who frequently served as models and ideals for artists' visions of vulnerable beauty, the Radmall girls were expected to play their parts in homemade dresses of peacock blue serge and in bonnets of medieval shape. The roles assigned to them keep the girls in sexual ignorance. The novel evokes well a society where young girls are humiliated when their "stomachs" are alluded to in public, and even the word "love" is to be circumvented when applied to real people rather than characters in books. ⟨. . .⟩

Christina refuses to be like either the conventional Virgilia or the repressed Orinthia. Blessed with literary ability and an independent spirit, she seems to be born between two worlds, too late to be a Pre-Raphaelite "stunner" and too soon to be a "New Woman." She is driven by a desire to leave behind the powerless world of childhood and exploits her position as eldest to distance herself from her two sisters. ⟨. . .⟩

Their Lives develops the shaping influences on the Radmall sisters from their Pre-Raphaelite childhood to the marriage of Virgilia; *Their Hearts* shows the consequences of that childhood upon them as they become fully adult. Here is no sensitive young man coming to terms with his environment, no artist on the brink of achievement, no successful struggle for identity and independence. Such masculine dreams of fulfillment are impossible for Victorian girls like the Radmall sisters. Instead Violet Hunt's young women, conditioned by their Pre-Raphaelite upbringing, struggle separately and with each other to define their feminine roles in the context of ordinary life. Their lives consist of weddings, courtships, births, deaths, and family tensions, rather than extraordinary achievement, and their hearts are engaged in the pursuit of sexual and social adjustment. ⟨. . .⟩

Unlike the submissive Orinthia, Christina in *Their Hearts* is a woman with a latch key, a symbol of liberation from Victorian parental supervision. She moves into the Bohemian world of artists and journalists, where laws of chaperonage are relaxed and "there were no proposals, strictly speaking—you did not speak strictly in Bohemia, where everyone was in love with Christina almost as a matter of course" (*TH*, p. 126). Here Christina is noticed, admired, and regarded as a pleasant attraction in otherwise drab offices. She comes and goes as she pleases, muddies her skirts and her reputation, and succumbs to the facile charm of her editor, Euphan Balfame. She is, however, neither proposed to nor taken seriously as an artist, and she does not take her own career very seriously. Despite herself she is a victim of what Rebecca West calls "the Victorian order of things," where for a young girl:

> There was no escape from this inadequate society into intellectual activities, for the pre-Raphaelite and the aesthetic movements described here with such gentle malice had nothing more to do with a woman than put her on a brocade settee with a sunflower. So all a girl could do was sit up in the "Trust" position till a husband was given one, and one could drop into the happy relaxation of "Paid For."

—Robert and Marie Secor, "Lives and Hearts in Pre-Raphaelite England: The Autobiographical Novels of Violet Hunt," *The Pre-Raphaelite Review* 2, no. 2 (May 1979): 60–64

B I B L I O G R A P H Y

The Maiden's Progress. 1894.
The Celebrity at Home. 1894.
A Hard Woman. 1895.
The Way of Marriage. 1896.
Unkist, Unkind! 1897.
The Human Interest. 1899.
Affairs of the Heart. 1900.
Sooner or Later. 1904.
The Cat. 1905.
The Workaday Woman. 1906.
The White Rose of Weary Leaf. 1908.
The Wife of Altamont. 1910.
The Doll. 1911.
Tales of the Uneasy. 1911.
The Celebrity's Daughter. 1913.
The Desirable Alien. 1913.
The Governess. 1913.
The House of Many Mirrors. 1915.
Their Lives. 1916.
Zeppelin Nights (with Ford Madox Ford). 1916.
The Last Ditch. 1918.
Their Hearts. 1921.
The Tiger Skin. 1924.
More Tales of the Uneasy. 1925.
The Flurried Years. 1926.
The Wife of Rossetti: Her Life and Death. 1932.

STORM JAMESON

1891–1986

MARGARET STORM JAMESON was born in Whitby, Yorkshire, England, on January 8, 1891. Though her parents, Hannah Margaret and William Storm Jameson, a sea captain, were extremely poor, Margaret was able to attend Leeds University on a competitive scholarship, earning a bachelor's degree with honors in 1912. Rare among British women of her generation, she also earned a master's degree from King's College, London, in 1914. Drama, literature, and history were her primary interests, and she later would write academic studies and literary criticism in addition to over 40 works of fiction.

After graduating from King's College, Jameson worked as an advertising copywriter and entered into a marriage that proved violent and unhappy. Though the couple only lived together for brief periods, they had one son before eventually divorcing in 1924. In spite of her personal hardships during this time, 1919 signified the start of an influential career: Jameson published her first novel, *The Pot Boils*, and became editor of the *New Commonwealth*, a post she held for three years. Her second marriage, to Guy Patterson Chapman, a writer and historian, proved happier. They were together from 1926 until his death in 1972.

Jameson's novels often focus on Yorkshire life, its shipyards and characters. The conflicts in many stem from unresolved issues in her and her family members' lives and revolve around shipbuilding or sailing. Jameson loved to travel and declared in her autobiography, "Writing is only my second nature. I would infinitely rather write than cook, but I would rather run around the world, looking at it, than write." This passion surfaces again and again in the actions of her characters as they break away from Yorkshire to the cities of England or the United States.

The 1930s found Jameson in an intense period of writing. Increasingly drawn to write political novels, she adopted two pen names, James Hill and William Lamb, and used different publishers for three resulting books. While her first dozen novels were fair successes and noticed by critics, recognition of her intelligence and flair for social satire followed in the second half of her writing career, with such novels as *Cousin Honoré* (1940) and *The Green Man* (1952). In addition to fiction and scholarly works, Jameson wrote plays and short stories and published translations of the works of Guy de Maupassant.

Jameson's role in the world of letters was more diverse than that of writer, however. From 1925 to 1928, she ran the British office of the

Alfred Knopf publishing company and in 1934 wrote reviews for *New English Weekly*. She was also a vocal and active member of the English Centre of International P.E.N. During her seven-year presidency (1938 to 1945), she traveled throughout Central and Eastern Europe to aid writers. Openly anti-Nazi during World War II, Jameson protested Germany's burning of books and spoke out in support of exiled writers.

Jameson's honors include the Calabrian International Prize in 1972; a P.E.N. Award in 1974 for *There Will Be a Short Interval* (1973); and honorary membership in the American Academy and Institute of Arts and Letters in 1978. One of the last projects she published before her death on September 30, 1986, was an edited version of her husband's autobiography.

CRITICAL EXTRACTS

REBECCA WEST

The Clash suffers from a stridency of mind and imagination which prejudice the reader against recognising that there is some very fine stuff in this novel. Throughout the book the action is constantly held up while there enters Tilburina, mad, in white satin. Miss Jameson is a person of enormous horse-power, and she occasionally puts this extraordinary force into drawing the conventional figures of the worst sort of fiction. With a gesture of energy that leads one to expect another *Wuthering Heights* she trots out again that cursed beautiful brave child, who steps forward from the shadow of the curtains when the vicar is attempting to comfort the bereaved family with talk of the will of God, and says in her clear treble, "He is a beast, that God," and who rushes out on the moors after she has heard the Moonlight Sonata played for the first time and is found at dawn high on the crags sleeping in the arms of the village harlot. Later on she writes of an aviator who "flew drunk rather than sober and he flew always with genius. He was swarthy and dark-browed, a giant with the ankles and wrists of a dancer. Women adored him for his insolent courtesy and for his eyes, which were the blue of rain-wet hyacinths." A girl's dream, a girl's dream. Nevertheless, in spite of a deal of this sort of thing (even including a Spanish dancer) there is real talent here. There is a description of the life that centred round an aerodrome where both American and English pilots were stationed which is brilliantly astute. The account of the Senator trying to unfurl the Stars and Stripes and keep command of his patriotic relative clauses is a curiously humorous production for a writer who elsewhere seems to have no sense of humour whatsoever. And the core of the story, the passion for a base and noisy man with power, which visits like a plague a woman who is married to a good and fastidious man who is without power, is described with great wisdom. There is a specially remarkable passage when the loquacious Texan picks up a pamphlet in Elizabeth's drawing-room and rants about it ("This country is rotten with Socialism," he observed, "your traditions are about to be strangled and turned out of their old home by a gang of sexless, immoral eaters of filth. To me a Socialist is a cross between a rattlesnake and a damned fool. And to all decent Americans. If we had the writer of this— indecency—over there we'd know how to deal with him.") and Elizabeth loathingly looks down on the bottomless pit of his folly, and at the same time sicklily recognises that even this knowledge of him does not break his power over her. Miss Jameson is a writer without literary taste, and that is a defect which does not correct itself. But it looks in this book as if she was develop- ing a curious emotional clairvoyance which would make her novels worth reading.

—Rebecca West, "Notes on Novels," *New Statesman* (27 May 1922): 213

THEODORE PURDY JR.

A nicely contrasted feminine triptych is exhibited in Miss Jameson's new book. As her rather combative title implies, the heroines of the three long stories which make up "Women Against Men" are arrayed against a masculine world, which according to the author dominates without much trouble their lives and actions, no matter what their social standing or mental equipment may be. Yet, while admitting that Miss Jameson's case histories are well chosen and in the main admirably told, it seems obvious that most readers will consider this an arbitrary and unproven,—not to say unprovable,—thesis, and will prefer to read her book as pure narrative, without attempting to connect the three sto- ries by any such unnecessary links.

The first ("Delicate Monster"), in fact, while presenting the portrait of a successful lady sex-novelist, who turns her affairs into royalties with a rapidity and ease only observable in fiction, has little to do with men, since it is Victoria Form's relationship to the autobiographical narrator which lends point to the whole. Less artificial is "A Single Heart," the straightforward his- tory of a Laborite M. P. and his almost too long-suffering wife. Miss Jameson is triumphantly successful in the difficult task of making the reader believe that Emily's devotion, which has nothing to do with Evan's faithfulness, is never- theless explicable. Undoubtedly the best of the three, this touching story will be found worthy to rank with the author's most characteristic work, such as the trilogy of Mary Hervey.

Third in the assortment is "A Day Off," a bitter and excessively veristic study of a prostitute on the decline. This sort of thing has been done so often and so well in recent years that only Miss Jameson's accuracy in minute observation of details and shades of feeling makes it unusual. Still, its acid tone serves as contrast to the over refined atmosphere of "Delicate Monster" and the lush sentiment of "A Single Heart," while the introduction of a mildly Joycean technique in dealing with the chief character's thoughts shows that the author is well able to adapt herself to new manners and methods. The entire book serves to demonstrate Miss Jameson's great capabilities anew.

—Theodore Purdy Jr., "A Feminist Triptych," *The Saturday Review of Literature* (31 December 1932): 353

DOROTHEA BRANDE

In a fine, formal, eighteenth-century prose, with fewer adjectives to the book than the average writer uses in a chapter, Storm Jameson has written three long stories and issued them under the title *Women against Men*. The title holds the only misleading words in the volume. The women of these stories are no more against men than they are against other women, or against the scheme of the universe, and the title, with its hint of fusty feminism, gives no promise of the real character of the book. For at last here are stories about women by a woman which are honest and unsentimental.

Miss Jameson may have to suffer for "speaking out" like this. She has been as plain-spoken about her heroines as about those at whose hands they suffered. This means that none of the stories offers any restful oasis for illusions, no nook in which the tender-hearted can rest. The tawdry vulgarian of "Delicate Monster", a woman novelist who turns her lovers and friends into "copy" and uses lovers, husbands, child, and friends without scruple is one thing. We have all had the pleasure of disliking these villainesses before. But what of the heroine—herself a writer, the childhood friend of the "monster", the narrator of the story? She is drawn as relentlessly as Victoria. Belonging in many ways to a higher order of being, more sensitive, frequently scrupulous, by preference fastidious, when she is robbed of her husband by her predatory friend she shows traits as inadmirable as any of Victoria's own: under jealousy she sets traps, indulges in hysterics, reads letters and notebooks. But how dreadful! you may exclaim. Does Miss Storm Jameson believe that decent women are like this? Read the story; if at the conclusion you still hold that Storm Jameson is unfair or inaccurate you are one of two things: one of them is "remarkably fortunate".

The second story is as unlike the first as possible. "The Single Heart" is a love story of a girl who, falling in love with a young workman after her marriage, spends the rest of her life and all her strength to get the man she loves, and to keep him. It is unbearably poignant; Storm Jameson has done studies of jealousy before, but none as good at this. The lover, whom Emily marries after her husband's early death, and whose career she promotes to her own last breath, deceives her again and again; and again and again she takes him back to her arms in spite of her agonizing jealousy. If that were all, we should feel that we had heard this story of a betrayed and noble woman more than once before: but Miss Jameson goes on to tell us that Emily had steadily deceived both her lover and her husband, feeling not the least scruple about it, hardly realizing that she was doing it, since she felt that she was acting to her lover's advantage. Yet her heart is very nearly broken when she discovers that Evan has been consoling himself trivially while she travels in America with her husband.

This is abandoning conventional novel psychology with a vengeance; yet it is done so well that you accept all the testimony. The three main characters are, under different aspects, detestable, admirable, and pathetic. Miss Jameson tells what one woman in love was like, and draws a good portrait. Again, if you are able to finish "The Single Heart" convinced that Emily is not recognizably feminine, you are, to say the least of it, lucky.

The last story in the book is "A Day Off." In its way it is as successful as the other two, and, since the specimen of femininity being examined in this case is an aging streetwalker, it is likely to get more wholehearted approval than the other two tales. For some time it has been a literary fashion to be frank about such poor drabs: so much so that the critics know now that such honesty is all right, and one of every two reviewers will undoubtedly hold that Miss Jameson has been at her most effective in capturing the essence of the dimwitted, distraught creature whose last lover has deserted her. It seems to me to have less of the bitter, tonic and bracing after-effect than either of the other two.

—Dorothea Brande, "Five Novels," *The Bookman* (January 1933): 86–87

PETER QUENNELL

Company Parade is a novel of the peace, or—as Miss Jameson would probably prefer to describe it—of the lull between European wars. Its background could scarcely be more depressing; Miss Jameson and her characters seem to live and breathe under the shadow of an approaching conflict, and can talk and think of little else. The idiocy of politicians, and villainy of armament manufacturers, the apathy and criminal stupidity of the upper and middle classes haunt the narrative like a bad dream or a bad smell; and it is only now and then, with the slightly shamefaced air of a dilettante caught in the act, that the reader is able to remind himself that human beings, even today, still experience moments of rare and precious happiness, and that so illogical is our human composition that it is still possible to derive pleasure from these moments, though the were- or war-wolf scratching at the door and every newspaper that slips through the letter-box contains an account of some fresh revolting atrocity. ⟨. . .⟩

Thus speaks the "bourgeois intellectual." There are some of us for whom the mind is its own place, for whom the most important events are still primarily subjective, and for whom personal salvation must come—not from without, from participation in a new and improved social order, but from within, whose "Kingdom of Heaven" (such as it is) will never quite merge its frontiers in any Union of Socialist Soviet Republics. But Miss Jameson is a novelist with a message. Her message is one with which few readers of *The New Statesman and Nation* will find it difficult to sympathise; though I think they may agree that her indignation has not yet been assimilated by the literary medium through which it is set forth and that, so iterated and reiterated, used to colour paragraph after paragraph, line after taut resentful line, it tends to lose the immediacy of its first effect. On the Embankment, she scents a future cataclysm. ⟨. . .⟩ Well, granted the huddled, shapeless derelicts, heaped up on the benches, under the bluish glare of the arc-lamps, the reflection is plausible and does her credit; but when one of her characters is discovered eating chicken cutlets "in a restaurant in which even the plates witnessed to the death of society"—they had been "stamped by sweated Czech workers with patterns which satisfied the American importer's idea of French peasant art"—I cannot help wishing that she would allow society to expire in peace. Nero, with his Stradivarius on the heights of the Palatine, is the type of artist for whom personally I have a sneaking regard.

To stress the social and political side of Miss Jameson's narrative is to draw attention to a very important and perhaps slightly over-obtrusive aspect of her book, but does not help to explain the energy and resourcefulness with which the narrative itself is conducted. Miss Jameson is an extremely practised writer, and her account of Hervey Russell's struggle against poverty, obscurity and a foolish, weak-willed, unprincipled and unfaithful husband—the type of husband with whom feminine fiction has made us painfully familiar—is written in a convincing and lucid style. Yet the impression left by the book is disappointing. Miss Jameson has attempted to give us a panorama of contemporary life. Up to a point she has succeeded; but beyond that point—the point at which observation becomes interpretation and clever reporting art—her imaginative grasp of her subject-matter does not extend. The reader may agree with her dominant thesis; but he will close the volume in much the same state as he started reading it.

—Peter Quennell, "New Novels," *New Statesman and Nation* (31 March 1934): 488

WILLIAM C. FRIERSON

⟨Storm Jameson⟩ is easily placed as the latest exponent of the English family chronicle and the person who has probably brought that particular mode of narration to its highest perfection. In a series of five books she has delineated the affairs of a shipbuilding family and has maintained through successive generations the traditions of English pride, shyness, obstinacy, consideration, and general intrinsic worth. In many respects she is a modernized Galsworthy. Her people are truly complicated individuals, the tangles of sentiment are intricate, and the modern scene is described with some sympathy for its changed codes.

Mrs. Jameson's faults are closely linked with the exigencies of chronicle-writing. Since family traits and the opposition of temperaments are the essential elements, the novelist must "heighten our interest in the characters of his story, so that we care intensely what happens to them. He must introduce delays, surprises, bewilderments." What Mrs. Jameson says of one of Bennett's novels is applicable to her own characters:

> These men and women, so calmly and faithfully going about their little daily tasks, are the battlegrounds of terrific forces. Love, jealousy, passion, hatred, courage, daring—all the monstrous emotions of a Webster play are here at work.

It is obvious that for such dramatic effects as Mrs. Jameson desires, the psychology is likely to be synthetic, the pictures picturesque. And yet in her effort to catch the flavor of successive generations Mrs. Jameson is successful. Ford Madox Ford has guided her in understanding the period of the war and the postwar days. She states that in his four Tietjens novels (concluding with *The Last Post*, 1928) he has

> succeeded in creating a picture of the years between 1912 and 1926 which wipes out (as a flame from a furnace would wipe out the light of a candle) such a picture as that drawn by Mr. Galsworthy in *The White Monkey* and *The Silver Spoon*. No other work . . . has so imprisoned the restless and violent spirit of those years when the ground moved under our feet.

In her own delineations of postwar attitudes Mrs. Jameson is generally unsentimental and aware, though by no means bold. Like Ford she gives an intimation that integrity and the finer English qualities are their own justification. To make life "clear and meaningful," she holds, is as little as you can do for the average reader. He must be given "something to take away into his own private corner. Some word to live by. Some spark at which to warm himself."

—William C. Frierson, "Diffusion, 1920-1940," *The English Novel in Transition: 1885–1940* (1942), excerpted in *Twentieth-Century British Literature*, ed. Harold Bloom (New York: Chelsea House Publishers, 1985), 1430

NINA BALAKIAN

One of the most intelligent, sensitive, and learned critics in England today is a woman with the unfeminine name of Storm Jameson, who is better known to American readers as a novelist. Had she been born in the eighteenth century, she might have been another Lady Mary Wortley Montagu (she has traveled as widely and has as sharp a sense of the uniqueness of other peoples). Or, if she were a Frenchwoman today, she might be leading a literary movement (for she can be passionate about ideas and literature). But in the England of our day, where, comparatively speaking at least, there is "no ferment of ideas, no excitement," she is content to write modest little essays, which appear from time to time in the few remaining journals. It is only when we read them in a collected and related sequence as in the present volume ⟨*The Writer's Situation and Other Essays*⟩ that we glimpse her real critical stature.

Written within a period of twelve years, the essays here deal specifically with the writer in a time of crisis. Miss Jameson, who has read widely in foreign literatures (especially the French) and is generally *au courant* with the output of her contemporaries, is distressed by the current state of the novel with its emphasis on "little jets of [the author's] personality." Perhaps because as a novelist she is acutely aware of the dilemmas of the modern artist, she does not scold or exhort, but only tries to analyze and understand.

As a humanist (she exemplifies the word in her insistence on the dual attributes of mind and heart), she is naturally drawn to the tradition of French culture with its emphasis on the individual's worth. She has only contempt (though perhaps the word is too strong for her tolerant mind) for a system which controls the minds of its writers. Yet she is aware of another, subtler kind of censorship which operates outside of Soviet Russia—with the possible exception of France—the self-imposed censorship of writers who are so overwhelmed by the sheer ugliness and chaos of their world that they cannot write about it. And it is these same writers who lack the necessary detachment to write strictly about the human heart.

What hope, then, does Miss Jameson see for literature and for mankind since the two are so closely related? ⟨. . .⟩

⟨. . .⟩ Miss Jameson can take heart because she has talked to young Polish writers in Warsaw who, with a crumbled world at their feet, are still fervent about life and literature.

But most of all Miss Jameson takes heart in the knowledge that there is still a France, with its symbols of eternity—a place where, no matter what the circumstances, people continue to live "with a passion, almost with joy." Only a French writer, André Malraux, she says, has so far asked—and answered—the terrible question of our age: "Can Man survive?"

She suggests further, provocatively, that we test the greatness of our writers by asking of them: are they able to tell us about the destiny of Man, our destiny, in such a way that we have "the courage to live it, and gaily"?

—Nina Balakian, "Critical Dilemmas," *The Saturday Review of Literature* (2 December 1950): 23

MARTIN LEVIN

The latest novel by the indestructible Storm Jameson offers a stretch of social history—1890–1942—a period the author has traversed many times before in pursuit of cosmic questions. In this partly metaphysical journey, she seems to be asking why man remains stubbornly inhumane. And the answer, provided by a spectral presence from hell, is that "in hell as on earth it is the helpless and innocent who are punished, who suffer."

This theorem is explored by winnowing the life and times of John Antigua, a Portuguese-English foundling who is born without the necessary human ingredient of malice. Antigua is malformed from birth, cruelly abandoned when his English stepfather dies, cuckolded by a trusted friend and nearly extinguished in the Blitz. Yet his cheerful, exemplary life is a testimony to the necessity of kindness. Unfortunately, Antigua's virtues are encased in a character that remains inert throughout the Galsworthian dialogues and strange interludes that comprise a decidedly static novel.

—Martin Levin, [Review of *The White Crow*], *The New York Times Book Review* (1 June 1969): 24

JAMES GINDIN

A chronicle, more shapeless than most, written in the 1920's and '30's, as yet little known or seldom discussed in this country, is Storm Jameson's series of novels centering on the family that begins with Mary Hervey, born Mary Hansyke, who heads a large shipbuilding firm and shipping line on the north Yorkshire coast during a long stretch of late Victorian and Edwardian time. Within the past two years or so, Berkley Medallion Books has published seven of these novels in paperback: *The Lovely Ship, The Voyage Home, A Richer Dust, The Captain's Wife* (entitled *Farewell Night, Welcome Day* in England), *That Was*

Yesterday, Company Parade, and *Love in Winter.* The first three of the novels were planned as a trilogy. Later novels extended the series, three of them described by Ms. Jameson only a few years ago (she is now eighty-seven) as part "of an unfinished series." ⟨. . .⟩

Exciting plots through turbulent generations, in the manner of Taylor Caldwell, do not distinguish Ms. Jameson's chronicle. The episodes, particularly in the first novel, are simply a stringing together of exterior events, recordings of marriages, deaths, and careers that often seem too derivative of earlier novels (some of the first novel sounds like a pastiche of eighteenth century novels, a part of the second like a less compressed version of Sophia's disillusionment in the Paris portions of Bennett's *The Old Wives' Tale*). Not until *That Was Yesterday,* ⟨. . .⟩ when Hervey herself becomes the central character and perspective, does the treatment of character deepen and the connection of the individual with history develop a particular and complicated resonance. Ms. Jameson herself has, more tersely, recently written as much, that "My earliest novels are not worth reading," and she lists *That Was Yesterday* as the first to be written that is now "worth looking at." ⟨. . .⟩

Line by line, Storm Jameson's writing is sometimes untidy, uneven, especially in the earlier novels. The author sometimes loads the situation clumsily: "If she had been more experienced, she would have known that . . ."; sometimes, she engages in a form of premonitory melodrama: "It was, though she did not know it, the last time she would step out of the dark side-street into the Place Verte"; self-pity can occasionally dwarf a passage of the persona's recollections. A portrait of the writer and rambunctious intellectual with whom Nicholas's young wife runs off for a temporary affair seems too obviously, too long-windedly, and too vituperatively modelled on the physiognomy and character of H. G. Wells. Ms. Jameson is much better with long descriptions of landscapes, the history and composition of towns, and the succession of small houses and furnished rooms in which Hervey lives during her first marriage, following her husband to various military posts in England later in the war, and, on her own, after the war, with her child, working at an advertising job in London and beginning to write novels. Like Bennett, Ms. Jameson is a splendid materialist, conveying the fabric and textures of domestic life in the past. She also is at her best in detailing the long complexities of relationships, as in the penetrating treatment of the slow dissolution of Hervey's first marriage in *That Was Yesterday* and subsequent novels. Their marriage erodes through living in a shabby housing estate outside of Liverpool as he takes his first job as an indigent teacher in a bad school, through the upheavals of war and different attitudes toward it, through changing social and political convictions, through the hostility of his wealthier family sending him back to Oxford for another career, and through their mutual infidelities. Yet the process of unraveling is protracted by each partner's dependence, his on her competence and her vulnerability to his weakness and his feckless rebellions, hers on his exterior manner of smooth assurance, but even more deeply on her own guilt and her own control. The reasons for prolonging the break are given far more painful intensity than is the collapse of the marriage itself. Ms. Jameson achieves a similar acuity and density in depicting Hervey's relationship with her mother. Sylvia begins by treating her first-born with severity, taking out her resolve to be independent from her mother on her daughter. She breeds, in Hervey, a tremendous desire both to please others and to go her own way, developing into ambition that would compensate her mother for a thwarted life. As the two characters, in superficial ways very different, build their defenses against each other, they reveal an intense, grudging, deep, almost unspoken respect for one another. Hervey comes, with great difficulty, to understand the self-defeating mother so unlike herself, as she never understood the grandmother she resembled. Storm Jameson works all these generational complexities of her characters' relationships with considerable skill.

Since the characters are always both within and reacting against their worlds, the chronicle also achieves and communicates a sense of history, less intimately the history of the nineteenth century, more immediately and intensively that surrounding the First World War. ⟨. . .⟩ War, unlike energy crises, imposes necessary conditions for its duration, temporarily obscures individual effort or conviction. After the war, as the later novels in the series show, Hervey's generation retains its singularity, not that all its members are identical (some respond by retreat, some by devotion to Communism as the force of the future, some by aggressive admiration for the new tyrants who, like Mussolini or the National Socialists in Germany, seek to control and impose themselves on history—the most difficult response to maintain is sane and liberal concern), but that all have been so indelibly marked by the war.

—James Gindin, "Storm Jameson and the Chronicle," *Centennial Review* (Fall 1978), excerpted in *Twentieth-Century British Literature*, ed. Harold Bloom (New York: Chelsea House Publishers, 1985), 1432–33

BIBLIOGRAPHY

The Pot Boils. 1919.
The Happy Highways. 1920.
Modern Drama in Europe. 1920.
The Clash. 1922.

The Pitiful Wife. 1923.

Lady Susan and Life: An Indiscretion. 1924.

Three Kingdoms. 1926.

The Lovely Ship. 1927.

Farewell to Youth. 1928.

The Georgian Novel and Mr. Robinson. 1929.

The Decline of Merry England. 1930.

The Voyage Home. 1930.

A Richer Dust. 1931.

The Triumph of Time: A Trilogy. 1932.

That Was Yesterday. 1932.

The Single Heart. 1932.

No Time Like the Present. 1933.

A Day Off. 1933.

Women against Men (includes A Day Off, The Delicate Monster, and
   The Single Heart). 1933.

Company Parade. 1934.

Love in Winter. 1935.

The Soul of Man in the Age of Leisure. 1935.

In the Second Year. 1936.

None Turn Back. 1936.

Delicate Monster. 1937.

The World Ends (as William Lamb). 1937.

Loving Memory (as James Hill). 1937.

Moon Is Making. 1937.

No Victory for the Soldier (as James Hill). 1938.

The Novel in Contemporary Life. 1938.

Here Comes a Candle. 1938.

The Captain's Wife. 1939.

A Civil Journey. 1939.

Europe to Let: The Memoirs of an Obscure Man. 1940.

Cousin Honoré. 1940.

The Fort. 1941.

The End of This Year. 1941.

Then We Shall Hear Singing: A Fantasy in C Major. 1942.

Cloudless May. 1943.

The Journal of Mary Hervey Russell. 1945.

The Other Side. 1946.

Before the Crossing. 1947.

The Black Laurel. 1947.
The Moment of Truth. 1949.
The Writer's Situation and Other Essays. 1950.
The Green Man. 1952.
The Hidden River. 1955.
The Intruder. 1956.
A Cup of Tea for Mr. Thorgill. 1957.
A Ulysses Too Many. 1958.
Days Off: Two Short Novels and Some Stories. 1959.
Last Score: Or, the Private Life of Sir Richard Ormston. 1961.
Morley Roberts: The Last Eminent Victorian. 1961.
The Road from the Monument. 1962.
A Month Soon Goes. 1963.
The Blind Heart. 1964.
The Early Life of Stephen Hind. 1966.
The White Crow. 1968.
Journey from the North: Autobiography of Storm Jameson. 1969, 1970.
Parthian Words. 1970.
There Will Be a Short Interval. 1973.
Speaking of Stendhal. 1979.

F. TENNYSON JESSE

1888–1958

FRYNIWYD (OR WYNIFRIED) MARGARET TENNYSON JESSE was born on March 1, 1888, in Christelhurst, England, to Edith Louisa and Reverend Eustace Tennyson d'Eyncourt Jesse, a distant relative of the poet Alfred Tennyson. Because Reverend Jesse had trouble obtaining a ministry post, the family was obliged to endure relative poverty and to move from one dismal lodging to another. His frequent absences, Edith Jesse's antipathetic disposition, and the trauma of wearing iron braces on her legs for rickets made Jesse's childhood an unhappy one. During a particularly difficult period, when her mother's health required "silent play," Jesse at the age of nine created her first book filled with drawings and character sketches.

At 19, Jesse escaped the family discord to the tranquillity of the Stanhope School of Painting in Cornwall. There she studied painting, exhibited her artwork in local galleries, began writing a novel, and became editor of the school's magazine. A year later, she moved to London, beginning her literary career as a journalist for *The Times*. "The Mask," her first short story, was published in 1910 in *The English Review* and created a sweeping sensation. The menacing thriller about an unhappily married couple climaxes with the accidental death of the wife's lover. Soon after the story's publication, playwright H. M. Harwood approached Jesse, and the two cowrote a stage version that was successfully produced in both England and America.

Jesse continued publishing short fiction and was approached by publisher William Heinemann, who hoped to print the young author's first novel. The light-hearted *The Milky Way* appeared in 1913, followed by the sexually frank short-story collection *Beggars on Horseback* (1915), which together paved the way for what Jesse considered a more serious novel, *Secret Bread*. Published in 1917, this earned her critical praise from such contemporaries as Rebecca West. In a shocking accident shortly after publication of *The Milky Way*, however, Jesse's hand was severely mangled as she waved, unaware of the whirling propeller, out the window of a small plane. Six operations and morphine given for pain precipitated the author's lifelong struggle with addiction.

At the outbreak of World War I, Jesse, who had been traveling throughout the Caribbean, returned to London and to journalism. Her regular war reports appeared in the *Pall Mall Gazette*, *The English Review*, and the *Tattler*, prompting the British Ministry of Information to send her to France to cover "The Women's Army." The experience generated a highly praised book, *The Sword of Deborah* (1919), and sparked Jesse's concern for women's rights on issues of divorce, abortion, education, and employment outside the home.

In 1918, Jesse and H. M. Harwood were married, though the union remained a secret from the general public for most of their lives. The couple continued to collaborate on numerous plays and many adaptations of Jesse's stories, including "The Pelicans," produced in 1924. By the 1930s, they were living comfortably, often hosting writers like Noel Coward and W. Somerset Maugham at their home, Cut Mill.

Despite failing health, Jesse's lifetime interest in criminology fueled her next few writing projects. Having attended many murder trials and visited numerous prisons throughout her life, Jesse was a skilled, self-trained criminologist. She published her first book about crime, *Murder and Its Motives*, in 1924, to praise in literary reviews and police journals alike; she wrote stories featuring a clever female detective, Solange Fontaine; she edited and wrote the introductions for six volumes in the *Notable British Trials* series. In 1934, she published *A Pin to See the Peepshow*—a chilling, vivid novel based on the infamous trial and execution of Edith Thompson and her lover for the murder of her husband (a subject also treated by E. M. Delafield). The book received an enthusiastic response from readers and critics.

Jesse's health rapidly deteriorated in the 1950s. On August 6, 1958, she died of a heart attack.

CRITICAL EXTRACTS

THE TIMES LITERARY SUPPLEMENT

In the Book of Proverbs it was the foolish woman who cried out to the passer-by that stolen waters are sweet, and bread eaten in secret is pleasant. And the dead were there, and her guests were in the depths of hell. Opening Miss Tennyson Jesse's new novel, SECRET BREAD ⟨. . .⟩, we expect, therefore, to find some tale of sin and its wages; and are surprised—agreeably surprised—to find something different, a new turn given to the old phrase. Ishmael Ruan's secret bread was Cloom, the Cornish estate which he had inherited from his father and was to pass on to his son and grandson. At least, that was what Ishmael Ruan believed to be his secret bread, and we, as we follow his long life, from birth to death, in and about Cloom, believe as he does. Before the close of the book we know better, and so does Ishmael. The pattern of life, roughly and smoothly, through many changes and much apparent futility, works itself out before him. In the end, Cloom passes to one who, though in blood a Ruan, was not Ishmael's son; but by that time Ishmael had a clearer view of what his secret bread truly was; and it was pleasant.

The book is long. It covers the eighty years of Ishmael Ruan's life. It is very generously planned, like the English novels of an earlier day. And now and then we find Miss Jesse straying a little too widely from her main theme, digressing so far into the lives of others than Ishmael and into regions in those lives which did not touch Ishmael's life that the progress of the story gets clogged. This occasional uncertainty or slackness of planning is a fault easily forgiven, because the digressive parts are often interesting in themselves; more, because they do, in their manner, keep alive the subject of the story. That subject is not Ishmael's life so much as human life. With admirable and justified courage this young author has "bitten off" a very big piece. She has many thoughts about love, life, and death to work out; and if some of them cannot be worked out in relation to Ishmael, they do not lure us inexcusably far from him. For Ishmael himself, he is well worth following through his eighty years. The author's grip on his queer, attractive nature is firm throughout. Miss Jesse has "got to know him" thoroughly, and therefore can lay plain before us remote elements in a shy and rather difficult spirit. We are continuously interested in this deep-thinking, inarticulate Cornish squire, as the pattern of love and life and death works itself out in him and before him.

—N. A., [Review of *Secret Bread*], *The Times Literary Supplement* (7 June 1917): 272

THE NATION

"Secret Bread" is ⟨. . .⟩ a sober and somewhat sombre interpretation of individual character in its relations to the family and to society at large. It gratefully lacks the famous brilliancy of the "younger British school" of novelists. It has solidity, not only in its portraiture, but in its embodiment of a truth, or, if you will, a moral, as contrasted with the expression of an "idea" in the Wellsian sense. And this spiritual truth is akin to that embodied in "The Twilight of the Souls." Parson Boase puts it in a nutshell for us: "There's only one thing certain—that we all have something, some secret bread of our own soul, by which we live, that nourishes and sustains us. It may be a different thing for each man alive." Here, more narrowly, is the "life story" of a Cornishman, Ishmael Ruan. ⟨. . .⟩ The process of growing old, the gradual slackening and decay of the faculties, are dwelt upon here with something of the ruthlessness that disconcerted many a sensitive reader in "The Old Wives' Tale." But our last vision of the soul of Ishmael, as, from his stricken and dying body, it surveys the course of its mortal experience, is not a vision of despair. It perceives that the nature of that secret bread by which it has lived has changed with the changing years: "In his childhood he had lived by what would happen in a far golden future, in his youth by what might happen any dawning day; but in his years of manhood, and from then till he began to feel the first oncoming of age, he had lived by what he did." Since then, "he had lived, as all men do, knowingly or not, by death. This was the secret bread that all men shared. . . . If, then, men lived by death, what was death? Not a mere cessation—then a going-on": an escape from the lesser life to the greater. And his soul perceives that, in the light of this truth, none of its earthly experience, none of its suffering or even its errors, have been wasted, as preparation for the "going-on." This is a book of rich texture, both in form and in substance.

—N. A., [Review of *Secret Bread*], *The Nation* (8 November 1917): 515

THE TIMES LITERARY SUPPLEMENT

Miss Tennyson Jesse, who writes when she has a mind to, when she has something to say and no oftener, never says the same thing twice. In this, as in other qualities, she differs considerably from many of her contemporaries, whose "message," varying only in key, is repeated with each new novel as the publishing seasons roll round. She is an adventurer and an explorer; poetry may persuade her, crime or ancient romance take her by the hand for a time, or the West Country call to her—whatever it is possesses her until it is written down, and she compels her readers to share her fine excitement. Her books, widely as they differ in subject, have in common a distinction of workmanship and a considered beauty of thought.

The sea is her theme in her new novel—a "Romance" she calls it—TOM FOOL ⟨. . .⟩, the sea and sailing ships; the sea viewed first by a little boy, one of a family of Lancashire cotton-spinners emigrating to Australia, then by the boy grown older, when it becomes his life. Miss Tennyson Jesse gives Tom Fould a dash of Cornish to explain his passion for ships and the poetry they quickly awake in his nature. No hardship, no brutal experience can beat down the craving he has for the sea, or his lust for high and dazzling moments of danger. The dead level of safe days makes him morose and unhappy, but the need for instant action sends him blazing at it, unconquerable. We are shown him at many such moments in his life, not destined to be a long one, as he works up to his master's certificate. The book is, very curiously, a one-character study, although the figure of Tom Fool stands out against a background of living people: Tom's family, sketched on their way to Australia and afterwards in the goldfields, passengers whose influence to some extent colours his life, and, later, his friend John. He is the well-to-do son of a shipowner, sent round the world on a cruise for his health; and he and Tom are as David and Jonathan, although Tom in his secret soul is aware that no human love can hold him when his "moments" call him to an ecstasy of physical effort. He saves John's life and is ashamed to realize that in doing so he has forgotten his friend and been mad only to get at grips with danger in the mountainous seas. Not only in its technical detail—that possibly only a master mariner could suitably review—⟨is⟩ this romance a fine performance, but in the intensifying and growing mind and character of the young man, romantic certainly, but positively alive. Fleeting episodes with chance women scarcely touch him at all, and he is twenty-eight when he loves and marries in Cornwall. The episode of Jennifer Constantine is beautifully related; but the brief idyll is over in a year, when she dies with her child, knowing perhaps that impatience with shore life is stirring up in Tom the eternal craving for the intoxication of danger, and leaving him free to seek it. Free, too, for ever of some slavery of the flesh;

> something that had always checked and tugged at him had snapped.
> . . . Jennifer had for ever, confidently in her keeping, the questing
> spirit that had driven him to a physical outlet for its hopes and
> curiosities. He was free to go back to the life where his own
> moments, untouched by any grosser thing, might yet fall his way in
> the natural changes of it. . . . Free to be free.

He sails to Australia with wheat which becomes symbolic to him, and with him goes John—with whom is the last word. For fire breaks out and the crew mutiny. They are quelled, but presently put off in the boats. John goes too, and at the last moment realizes that Tom Fool, true to his name, means to stay with his ship, the Happy Return, and take one final, insane chance to save her. The brilliantly contrived climax shows him heading direct into a waterspout in order to put out the fire in the hold.

—N. A., [Review of *Tom Fool*], *The Times Literary Supplement* (27 May 1926): 354

THE NEW YORK TIMES BOOK REVIEW

This graceful and colorful writer—F. Tennyson Jesse, the grandchild of Alfred Tennyson—has joined in the production of "Tom Fool" the seagoing school of romantic realists. It is in the Conrad tradition. It has the spirit of going down to seas in ships and is observed with minute detail. This accumulation of detail has been set down in a method that is both delicate and robust in its impressionism. For Miss Jesse in recording—with her feeling for the lovely word—the beauty of ships bending before the wind in full sail, also includes in her picture the brutality and ugly aspects that attend the service of the sea. ⟨. . .⟩

"Tom Fool" is a novel fused with a fine imagination. It is colored with the glamour of the diverse ports of call, scattered about the world, for a background to an intense and dramatic conflict that is the inward life of Tom. It has the stimulating insight of poetic vision. It has a dreamy grace and the inferno of a man's soul that is constantly on the rack. It is austere of manner and yet a passionate tale. It has visualized an individual man and set him down in entirety. In the projection of this character "Tom Fool" stands superior to romantic fiction. Here has been presented a latent poet who couldn't escape his own personality. A curious, impalpable, shy and alluring novel, this "Tom Fool," that will haunt your imagination and color your fancy with its feeling when many things of import have come and gone and been forgot.

—N. A., [Review of *Tom Fool*], *The New York Times Book Review* (20 June 1926): 8

DONALD DOUGLAS

Whenever a writer binds himself over as apprentice to a pirate story he seems to find it necessary and proper to follow a routine of art as fixed and rigid as any articles of trade. There's the inevitable young man who runs away to sea and is worked pretty hard either by a nice captain or by a horrid captain; and after a few descriptions of life on the ocean wave (heave ho, my hearties!) with technical sea terms, thrown about careless-like and a few picturesque tars who refer to themselves in the third person and perhaps a storm or two you know just what you are in for in the next chapter. You just can't go wrong ⟨. . . .⟩

It's the fault of Stevenson in his healthy-minded "Treasure Island," where even the most vituperative rascal never does much more than shiver his timbers and the carnage is made altogether a delightful and rather jolly lark for cabin boys to observe with young, clean eyes. Long ago Smollett gave us the real thing in tough sailors; nor were his heroes the immaculate tarradiddles through whose eyes the whole scene develops. Since "Roderick Random" and the other tough guys we have had very little except stories which young boys may read in Boston; and in "Moonraker" Miss Jesse writes all the way through as if she were writing for boys and nice people who like to fancy pirates just a lot of good fellows getting together on the forecastle and now and then using a naughty word and at times killing a man, but all in a picturesque and exciting way. Now why (oh, why?) doesn't some one let us see a pirate ship through the eyes of its captain? We are getting a little weary of seeing resolute and bloody-minded men only through the philosophy of a cabin boy who in himself has no character.

There's no intention here to deny the vivid scenes which Miss Jesse unrolls like bright flags. It's a story of the most pleasant kind, and it has skill and subtlety and excitement. It chooses to follow a pattern with only a variation of sex which makes Captain Lovel turn out to be a woman; but the disclosure takes place at the very last, and we have only one chapter or so to learn the emotions of a woman who commanded ruffians for years and cowed them with her bravery and knowledge without their ever knowing or suspecting her to be a woman. That is too much to believe, but had Miss Jesse begun at the beginning and shown us all the successive stages whereby Captain Lovel was trained by her father to act like a man and her emotions at various stages of her career and her jealousy of one of her captives when she saw him love a girl with a baby-doll face: that would have been a story! Instead, Miss Jesse contents herself rather than ourselves with a trick ending (implied, of course, in the context), and has the whole meaning of the tale explained in one tragic scene. She does that scene very well, but it ought to have been a book. It's never been done before and by a great writer who is also a woman it ought to be done. Miss Jesse dodges her duty like a merchantman flying before the sinister hulk of a pirate ship.

—Donald Douglas, "Fie Upon This Puny Life!" *New York Herald Tribune Books* (29 May 1927): 6

THE TIMES LITERARY SUPPLEMENT

Miss Tennyson Jesse has chosen for the theme of her new novel A PIN TO SEE THE PEEPSHOW ⟨. . .⟩, the life and death of a girl who by trying to escape from dull reality into a glamorous world that she dreamed of fell into a dismal pit. There is something a little old-fashioned about this story of a dressmaker's *dégringolade;* for, although the date, the detail and the approach to the sexual element are modern enough, it belongs essentially to the classic period of realism, the nineteenth century.

Julia Almond, daughter of a clerk in an estate office, had two gifts—a business capacity and "the finely attuned orchestra of her body"—but she had no stability or depth of mind to keep her feet from following a will-o'-the-wisp. The magic of life, sensibility to which is the strength of the creative artist, thrilled her too profoundly; and this quality in her heroine the author brings out very skilfully. From loving to gaze into the lighted windows of other people's houses she learned the fatal habit of *dédoublement*, by which the Julia of everyday life was accompanied by a spectral Julia, brilliant, successful and marvellously loved by a perfect lover. Her first romance, frustrated of consummation by her lover's death in the War, awoke her body. Urged by her senses and by the uncomfortableness of home, she married a stupid, honest and sensual shopman, while still carrying on her life as the successful chief assistant in a fashionable dressmaker's establishment. The inevitable happened when Leonard Carr, a naval airman, seven years her junior, masterfully made her his. She believed that her dreams had come true, and as Leonard's mistress she saw herself full in the magic peepshow. Leonard and her husband saw differently: jealousy, quarrels, and finally a murder ensue. Julia's dream ends in the

Central Criminal Court, in the condemned cell and on the scaffold, the sordid horrors of which are conscientiously piled upon the reader.

At the end there are a few pages of commentary on Julia's life as reflected on by two doctors, her counsel, and the prison chaplain, which so shrewdly sum up the whole tragedy that it is superfluous for a reviewer to do so further. It is, rather, his privilege to point out the solidness of Miss Tennyson Jesse's construction, her intense sympathy with her characters, and the vividness with which she paints the scene of London life during the present century—the speech and sights and smells, and the multitudinous self-adjustments of ordinary people to the cataclysmic change. But Julia herself, if pitiful, is not new. A Frenchman who met her in Paris told her that, had she been born a Frenchwoman, she would have been the mistress of a millionaire. Perhaps he forgot that Flaubert drew a Julia in Madame Bovary, whose end and its cause were, in essentials, similar. It is a theme that can never grow old, and to take it up is an enterprise calling for every gift at a novelist's command. Miss Tennyson Jesse carries it through with bravery and distinction.

—N. A., [Review of *A Pin to See the Peepshow*], *The Times Literary Supplement* (11 October 1934): 692

PETER QUENNELL

Following a practice that seems to be growing quite common among modern English novelists, Miss Tennyson Jesse has founded her new book, *A Pin to See the Peepshow*, on the story revealed by a notorious murder committed in London some years ago. Unlike Miss Elizabeth Jenkins, whose *Harriet* struck closely to the outlines of the Penge Murder Trial, Miss Jesse has taken considerable liberties with the simple, squalid and yet somehow supremely moving drama that culminated in the murder of a harmless unwanted husband, late one evening, beneath the gaslamps of a prim suburban street. Julia was a more cultivated and thoughtful being than Edith Thompson; Leonard Carr a more engaging gallant than the young ship's-steward whom Mrs. Thompson—at least, according to the prosecution; for this view is disputed by criminologists—incited to take her tedious partner's life. But the main facts of the story are the same. A woman with the temperament of a *grade amoureuse* pursues the career of small businesswoman and of faithful wife to the dull unimaginative man she has never loved. Passion reaches her in the shape of a man much younger than herself. It is very difficult—it is often impossible—for them to meet. Respectability dogs their footsteps at every turn; and the woman seeks refuge in a world where the pleasures of the imagination—the joy of writing and receiving passionate letters—deputise for the concrete pleasures of which they are thwarted.

The book ends with a double execution. After a confused scuffle in the street between her husband and lover, Julia Starling wakes up to the knowledge that she and Leonard Carr—for the purposes of the story, his ship is not a liner but a naval aircraft-carrier—are suspected of having deliberately plotted and contrived Herbert Starling's death. Julia, too, begins by refusing to admit that her husband's injuries had been caused by her lover. She, too, is overwhelmed by the fantastic private universe that she has built up for her own and her lover's benefit; and her last mood is that of horrified incredulity. . . . Do ordinary people commit crimes? She herself is so ordinary that she finds it hard to picture herself as the romantic and infamous figure, popularised by the daily press and soon to be annihilated by the public hangman:

> She'd never had a chance of anything she really wanted. That was why she'd always pretended. She'd only pretended Herbert's death, and it had suddenly come alive in spite of her. Now her own death was here, and she couldn't pretend any more. If, when morning came, she were to stay lying on her bed, pretending something quite different, they'd pull her up; they'd make her stand on her feet, they wouldn't let her go on pretending. She had come to that place where dreams fail.

In the earlier sections of the novel, Miss Jesse, with some skill but, I cannot help thinking, at rather unnecessary length, sets to work to depict the background that had made Julia Starling what she was: a woman who dreamed passionately, vividly, even murderously, of pleasures to which her temperament had given her a right but which economic circumstance had denied. Not till the opening of Book Three, on page 267, is the real basis of the narrative allowed to appear; and the preparatory sections are somewhat conventional. It is a pity that the novel has not been telescoped; for, towards the middle, a reader's interest is inclined to flag.

—Peter Quennell, [Review of *A Pin to See the Peepshow*], *New Statesman and Nation* (13 October 1934): 518–19

JANE SPENCE SOUTHRON

The French Riviera has provided subject-matter for many books and has supplied scenery for many more. Fryniwyd Tennyson Jesse has, in "Act of God," made it the battleground of religious controversy.

The central theme has to do with a modern miracle vouched for by two children who announced, with a conviction nothing could upset, that the Mother of God had appeared to them on the lonely hillside where they were wont to tend their sheep. That was in 1929. By 1934, when the controversy started, Haut Fraxinet, where they said the Virgin had come to them "from nowhere" leaving the grass blades unbent by her passage, was firmly established as a place of constant pilgrimage, with a shrine, statues and other religious appurtenances blessed by the church; and with much besides that could claim nothing whatever of sanctification. "The *remote* mountain-top," we are told, "became a lively commingling of Benares and Margate," unspeakably distressing to the curé, Charles-Marie Cabadeus, a saintly Catholic whose love of his flock by no means blinded him to their faults and who saw them becoming daily more and more infected with the virus of commercial duplicity and avariciousness.

Cabadeus is highly cultured; and his faith has roots that strike down through world history. He is cognizant of the findings of modern science but his religion is on a separate plane, accepted implicitly and lived up to in an asceticism that has become second nature to him. When it is proved that the shepherd children had been deceived by a publicity-mad, feather-brained woman the shock to Cabadeus is terrific; but his faith is unshattered until his Bishop, in the interests of the church and of the pilgrims, decides to hush matters up. ⟨. . .⟩

Colonel Toby Erskine, the second most important personage introduced to us, is at once a man of the world and a scholar who finds it impossible to square the knowledge he has acquired with any but a material explanation for human existence. He and Cabadeus have a real regard and love for each other based on the integrity that is the most distinguishing characteristic of both of them and on a mutual delight in historical and antiquarian lore. They are well-drawn, being as convincing in their straightforward way as is Vera Fanshawe, Erskine's cousin, in her exhibitionism and neurotic tortuousness.

The discovery of this woman's diabolic deception and Erskine's failure to prevent her from "sharing" her sin publicly with the Oxford Groupers who are visiting Fraxinet are high lights in a strongly dramatic situation written of with directness and force. But the long stretches of controversial dialogue as well as the argumentative thesis-making indulged in mentally, by Erskine, are hard to accept as integral parts of an artistic whole. To those who have endeavored to keep more or less abreast of twentieth century scientific investigation and who are deeply enough read in history it is old news, with the viewpoint of scientists who do not reject religion omitted from count; while people who are just beginning to think things out for themselves will, almost certainly, prefer to do it first-hand; it is, in any case, matter more suited to midnight conversations in real life than to inclusion within the framework of a prose tragedy.

The book is marked by a world weariness that lies heavily upon it despite the author's stylistic excellence, the freshness of her sea-scenes and the beauty of her verbal landscapes.

—Jane Spence Southron, [Review of *Act of God*], *The New York Times Book Review* (19 September 1937): 4–5

VIRGINIA B. MORRIS

Its ⟨*A Pin to See the Peepshow*'s⟩ power evolves from the skillful characterization of the doomed Julia, who could bear to live in the world where she belonged only by filtering reality through the romantic haze of her fantasies. Though she is selfish, myopic, and unwittingly destructive, she is profoundly sympathetic, a woman whose punishment so far exceeds her crimes that she becomes a symbol, for Jesse, of the class and gender discrimination endemic in Britain in the 1920s and 1930s. ⟨. . .⟩

In a novel filled with ironies, Jesse gives Julia's attempts at conventional behavior the most devastating consequences. To escape from the family's encroachment on her privacy at home, Julia turns to marriage without considering the loss of privacy implicit in being a wife. She marries a family friend, an officer in a dashing uniform, forgetting until too late that he is a very ordinary men's shop manager and a widower eager to be cosseted by a devoted and faithful young wife. More like Julia's father than her husband, he is as incapable of understanding her needs as of satisfying them. Yet she is terrified of risking the poverty and disgrace implicit in divorce to gain the independence she craves. The bitterest irony Jesse hammers out, by contrasting her heroine with other characters in the novel, is that Julia would have been an overwhelming success had she been a member of the upper class, among whom divorces were affordable and socially acceptable, or had she been a man, allowed the indulgence of adultery.

The novel brilliantly plays out the counterpoint between Julia's aspirations and her fate. Never understanding what it means to love or be loved, she craves adoration and sexual excitement. Imagining that secret meetings and passionate letters are the essence of romance, she creates a fantasy world of assignations and promises that lead ultimately to Herbert Starling's murder and her own execution. That she never really meant the promises she made in those letters or used any of the poisons she described to get rid of Herbert was clear enough to her. She was more surprised than anyone when Leonard Carr killed him; murder had nothing to do with romance. But neither judge nor jury believed her, as they had not believed Edith Thompson.

At the arrest, throughout the trial, and into the grueling final hours when her appeal is denied, Julia struggles to grasp the reality that has caught her and destroyed her dreams. Meaning no real harm to anyone, frustrated still by never having "had a chance at anything she really wanted," she collapses into screams, heavily sedated and scarcely human. The novelist's message is horrifyingly and didactically clear: nothing Julia Almond has ever done deserves such a punishment.

By making Julia technically innocent yet unwittingly guilty, Jesse took an artistic risk critical to the novel's success. Had her protagonist been either as blameless as she thought herself or repentant for the self-absorption that precipitated the murder, the story would be maudlin. Instead the novel becomes an indictment of the society in which Julia lived and died, because she is punished for refusing to conform to the standards demanded of women of her class. In writing Julia Almond's story, Jesse is advocating equality for women in every social and political sphere. Ironically, of course, Julia is not interested in equality, but in love. That too is part of Jesse's point: her character is tragic because she is so inescapably the product of her time and place.

—Virginia B. Morris, "F. Tennyson Jesse," *Dictionary of Literary Biography*, vl. 77. *British Mystery Writers, 1920–1939*, ed. Bernard Benstock and Thomas F. Staley (Detroit: Gale Research Inc., 1985), 179–80

BIBLIOGRAPHY

The Milky Way. 1913.

Beggars on Horseback. 1915.

The Man Who Stayed at Home (as Beamish Tinker). 1915.

Secret Bread. 1917.

The Sword of Deborah: First-Hand Impressions of the British Women's Army in France. 1919.

The Happy Bride. 1920.

Billeted (with H. M. Harwood). 1920.

The White Riband; or, A Young Female's Folly. 1921.

Murder and Its Motives. 1924.

Anyhouse. 1925.

The Pelican (with H. M. Harwood). 1926.

Tom Fool. 1926.

Three One-Act Plays (with H. M. Harwood). 1926.

Moonraker: or, The Female Pirate and Her Friends. 1927.

Many Latitudes. 1928.

The Lacquer Lady. 1929.

How to Be Healthy Though Married (with H. M. Harwood). 1930.

The Solange Stories. 1931.

A Pin to See the Peepshow. 1934.

Sabi Pas: or, I Don't Know. 1935.

Act of God. 1937.

Double Death (with Dorothy L. Sayers, Freeman Wills Crofts, and others). 1939.

London Front: Letters Written to America (August 1939–July 1940) (with H. M. Harwood). 1940.

The Saga of San Demetrio. 1942.

While London Burns: Letters Written to America (July 1940–June 1941) (with H. M. Harwood). 1942.

The Story of Burma. 1946.

Comments on Cain. 1948.

The Alabaster Cup. 1950.

The Compass, and Other Poems. 1951.

The Dragon in the Heart. 1956.

PAMELA HANSFORD JOHNSON

1912–1981

PAMELA HANSFORD JOHNSON was born in London on May 29, 1912. When she was 11, her father, Reginald Kenneth, died, leaving her mother, Amy Howson, poor and burdened with debts. Instead of continuing her formal education after graduating from Clapham Secondary School, Pamela took a secretarial job at a bank at the age of 16 to help ease her mother's financial burden. She continued to educate herself, however, and developed many intellectually fertile friendships with other young writers.

One such friendship was with poet Dylan Thomas, with whom Johnson became romantically involved around the same time that her first collection of poetry, *Symphony for Full Orchestra*, was published (1934). Thomas is in fact credited with suggesting the title of her first novel, *This Bed Thy Centre* (1935), published when Johnson was just 22. Although mild by today's standards, its forthright examination of sex caused a sensation when it appeared. The novel also proved such a lucrative commercial success that Johnson was able to leave her bank job.

In 1936, Johnson married Neil Stewart, with whom she would have two children. Like other writers of her generation, Johnson was politically active, supporting the Spanish loyalists and working for other left-wing organizations. She edited the weekly *Chelsea Democrat* and during the 1940s became a frequent contributor to the BBC. The marriage to Stewart ended in 1950, when she married novelist C. P. Snow, with whom she would coauthor six plays and have one son. Theirs was a literary marriage full of mutual admiration for each other's work and frequent travel throughout the Soviet Union, United States, and Canada.

Johnson's early novels were psychological examinations of people debilitated by one or another aspect of their lives. In the 1940s, her writing took a new direction and she produced the "Helena" trilogy—*Too Dear for My Possessing* (1940), *An Avenue of Stone* (1947), and *A Summer to Decide* (1948)—which are considered among her best novels. From the 1950s through the early 1960s, she shifted to more classic models, writing a series of satirical novels often compared to the works of George Eliot and Marcel Proust. Among them is the "Dorothy Merlin" trilogy, initiated with the 1959 publication of *The*

Unspeakable Skipton, a story about the complex psychology of a para-noid artist.

In addition to writing 30 works of fiction, Johnson was a highly regarded critic, contributing articles to many journals and magazines and publishing studies of Thomas Wolfe and Marcel Proust. She received numerous honorary degrees and was made a Commander of the British Empire in 1975.

C. P. Snow died in 1980. After the publication of her last novel, *A Bonfire*, Johnson died on June 19, 1981, at the age of 69. Her obituary in *Publishers Weekly* described her as "one of England's best-known nov-elists, whom many American critics regarded as greatly underrated in the United States."

C R I T I C A L   E X T R A C T S

GILES ROMILLY

⟨T⟩here have been major-domos in the English novel, of whom Dickens was only the greatest, and they were of a tradition that was not discredited until after the 1914–18 war. Miss Hansford Johnson vigorously reasserts it. In her title, *An Impossible Marriage*, she tells you what you are going to receive, and thereafter is continually at your side, explaining and embellishing, in case some beauty should be missed.

> "You know I like you, don't you, Chris? You know that what I'm saying's really for the best?"
> "Things that are for the best always means the worst for some-body," I said, and was astonished by my own epigram.

From that short passage, how many novelists would have struck out the last seven words? Yet the effect of them is delightful; and Miss Johnson creates equally successful effects, by the same method, in passages of serious emotion. For instance, she makes her heroine, Christine, tell how Ned, the "impossible" husband, "put his head on my shoulder and began to cry." And this is not only a matter of how Christine felt, but also of how Miss Johnson's readers, of what-ever sex and culture, ought to feel about a man crying. Miss Johnson tells them. She does it very well.

To risk such a method today you have got to be able. This author's special ability is a buoyant sense of situation. Her period here is the no-man's-land between the Twenties and Thirties, and a particular pocket of that territory: not the Bright Young Things, but the Nice Young Things. The BYTs had parents who had already despaired, but the NYTs were still growled at—"You young people want everything your own way," and "You young people think you can break marriages as easily as breaking teacups"—when, primly and dimly, they edged towards emancipation. Miss Johnson has a set of them, middle-class and moderately impoverished, in Clapham; the "blind date" their novelty, the Charleston their mania, the ukulele their fashion. This is all tremendously real; and the hierarchic travel-agency office in which Christine works as "Junior" is not less real.

Miss Johnson fails to check in herself a suave prodigality of style that was one cause of the revolt against the major-domo succession. She has "jewelled pincers" (of Outer London), "a moment of drenching terror and joy" (love), "the lightning-edged scarlet of pain" (pain). Often she lingers when she *ought* to hurry away. This is only a sort of carelessness. Yet it has allowed her to end this carrying and vital novel on a commonplace note. Christine has a new husband, and is happy. That is all right. But the language in which Miss Johnson makes Christine describe her good fortune is so careless—"blobby," I kept thinking—as to produce a commonplace and smug effect, that seems to ask for a closer type, a narrower column, and a shinier page.

—Giles Romilly, [Review of *An Impossible Marriage*], *New Statesman and Nation* (3 April 1954): 445–46

ARTHUR MIZENER

Of the half dozen of her novels I have read, *The Sea and the Wedding* comes close to being the best: everything in it is sharply observed and finely ordered, down to the very title—that is, the real title, *The Last Resort*, which refers equally to the book's world, a seaside resort hotel filled with the left-overs of a dying middle class, and its chief character, a girl who ends by marrying a homosexual for a reason the author drives home in the book's last sentence: "She had added beneath her name [on a post card] . . . in a spurt of unquellable pride in having some kind of country she could call her own, "Evans.' " There is real pathos and irony in this ending, and it illuminates the book's social judgments in a variety of ways, but it has an even greater interest than those.

It was, I think, Virginia Woolf who pointed out that, since most of the novels have been written by men; women are in much the situation of Samuel Butler's Devil in his quarrel with God, who, as Butler pointed out, had also written all the books. This is as much a woman's book as a Hemingway novel is a man's. Its men, for all that they are extremely convincing externally, are emotionally about as convincing as Hemingway's women; they are, I take it, women's men. Its women strike me as terrible beyond belief, but I am prepared to believe they are what women really are, creatures with an "unquellable pride in having some kind of country [they can] call [their] own." The most impressive instances of this need are given by the narrator, because she is a normative character whose experience presumably enters the book only to provide occasions for the main characters. We are not, therefore, to consider it abnormal that, when her husband writes her that he is mildly ill in New York with virus pneumonia, she is reduced to hysteria and can only be calmed by a trans-Atlantic telephone call. On another occasion she has a miscarriage; "after that I wanted . . . simply to be alone with Gerard and to assure myself that this failure had not spoiled me for him." Any man's blood must, I think, run cold at the thought of being Gerard, faced with the appalling possessiveness of a demand to be needed which is so exclusive as that.

All the women in the book are like that. They feel on the grand scale, feel largely in relation to the minutely analysed battle of conquest for their chosen countries, and, in the last resort, choose to live with men who hate them, as the heroine's mother does, or to marry a man whose need for them is marginal, as the heroine does, rather than to have no country to call their own. It seems to me a terrifying vision, and it is made more terrible by the sanity and the supreme intelligence with which the novel represents the world in which these women live.

—Arthur Mizener, [Review of *The Last Resort*], *Kenyon Review* (Summer 1957), 488–89

THE TIMES LITERARY SUPPLEMENT

Miss Hansford Johnson belongs to that group of writers—they are perhaps most to be envied—whose fame has climbed slowly on the wings of each new achievement. In the past ten years she has become well known to the reading public as a novelist of great craftsmanship and distinction and to readers of the weeklies as one of the best contemporary reviewers of novels in the language. She is a profound moralist, though of a deliberately unpretentious kind, and each of her books is at bottom concerned with a moral situation. Yet each, at the same time, has been an attempt to master some technical problem. For, in spite of her great gifts as a critic and her deep involvement with the theatre—her essay on "The Future of Prose Drama," published as an introduction to her play *Corinth House*, is the best thing that has been written on the aesthetics of contemporary drama—it is with the art of fiction that she is primarily concerned. Where others have merely dogmatized, pooh-poohed or aired their fancies about the novel, she has genuinely mediated and practised.

Though her own interests in literature lean towards the bizarre—she had given us the most perceptive criticism of Miss Compton-Burnett's novels that has ever been written—it is in her comments on life as lived out by her characters that she excels. She has done this nowhere better than in *An Avenue of Stone* and its successor, *A Summer to Decide*, and also in her last book, *The Last Resort*—a novel conceived on a smaller scale but containing much superb characterization with its accompanying and unique gloss on the fruits of human action.

An Avenue of Stone lies at the centre of all Miss Hansford Johnson's fiction. In this novel and in its dying tigress of a heroine, Helena Archer, all her energy as an artist and her moral attention as an observer are concentrated. It is a book filled with a great urgency, like an angry sky, and its background—the strange post-war London of scarcities and points, regrets for lost *camaraderie* and good times—is brilliantly filled in and related to the immediate human situation. The theme—betrayal of the first-rate or the good in heart by the warped, the hangers-on or the discomfited—is one that absorbs this writer; she has returned to it many times, particularly in the play, *Corinth House*, in which a basic situation similar to Balzac's immortal *Le Curé de Tours* is lifted into metaphysical melodrama of a high order through the two antagonists' agreement to share their complementary guilt together. *An Avenue of Stone* is in no sense melodramatic: it is a plain, unvarnished study of human temperaments acting out their needs and jealousies on one another.

—N. A., "A Corvo of Our Day," *The Times Literary Supplement* (9 January 1959): 18

FREDERICK R. KARL

The novels of Pamela Hansford Johnson are the basic material of the publisher looking for a well-made, intelligent novel that stands the chance of a book club selection and will go well with a public that wants its fiction neither light nor heavy. It is the kind of fiction that keeps the novel going in between the valleys and the peaks. It handles ideas in terms of the people involved; it rarely aims at abstractions, and the conflicts themselves are those one encounters in daily life. Emotions are of course played down; there are few powerful climaxes, few dramatic intensities that would weight the novel unduly. In brief, the novelist makes no attempt to exceed the tight, well-controlled world over which he or she is a master.

The themes of Miss Johnson's novels demonstrate the ordinary world in which her characters are immersed. In *An Impossible Marriage* (1954), for example, she is concerned with a marriage that does not work; the situation, the characters themselves, the incidents that display their incompatibility are all commonplace. What significance the novel does have is simply its toned-down, day-to-day cataloguing of why and how a marriage fails—the direct appeal to a middle-class female audience is clear. In *The Sea and the Wedding*, published two years later, Miss Johnson centers on the relationship between Celia Baird and Eric Aveling, principally their hopeless love affair while Eric's wife is slowly dying, their inability to marry once she has died, and Celia's attempt to find happiness at any price, which she does by marrying a homosexual friend, Junius. This novel is somewhat spicier than the previous, including as it does the illicit affair and the homosexuals around Junius.

To take one more of Miss Johnson's novels, the one with perhaps the most exotic content: *The Unspeakable Skipton* (1959) features a rogue who lives in Bruges and tries to cadge his way through life, much as Cary's picaresque Gulley Jimson in *The House's Mouth*. Miss Johnson has turned the painter Gulley into the writer Skipton, a man who must live by his wits. The central character is a man who believes so strongly in himself that he will do anything to insure the opportunity for his art to mature. In presenting Skipton and his world, however, Miss Johnson avoids the larger issue suggested by the introduction of a confidence man: that is, coming to terms with the confidence man as he tries to disguise his various shifts from illusion to reality.

—Frederick R. Karl, "Composite," *A Reader's Guide to the Contemporary English Novel* (1961), excerpted in *Twentieth-Century British Criticism*, ed. Harold Bloom (New York: Chelsea House Publishers, 1985), 1442

WALTER ALLEN

Such novels as *The Last Resort* (1956) and *The Humbler Creation* (1959), render beautifully the complexities, the discontinuities, the contradictions of human behaviour and the necessary recognition of the frustrations attendant upon it. They seem to me to have the sad, honest, lucid acceptance of life we find in George Eliot, and, like George Eliot, Pamela Hansford Johnson is concerned, in her later novels at any rate, with the problem of right doing, of duty. The central character of *The Humbler Creation* is an Anglican parson, vicar of an unfashionable London parish, saddled with a silly neurotic wife and with too many family burdens, a good man tempted into the sin of love outside his marriage. But this is very much to over-simplify, for in these novels complexity of detail is everything, and it is through the complexity that the author's discrimination asserts itself.

So, in *The Last Resort*, it is possible to isolate the moral element that sunders the two lovers in the words of one of them:

> 'Underneath it is all the undertow of the Ten Commandments. They make dreadful fools of us. They're like our grandmother's sideboard, which we don't use any more, but can't bring ourselves to sell. There it is, all the time, weighing us down from the attic or biding its time in the cellar.'

But beyond this is the whole intricate pattern of character-relations and the events that spring out of them, a pattern that has to be intricate in order acceptably to suggest the complexity of life itself. This is essential to Miss Hansford Johnson's purpose, and she achieves it. In *The Last Resort* particularly she is, one is persuaded, seeing life steadily and, if not whole, seeing sufficient of it to stand for the whole. She persuades us of this by the sobriety of her realism, her ability to render specific places and their inhabitants, by her sure grasp of her characters, who are many and diverse and who are never seen statically but are always capable of surprising us with new facets of their personalities, and, not less important, by her tone. ⟨. . .⟩

In *The Last Resort* it became apparent that she was steadily extending the range of her fiction. It is not that the types she describes, or their milieus, are new; but she makes them new: the retired, angry, self-absorbed doctor, his wife neurotically possessive of her daughter, the homosexual architect, and the rest. She sees all round them and catches them in a new light, in a new significance, so that in the end they are somehow bigger, richer as emblems of the human condition, than one might expect them to be. And what is strikingly absent from their delineation is what Norman Douglas called 'the novelist's touch', the falsification of life through failure to realize 'the complexities of the ordinary human mind'.

How much Pamela Hansford Johnson is extending her range may be seen in the novel that followed *The Last Resort—The Unspeakable Skipton* (1959). Her subject here is the paranoiac artist. Familiar enough in life, in fiction treatment of him has been mainly marginal. In life the great exemplar is Frederick Rolfe, 'Baron Corvo', and Miss Hansford Johnson has admittedly drawn on him for her portrait of Daniel Skipton, Knight of the Most Noble Order of SS. Cyril and Methodius. But Rolfe is no more than the starting-point: Skipton exists in his own right and in our time, a separate creation.

Skipton is a monster. We see him in his austere garret in Bruges writing blackguarding letters to his long-suffering publisher even while trying to borrow from him; we see him attempting to blackmail the elderly cousin who has never met him and who makes him an allowance out of sheer kindliness. He scours the town for English tourists to pimp for. He is a monster of satanic egoism, and with diabolical glee he translates all who offend him—by their mere existence—into figures of fun, effigies of depravity, that go straight into his interminable, unpublishable novel. A monster—and yet, as Miss Hansford Johnson reveals him, the mind, called to pass judgment, wavers. That ferocious anal-eroticism, that passion for cleanliness, that revulsion from the contacts of the flesh, don't they come very near to a perverted saintliness? And certainly the intransigence of his appalling lunatic self-regard makes him almost one of the saints of art.

Skipton is a splendid comic creation; and yet, without abating the rigour of her sardonic comedy, Pamela Hansford Johnson brings out the full pathos of the poor wretch and his fate, which is in essence that of the dedicated artist who is devoid of talent. She embodies his fate in a plot marked by continuously amusing invention and by a set of characters that are excellent foils to him. And the setting of the novel, Bruges with its bells and its canals, places the comedy in a further dimension of poetry.

—Walter Allen, "War and Post-War: British," *The Modern Novel* (1964), excerpted in *Twentieth-Century British Criticism*, ed. Harold Bloom (New York: Chelsea House Publishers, 1985), 1442–43

ANTHONY BURGESS

Admirers of the work of Pamela Hansford Johnson (Lady Snow) have not always seen a preoccupation with the problems of right-doing, sometimes resolving itself into questions of the final sanctions of morality, which lies hidden under the complexities of her novels, as well as their wit, accurate reportage, and delight in the surface of life. Her first book, *This Bed Thy Centre*, appeared when she was only twenty-two, but its recent reissue reminds us that she has been pretty consistent in her preoccupation with moral dilemmas. *The Humbler Creation* presents an Anglican clergyman who is saintly but, driven by the intolerable frustrations of his family life, falls into adultery. As with Graham Greene (whom she in no way really resembles) we are tempted towards moral judgements that orthodoxy would not condone. *The Last Resort* seems to touch a theological level with its rumination (in the person of the narrator) on the difference between ourselves and the company of the saints and martyrs: they commit themselves to the big terrible decisions; we hold back. And however amoral and free we like to think ourselves, there are always nagging doubts about the religious furniture that lies, gathering dust but still very solid, up there in the attic. *An Error of Judgement* deals with a consultant physician who has done fine work and is revered by his patients. But he is aware that he took up medicine only because pain fascinates him: his profession could be a means of inflicting it, or at least withholding its palliatives. He abandons his practice and takes to a job whose altruism seems obvious—trying to rehabilitate delinquent youth. But he meets one young man who has committed a sadistic crime of particular ghastliness; he has not been caught, he is quite ready to commit the same crime again. Like a vet, the doctor 'puts down' the young brute with brandy and sleeping tablets. What sort of judgement do we make? The orthodox answer is not satisfactory, but could any answer be? No novel of any complexity can ever have the directness of a moral tract, but the virtue of Pamela Hansford Johnson's work often lies in its power to present the great issues nakedly—forcing us not so much to a decision as to a realization of the hopelessness of decisions. If, that is, we are not saints and martyrs.

I ought to stress that all Miss Hansford Johnson's novels are notable for a kind of grave lightness of touch, they are never without humour. Her comic gifts are seen as well as anywhere in *The Unspeakable Skipton*, whose hero is a mad, egoistical novelist working on a book that will never end and never be published. All kinds of beastliness are, to him, in order if they provide material for his fiction: like Dante, he puts his enemies in hell. There is nothing good about him, and yet there is this monstrous dedication of art which lifts him to a kind of empyrean: he is as far above ordinary decent plodders through life as the saints and martyrs are. He is, perhaps, a devil, and is not a devil a perverted angel—having more traffic with the divine order than people who are not Skipton and are all too speakable?

—Anthony Burgess, "Good and Evil," *The Novel Now* (1967), excerpted in *Twentieth-Century British Criticism*, ed. Harold Bloom (New York: Chelsea House Publishers, 1985), 1443–44

GERDA CHARLES

As the man said . . . all criticism in the end is subjective. Bend over backwards as he may, the critic's judgment ultimately depends on whether his personal experience, temperament or vision chimes with that of the artist. A writer who for me possesses this precious, chiming quality is Pamela Hansford Johnson. She notices and tells precisely what I would wish to be noticed and told.

The Survival of the Fittest is a long novel, spanning the last thirty-odd years, but though it traces much of the history of the period it is really a study of a group—in the more enclosed sense of the word. It is a fascinating theme. The group, the gang, our lot . . . how much of human destiny, one wonders, depends on the particular set one chances to find oneself in; college, rooming house, relatives—or simply street? One hard glance at this question is almost enough to make fatalists of us all.

The group in this novel are primarily linked by neighborhood. Two young men grow up together in the narrowly respectable district of Clapham in South London. It is a region of Edwardian suburbia already beautifully conveyed in an earlier novel, *An Impossible Marriage*. Miss Hansford Johnson is as much the poet and chronicler of this area as John Betjeman is of his; the "soft, violet evenings" on Clapham Common; the houses, "mean and flashy"; the grayly facetious quality of its social occasions. No wonder the young men long to escape. Both have literary ambitions, both are in love with the idea of Bohemia, Chelsea, Soho pubs. Undergraduates *manqué*, not untouched by sophistication, they nevertheless pursue with an absurd and touching innocence, "the wild time." ⟨. . .⟩

In this long novel, never less than supremely readable, often shot with pure and marvelously fresh perception, it is the character of Jo which, standing at the center, holds (or should hold) the moral heart of the book in his hands. Always courageous, Miss Hansford Johnson in this as in other fields has chosen to illuminate and indeed to bless such unfashionable virtues as endurance, acceptance, the settling, without screaming, for less; the not-so-bad-after-all. Yet it must be admitted that this fine purpose does not quite come off. For all the deaths and disgraces, the minutely observed bliss and anguishes of love, what is lacking (and what, perversely, the reader *wants*) is the sense of tragedy. As Belphoebe says (Belphoebe is the gorgeous name chosen for a most charming and affectionately drawn little portrait of Edith Sitwell): "Be grandiose. It is a great shield, grandiosity."

But if grandiosity is missing it is the only real flaw in this otherwise witty, melancholy, beautiful and generous novel.

—Gerda Charles, "The Moderately Content," *The Nation* (19 August 1968): 124–125

ELIZABETH JANEWAY

Pamela Hansford Johnson was once beloved of Dylan Thomas and is now the wife of C. P. Snow. And why, you may well ask, should I start a review of her book, subtitled "A Personal Record," with this sexist description instead of noting that she has published 14 novels, a play, a critical volume on Proust and a moral essay, "On Iniquity," inspired by a particularly nasty British murder case of some years ago? Because her book is much more interesting when she is recalling her experiences with friends and family, acquaintances and lovers, than when she is communicating her ideas and opinions. That's not too surprising, after all, for someone who's a novelist by trade. Novelists don't need opinions, indeed it can be argued that they're better off without: think of Céline and Dostoevsky, think of those essays of Tolstoy on history. Let us, therefore, thank Miss Johnson for her reminiscenses but not for her views, which run from the banal to the curmudgeonly. 〈. . .〉

〈. . .〉 Her sketch of Dylan Thomas is wry and objective and warmly affectionate at the same time, a portrait of the artist as a *very* young man . . . A magnanimous Edith Sitwell appears and, most amusing of all in its sharp observation, a picture of Ivy Compton-Burnett as fabulous monster in her ogress's den. But the further Miss Johnson strays from the immediate reality of people in their setting, especially known people in a known setting, the less well does she persuade us of the value of her observations. When she describes an air-raid shelter in London where she and her mother waited out the bombing raids, we see it and smell it, we hear the sounds and voices of war. But enter politics, let the literary friends she is recalling be Russian instead of British, let her find herself a visiting lecturer on an American campus, and her vision blurs into generalities.

—Elizabeth Janeway, [Review of *Important to Me*], *The New York Times Book Review* (14 September 1975): 18–19

ISHRAT LINDBLAD

⟨The⟩ outburst of creative experiment just before and during the 1920s meant that, by the time Pamela Hansford Johnson began to write, the techniques of stream of consciousness and parallel plots had obtained general currency.

In *This Bed Thy Centre* and *Here Today*, Pamela Hansford Johnson's narrative focuses for a short period on a scene in the life of one of her characters before switching to another. The juxtaposition of the two scenes enhances the meaning of each, creating a unity that has a more complex significance than either of the two scenes could have had in isolation. Thus, for example, there is a brief scene in *This Bed Thy Centre* where Roly is full of apprehension after receiving a note from Gwen asking him to meet her because she has something important to tell him. Without actually expressing what it is he fears, the scene ends with his thoughts: "No, it couldn't be" (p. 219). The next scene opens on Leda and her lover together, and John asks her, "A child, my darling?" It proves that Leda is pregnant. Her unwanted pregnancy is thus immediately linked to Roly's fears, and John's distaste for the role of father is a reflection on Roly as well.

Another characteristic feature of her technique is the use of interior monologues and stream of consciousness. In the *New Republic* a reviewer writes slightingly of her use of this method, describing her characters as "wading many a sluggish stream of consciousness." In fact, the stream does not flow sluggishly at all. Elsie's fear of sex is built up into a kind of crescendo by the constant use of the phrases "Perfect love casteth out fear" and "Oh God, I don't want to get married" in the middle of her fervent efforts to think about something else. Mrs. Maginnis's fear of cancer is also best expressed by rendering the flow of her thoughts.

In *Here Today*, Miss Waghorn's fear of her guilty secret being discovered, Mr. Doppy's malevolent delight in persecuting his victims, Bert Pereira's despair at the thought of his wife's finding out about his infidelity, and Phil's emotions as he stands waiting to meet Connie are all conveyed directly to the reader by using a technique that gives the impression of their innermost thoughts being recorded.

Related to this technique is the frequent use of *erlebte rede*, or indirect direct speech. For example, Mrs. Maginnis returns to her lonely room after an attempt at forced gaiety in the pub. She bumps into a gramophone: "As the instrument crashed down, the needle gave a last scream up the record. I hope no one heard. They'll be coming to ask questions, and I can't talk to them. She touched herself with fearful fingers" (p. 98). Here the word "scream" indicates how it sounded to Mrs. Maginnis, and "I hope no one heard. They'll be coming to ask questions" is a direct transcription of her thoughts without the use of quotation marks, and it imperceptibly gives way to the third-person narration of "She touched herself with fearful fingers." Thus the description of a simple episode like a gramophone falling to the floor assumes the same proportions for the reader as it has for the person involved. The use of lines from songs and poems as refrains that stick in the minds of her characters and suddenly interrupt their thoughts, and the frequent recounting of dreams and nightmares are other ways of rendering events of internal rather than external importance.

In both these early novels the prose is frequently poetic. Thus Mr. Doppy in his flower shop is described: "He touched his great stone jar full of delphiniums, evil blue, wedding blue, sleeping purple. Nice" (p. 14). There are several lyrical descriptions of the Common where Roly and Elsie take their walks and, in both novels, poetic images abound. In *Here Today*, for example, a passage of description uses the image "wands of light lengthen with the green evening" (p. 13). This use of language reveals Miss Hansford Johnson's early interest in poetry and her use, in prose, of many of the stylistic techniques of the poet.

—Ishrat Lindblad, *Pamela Hansford Johnson* (Boston: Twayne Publishers, 1982), 34–36

B I B L I O G R A P H Y

Symphony for Full Orchestra. 1934.
This Bed Thy Centre. 1935.
Blessed Above Women. 1936.
Here Today. 1937.
World's End. 1937.
The Monument. 1938.
Girdle of Venus. 1939.
Too Dear for My Possessing. 1940.
Tidy Death (with G. N. Stewart). 1940.
The Family Pattern. 1942.
Murder's a Swine (with G. N. Stewart). 1943.
Winter Quarters. 1943.

The Trojan Brothers. 1944.
Thomas Wolfe: A Critical Study. 1947.
An Avenue of Stone. 1947.
A Summer to Decide. 1948.
The Duchess at Sunset. 1948.
Hungry Gulliver: An English Critical Appraisal of Thomas Wolfe. 1948.
The Philistines. 1949.
Corinth House. 1950.
Ivy Compton-Burnett. 1951.
Family Party (with C. P. Snow). 1951.
Her Best Foot Forward (with C. P. Snow). 1951.
The Pigeon with the Silver Foot (with C. P. Snow). 1951.
Spare the Rod (with C. P. Snow). 1951.
The Supper Dance (with C. P. Snow). 1951.
To Murder Mrs. Mortimer (with C. P. Snow). 1951.
Catherine Carter. 1952.
Swann in Love. 1952.
An Impossible Marriage. 1954.
Madame de Charlus. 1954.
Albertine Regained. 1954.
Saint-Loup. 1955.
A Window at Montjarrain. 1956.
The Last Resort. 1956.
Six Proust Reconstructions. 1958.
The Unspeakable Skipton. 1959.
The Humbler Creation. 1959.
An Error of Judgement. 1962.
Night and Silence, Who Is Here? 1963.
Cork Street, Next to the Hatter's. 1965.
On Iniquity: Some Personal Reflections Arising out of the Moors Murder Trial. 1967.
The Survival of the Fittest. 1968.
The Honours Board. 1970.
The Holiday Friend. 1972.
Important to Me. 1974.
The Good Listener. 1975.
The Good Husband. 1978.
A Bonfire. 1981.

MARGARET KENNEDY

1896–1967

MARGARET MOORE KENNEDY was born on April 23, 1896, the daughter of a distinguished London lawyer. She was educated at Cheltenham Ladies' College and then Somerville College, Oxford. After graduating in 1919, she lived with her parents while writing *A Century of Revolution* (1922), a textbook on modern European history.

Her next two books, *The Ladies of Lyndon* (1923) and *The Constant Nymph* (1924), established Kennedy as one of England's favorite popular fiction writers. Both novels are impelled by her criticism of Victorian convention in English society; both employ an unhappy love story to illustrate the author's ideas about artistry and morality; and both are excessively romantic. However, the latter captured the imagination of the public, earning Kennedy overwhelming success in both England and the United States, which in turn prompted several film adaptations.

In 1925, Kennedy married Sir David Davies. The couple lived mainly in Kensington, London, and had a son and two daughters. She continued to write while raising their children, publishing *Red Sky at Morning* in 1927 and a sequel to *The Constant Nymph*, *The Fool of the Family*, in 1930. Of her 11 other novels, *The Feast* (1950) and *Lucy Carmichael* (1951) were Literary Guild and Book Society choices, and *Troy Chimneys* (1952) won the 1953 James Tait Black Memorial Prize. Kennedy was also an accomplished pianist, and many of her novels reflect a wide-ranging interest in the arts. Recognized as a distinguished playwright, critic, and biographer, she also wrote a book on Jane Austen and several studies of fiction and film.

Kennedy's last novel, *Not in the Calendar: The Story of Friendship*, was published in 1964. Her husband died the same year, after which she lived alone in Oxfordshire until her death on July 31, 1967.

CRITICAL EXTRACTS

JOSEPH WOOD KRUTCH

Miss Kennedy has undertaken ⟨in *The Constant Nymph*⟩ to describe the conflict between the ferocious egotism of the creative artist and those who are the unfortunate victims of his love, and though she begins in the mood of sophisticated farce, with a description of the disorganized household of another artist, she means to rise to a considerable height in the description of passion and to achieve a moving pathos through presenting the fate of two women condemned to love this man of no passion save the passion for music. Yet she does not, so it seems to me, do either of these things supremely well. The desired fusion does not take place. What we get is only a preliminary farce succeeded by a tragedy which would be readily seen to be executed in a manner no more than reasonably competent were it not for the piquancy of the contrast and the fact that such a contrast happens to have a very definite appeal to contemporary taste. ⟨. . .⟩

⟨. . .⟩ The persons are all of heroic stature and they are mastered, so we are told, by volcanic passions; but it is difficult for the reader to feel them, and we are compelled—a fatal thing for a novel—to take the author's word for their existence. When we are told, for instance, that almost at first sight an English girl of conventional upbringing falls desperately in love with our hero and wishes to marry him a few days later we have nothing except the word of the author to make it seem credible, in spite of the fact that upon a belief in this passion hangs the whole effect of the story. Thus we are given the outline of a great novel, but that outline is not filled by living characters or surrounded by that atmosphere of convincing passion which alone could achieve the effect contemplated. ⟨. . .⟩

The trouble with Miss Kennedy seems to me not that she lacks talent but that she has very definitely fallen between two stools, that she has failed to make up her mind soon enough whether she wished to write a tragic farce or a genuinely heroic novel of the sort which she ends by attempting. Evidently she is familiar with the work of the contemporary English sophisticates; but if she has not already done so she might profitably read Jacob Wassermann's *The Goose Man*. It is a novel which deals with a theme almost identical with hers, and it does all the things which her novel does not. To read it is to believe it, as one must of necessity believe those things which one has experienced; to read *The Constant Nymph* is no more than to be told that certain things took place. The difference is the difference between a great novel and one which, whatever intelligence it may reveal, is not in the most important sense a novel at all.

—Joseph Wood Krutch, "A Minority Report," *The Nation* (15 April 1925), excerpted in *Twentieth-Century British Literature*, ed. Harold Bloom (New York: Chelsea House Publishers, 1985), 1526–27

MARY ELLIS OPDYCKE

Miss Margaret Kennedy writes a novel ⟨*The Constant Nymph*⟩ so fearlessly unrespectable in its sympathies, so alluring in its characterizations, so romantic and so true that all England buys it, reads it, and promptly bursts into smiles of wholesome bitterness. ⟨. . .⟩

It is not often that the author allows her thesis a naked demonstration, but in one scene the fiction is stripped down and the main issue shines out. Florence Dodd has traced her husband to the home of his old associates:

> Music, with all these people, came first; that was why they talked about it as if nobody else had any right to it. Once Florence had liked them all too well; now that she understood them better she was fright ened of them. She wanted to challenge them, to make a demonstration of her power, to call them back to that world of necessity and compromise which they so sublimely ignored, but with which they would ultimately have to reckon. After all she was the strongest. She had order and power on her side. They were nothing but a pack of rebels.

An author who can so clearly state one cause, and yet throw her sympathy and hero worship to the other has herself solved a compromise. She has written a satirical novel, and securely pinioned her subject to the wall for all to laugh at, and yet she has lured a public composed largely of such subjects to read her book and thus to laugh at themselves.

Given such a large order to fill, it is small wonder that Miss Kennedy has relegated literary style to the background. At her hands the English language becomes a serviceable medium, coin of the realm, useful as a means to an end. And if her shillings and pence transfer easily into marks or francs and buy for the reader convincing pictures of Munich and Brussels, she is tempted to satisfaction. Why should they also jingle as numismatic curios?

Though said to be under thirty, Miss Kennedy can bring to her characters a sympathy that magnifies its object without distortion. Her situations are developed with humor and her descriptions with restraint. ⟨. . .⟩

Similarly is her dialogue a significant and transparent lens by which her characters are elucidated. She refrains from saying things about people which they themselves do not say. A single exception has been found in the profanity of the young Sangers. The reader is continually told of their lewd habits of speech, but rarely given a chance to hear more than an isolated "damn."

One other fault casts a small shade on the book's importance: its inappropriate and banal title. *The Constant Nymph* suggests a pastoral lyric, a romantic glimpse into a postwar drawing-room, even a ballerina's tragedy, but it does not convey the bitter fight between talent and genius, the harsh contrast between orderly, constructive calm and high revolt. Is this perhaps another subtle bit of compromise, one final bait to invite the bourgeoisie to their own funeral? For its success, at least, whether accidental or intended, one must admit appreciation.

—Mary Ellis Opdycke, [Review of *The Constant Nymph*], *New Republic* (15 April 1925), excerpted in *Twentieth-Century British Literature*, ed. Harold Bloom (New York: Chelsea House Publishers, 1985), 1527–28

REBECCA WEST

I have with me in this shack in Cornwall exactly three books: "The Constant Nymph," by Margaret Kennedy; "Serena Blandish," by A Lady of Quality; "Piano Quintet," by Edward Sackville-West. ⟨. . .⟩ Now, I find these casually collected volumes amazing in one important respect. The level of their technical achievement is stupendously high. This is Miss Kennedy's second book; "A Lady of Quality" has done it but twice before; "Piano Quintet" is a first novel. But all these three writers know how to say what they want to say as in the past no craftsman knew till his life was nearly over. The most striking of the three in this respect is Miss Kennedy. ⟨. . .⟩

Yet there is another side to it. How comes it that the novel which of these three has attracted most attention by its dazzling dexterity, to which I myself in this article have devoted most space, is somehow the least pleasing? It is impossible for the reader of taste to derive from "The Constant Nymph" the same feeling of aesthetic satisfaction that he receives from "Serena Blandish" or even "Piano Quintet." At first the reason for this is not easy to discover. Obviously "The Constant Nymph" is a more massive book than "Serena Blandish"; and "Piano Quintet" is difficult to read and contains a character escaped from the lunatic asylum of Mr. D. H. Lawrence's fancy, who talks about his "abolished nature" and is possessed by the Lawrencian idealess and gloomy metaphysical system which is nothing but a piece of blotting paper which takes dark patches from its creator's spilt moods but remains blank elsewhere. It occurs to one that perhaps it was unfortunate for "The Constant Nymph" that one happens to read it at the same time as "Piano Quintet" since the special excellence of that novel, its treatment of the musical interests of the characters, is the special weakness of Miss Kennedy's work. ⟨. . .⟩

Now, it may be said that this is a trifle; that compared with the success Miss Kennedy has won in her main duty of the creating of character it is negligible. But indeed it is a very significant trifle. This business of writing about persons engaged in some other art than literature is one of the most difficult of all enterprises one can engage in during practice of the art of fiction. It takes a Goethe to write a "Wilhelm Meister." Writing a novel about ordinary characters is to translate into the terms of one kind of artistic consciousness the doings of persons in a state of normal human consciousness. Writing a novel about artists is to retranslate into the terms of one kind of artistic consciousness the doings of persons who have already translated themselves from a state of normal human consciousness into the terms of another kind of artistic consciousness. It is a task comparable to painting the picture of a figure reflected in a mirror. And like that it can hardly be done save by direct contact between the artist's attention and his subject. The group seen simply, with no distortion from the ordinary due to mirror or art, he may do by reference to the discoveries of others; but he must avoid these special cases, of which there are relatively few models for him to copy; in which guesswork is likely to land him in detectable inaccuracy. Sert will fill a wall as agreeably as may be by recalling how Goya or Tintoretto or Giorgione presented this and that particular aspect of nature. Edith Wharton will produce book after book whose tranquil majesty is based on observations made by Henry James concerning the processes of refined sensoria. Miss Kennedy reveals her inexperience only by presenting one of these special cases such as these more wily practitioners avoid; and thereby betraying that she is one of those artists who work on a substructure of the perceptions of others. There is not one moment of discovery in "The Constant Nymph." Never does one stop, as one does constantly throughout "Serena Blandish" and "Piano Quintet," because the author has helped one in the business of making a map of the universe by saying how this or that point in the landscape looks from their point of vantage. There is really nothing peculiar to Miss Kennedy in the whole book except its general power and competence. For it is based on certain romantic traditions that are the crystallization of the discoveries made by preceding artists; I should be inclined to guess that the particular progenitors of her imagination are Shakespeare and Mr. Galsworthy, for about Teresa there is very much of Cordelia, and the refusal to accept the validity of Florence's claims one suspects to be a consequence of the lesson of the Forsytes. That is to say that "The Constant Nymph" is a masterpiece of decadent art. One hastens, since there are so many fools about, to say that there is no touch of moral derogation about that term decadent. It simply expresses its position in artistic time; a lovely hour which shall have no successor. For when an artist makes no discoveries, adds nothing to the stuff of tradition, then his art, so far as he is concerned, is on the way towards decay, and he must be termed decadent.

Now, this is no reason why we should not appreciate "The Constant Nymph"; but there are very forceful reasons why we should not allow our appreciation to overbear our sense of its decadence. For now that the technique of novel-writing is so widely and so guilefully practised this particular kind of novel will be more and more often and more and more successfully achieved. It will be a pity if its essence is not recognized; if readers do not perceive that though it offers them harmony and suavity other books that lack these qualities may yet have the superior claim of being a part of living art.

—Rebecca West, "Notes on Three Novels," *The Saturday Review of Literature* (17 October 1925): 207–9

LEE WILSON DODD

⟨*The Ladies of Lyndon*⟩ is Margaret Kennedy's first novel. It made little stir in the world when published, and its appearance now in America is of course due to the great popular success of her second novel, "The Constant Nymph." All of which seems to me to prove that the great popular success of "The Constant Nymph" was very little due to its higher qualities, for there are literary virtues in "The Constant Nymph" which, to my mind, remove it entirely from the ranks of ephemeral best-sellerdom. And these virtues, though here a little clouded perhaps, are almost equally apparent in "The Ladies of Lyndon."

What the special virtues of Miss Kennedy as a writer are, may be briefly suggested by saying that they are also the literary virtues of Jane Austen. If Jane Austen had lived a hundred years later, in a freer environment, she might quite well have given us Sanger's Circus, or Mrs. Varden Cocks of the present novel, or her lovely daughter Agatha, who did want so to be a woman of something more than charm but could never quite conveniently manage it. Miss Kennedy knows her characters as few of us know our friends or ourselves; she brings them before us without fuss or difficulty or tedious parade of psycho-analysis; and she is just to them—she neither caricatures nor sentimentalizes the human scene. And finally, like glorious Jane, she has a pervading humor and also a dangerous wit which she holds severely in check. She escapes wonderfully from the snares set for her by her own exuberant liveliness of mind. It would be easy for her to be merely a satirist; but she is something better than that already—and may yet, if she will, become a novelist of distinctive rank.

—Lee Wilson Dodd, "The 'Nymph's' Precursor," *The Saturday Review of Literature* (14 November 1925): 291

L. P. HARTLEY

Here is Miss Margaret Kennedy's new novel ⟨*Red Sky at Morning*⟩, and one naturally asks oneself, Is it as good as *The Constant Nymph*, or less good, or better? A difficult question to answer. Certainly no book could make a more difficult debut than *Red Sky at Morning*, following and necessarily challenging comparison with a novel that was at once a popular success and a *succès d'estime*. The books have certain resemblances; *The Constant Nymph* opened, and its successor closes, with a large group of people compressed into surroundings too narrow for them. The friction engendered by this compression set in motion the earlier story and is instrumental in bringing about the catastrophe in this. For it is of the essence of Miss Kennedy's view of life that her characters are always in opposition to each other, and to intensify their mutual uncongeniality she naturally places them in circumstances in which they cannot possibly get out of each other's way.

Monk's Hall is a slightly more artificial rendezvous than Sanger's Chalet. The inmates of the latter were loosely bound together by ties of consanguinity; they lived under a patriarchal system. But Monk's Hall was a caprice of William Crowne's. He had plenty of money and little idea of what to do with it: so he bought the house which should have gone to his cousin Trevor, and established there not only Trevor, but a large company of unsuccessful and second-rate artists with their wives, mistresses and children. Not least important of these was his own wife Tilli, a sinister figure who seems to have married him out of an obscure wish to revenge herself on the whole male sex. A few miles away is the "other house," Water Hythe, the home of Catherine, Trevor's mother and William's aunt, a stronghold of Victorian respectability and intolerant conventionality. Catherine wishes that these leavings of Bohemia and riff-raff of the studios could be cleared out of Monk's Hall; but from convenience, from inertia, from positive malevolence, they continue to stay on. But they might have gone, and as the sufferings born of a distasteful contiguity grow apace, one asks oneself, Would they really have stayed, would common little Sally have lingered on to swallow Catherine's polite insults, would Trevor have stayed on, merely to be near Tilli, whom, though her lover, he really loathed?

Perhaps the answer to this lies in the consideration that while the World plays a part in *Red Sky at Morning*, and the Flesh a greater one, the Devil has perhaps the largest rôle of all. ⟨. . .⟩

⟨. . .⟩ Considered as a work of art the book shows its predecessor's merits, and shows them intensified. It creates a world of living people, who lend themselves to the imagination and at the same time compel it. They are people who can be talked about and discussed as though they were actually alive. They are so vital, so full of themselves at every moment, that their most casual encounter is a crisis. With the possible exception of William, they accumulate personality as the story goes on instead of shedding it, as happens to the characters of so many authors. They have immense momentum and solidity. But they seem to end with themselves.

Unlike Tessa, William Crowne is not a figure to which emotion naturally attaches itself, nor is there among the characters (as far as I could see) one who, by the possession of some universal, extra-personal attribute (such as Tessa's devotion) brings the whole bitter, melancholy, unforgettable story into a cadence which the lover of life can realize and take heart from. The antagonisms between human beings are presented with unremitting force, particularly the antagonism (if such it be) between the present and the previous generation. It is as though Miss Kennedy had been anxious to acquit herself of a charge of sentimentality, and gone to the further extreme. *Red Sky at Morning*, as its name suggests, is a book heavy with menace, doom and despair. It is intensely interesting and provocative; one's armour of emotional security is for ever being pierced by its darts, one's memory is dyed by its vivid colours.

It establishes Miss Kennedy's reputation on an even firmer basis than did *The Constant Nymph;* for here we are in no danger of being beguiled into the indulgence of those emotions which, while we have them, minister to our self-complacency, assure us of charitable impulses, and persuade us to see the author's greatness reflected in our own. Miss Kennedy does not tempt us to identify ourselves with her characters, and if we did we should get no self-satisfaction. We could no more project ourselves into the story, for the sake of increasing our self-esteem or living a denied romantic existence remote from our own, than we could insinuate ourselves into the marble of the Venus of Milo and conceive ourselves equally beautiful and equally adored. Certainly *Red Sky at Morning* extends no consolation for and escape from life. It stands on its own merits, and they are of the first order.

—L. P. Hartley, [Review of *Red Sky at Morning*], *Saturday Review* (5 November 1927), excerpted in *Twentieth-Century British Criticism*, ed. Harold Bloom (New York: Chelsea House Publishers, 1985), 1528–29

CYRIL CONNOLLY

Red Sky at Morning is not such a good book as *The Constant Nymph*, and yet it is a book that has certainly demanded progress to write. *The Constant Nymph* revealed a balance of qualities, a proportion very rare in that kind of work; it was obvious that Miss Kennedy could probably only proceed by stressing some particular side, her humour, her wit, her sentimentality, or her respect for life. *Red Sky at Morning* is about the same theme as *The Constant Nymph*, the sad fate of genius at the hands of vulgarity. The children of a brilliant murderer and of a successful critic are brought up together; all are literary, but the first two are rich and unpractical, the others scheming and poor. In post-War London, and at a country retreat, the genius is robbed by his cynical cousin whom finally he shoots for making love to his wife. There is no radical change to the moral of *The Constant Nymph*. There is even a transplanted Sanger's Circus, a brother and sister to play Lewis and Tessa, a husband like Jacob, a wife like Florence, and a great deal about implicit intimacy, destroyed by the second-rate contacts of life. The book has less charm, less economy, and less clearness than *The Constant Nymph;* the brother and sister are too unreal, the wife of one is too squalid, and the husband of the other too dull. The Sanger's Circus is almost intolerable when composed of needy grown-ups, transplanted to a Cotswold Valley. There is no character that is really sympathetic, but this one must excuse because it is the surest way in which the public will be discarded, the huge sentimental public, which it is a mark of genius to have bitten off but which it would be proof of a miracle to be able to chew.

Though the book as a whole is packed and blurred, the workmanship itself stands very high. The dialogue, the descriptions of English scenery, and the

Greek chorus reflections on the theme are really an improvement on *The Constant Nymph*, and the details of the book reveal infinite care. The management of the title and of the allusions to the toy theatre are perfect examples of tragic irony; and the humour and insight of the author are delicate and sure. The ugly ducklings are too ugly for this to be a popular book, but what is rare in this kind of sequel, it is undoubtedly a promising one.

> —Cyril Connolly, [Review of *Red Sky at Morning*], *New Statesman* (12 November 1927), excerpted in *Twentieth-Century British Literature*, ed. Harold Bloom (New York: Chelsea House Publishers, 1985), 1529

NICOLA BEAUMAN

To the eternal dismay of publishers, bestsellers are almost always chance creations and there is no obvious reason why *The Constant Nymph* was so hugely successful. Two things helped: the unforgettable Sanger family, and the intense passion with which the novel is imbued. Not the passion of sexuality, despair or longing but the passion of life (what used to be called spirit) and each individual manifestation of it. The underlying message of the book is that spirit and integrity are the only values worth holding out for, and the Sanger family are shown doing just that.

This same theme had already been explored by Margaret Kennedy in her first novel, written a year previously, called *The Ladies of Lyndon*. Considered as a novel, as a work of art, it is undoubtedly superior. ⟨. . .⟩

⟨. . .⟩ For a first novel, written by someone in her mid-twenties, it is extraordinarily rich in theme and subtle in overtone; in some ways Margaret Kennedy never did anything quite so accomplished again. The novel is one of social comedy rather than plot. The central 'lady' is Agatha Clewer, née Cocks, who married in haste and repents at leisure, a repentance that is activated partly by her own dawning self-knowledge and partly by her newly recognised love for her cousin. The other main character is James, her brother-in-law, who is a budding painter of genius treated by his family as not only beyond the pale socially but also as a near half-wit.

Reviewers at the time treated the Agatha theme as most important, but in Margaret Kennedy's mind James mattered most. ⟨. . .⟩

⟨After his success following the war,⟩ James resists attempts to turn him into the 'tame family genius' and baffles his family by living domestically in Hampstead rather than in romantic squalor in a one-room studio—which course of action would have been considered more conventional.

Agatha too tries to adapt herself, to bridge the gap between the two worlds she sees to each side of her. But the conflict between the artists and the moneyed, the sensitive and the insensitive, the cultured and the philistine is well-nigh inevitable. It is a conflict which has often been described in fiction, the most obvious parallels (because they too use a large house as hero/villain) being *Mansfield Park* and *Howards End*. The former explores the opposing pull of principles and worldliness, the latter, which was published when Margaret Kennedy was in her early teens, describes the struggle, either futile or dependent on compromise, to connect the world of 'telegrams and anger' with the world which holds personal relations paramount. Virginia Woolf too was ever conscious of the apartness of the two worlds believing that 'the gulf we crossed between Kensington and Bloomsbury was the gulf between respectable mummified humbug & life crude & impertinent perhaps, but living'.

It was this theme, as well as that of the 'genius' in society, which was re-explored with even more obvious point and such public success in *The Constant Nymph*. ⟨. . .⟩

Time after time Margaret Kennedy describes women who lack the inner strength to forge their own destinies, who are at the mercy of their circumstances, domestic responsibilities or inner natures. Agatha has been stifled by her mother and her life is subtly sabotaged by her mother-in-law's interference. ⟨. . .⟩

But it seems that Margaret Kennedy, although preoccupied with the imprisoned woman, did not have those feelings herself—she always put her work first and there is an element of contempt, certainly not of sympathy, in her descriptions of subjugated women. It is the rebels, the Sangers and James's of this world, who have her sympathy—they, as she, took their art deeply seriously.

> —Nicola Beauman, "Introduction" to *The Ladies of Lyndon* by Margaret Kennedy (1981), excerpted in *Twentieth-Century British Criticism*, ed. Harold Bloom (New York: Chelsea House Publishers, 1985), 1530–31

VIOLET POWELL

Troy Chimneys, published in 1953, was awarded the James Tait Black Prize for a work of fiction, one of the pleasantest prizes to receive. Margaret had come to recognize the sudden glow, as if the landscape had become clearer, as a signal that here was something in her mind about which she was going to write. In the case of *Troy Chimneys* one aspect of the plot came from a few sentences in two letters, written by Jane Austen to her sister Cassandra, during a visit to their brother Edward Knight at his imposing house at Godmersham.

The party, Jane Austen wrote, had been joined by a Mr Lushington, MP for Canterbury. With a characteristically sardonic note, she combined assurances that she liked him very much, with the opinion that she thought him to be insincere and ambitious. *Sense and Sensibility* had just gone into a second edition, and the irrepressible Henry Austen had been putting it about that *Pride* and *Prejudice* was the work of his sister Jane. It may be speculated that when Mr Lushington "got a volume of Milton and spoke of it with warmth", he was aware that there was an author of two successful novels in the company, even if it was impolite to refer to such an excess committed by his host's spinster sister.

This hint was a strong enough signal to set Margaret to work. She must have felt that she was sufficiently familiar with political life to be able to draw the portrait of an adventurer. Additionally, she could contemplate her husband's experiences in the Asquith circle when she wished to give details of the life of a court jester. The story she finally wrote was, however, very different from anything known to David Davies in the days when he was a most popular diner-out. In its essence it was the story of what Jane Austen might have felt, and how she would have behaved, towards a man she loved but whose worldly ambition would always offend her sense of the truly virtuous.

—Violet Powell, *The Constant Novelist: A Study of Margaret Kennedy, 1896–1967* (London: William Heinemann Ltd., 1983), 187

BIBLIOGRAPHY

A Century of Revolution, 1789–1920. 1922.
The Ladies of Lyndon. 1923.
The Constant Nymph. 1924.
The Constant Nymph: A Play in Three Acts (with Basil Dean). 1926.
A Long Week-End. 1927.
Red Sky at Morning. 1927.
Dewdrops. 1928.
The Game and the Candle. 1928.
Come With Me (with Basil Dean). 1928.
The Fool of the Family. 1930.
Return I Dare Not. 1931.
A Long Time Ago. 1932.
Escape Me Never! A Play in Three Acts. 1934.
Together and Apart. 1936.
The Midas Touch. 1938.
Where Stands a Winged Sentry. 1941.
The Mechanized Muse. 1942.
Who Will Remember? 1946.
The Feast. 1950.

Jane Austen. 1950.
Lucy Carmichael. 1951.
Troy Chimneys. 1952.
Act of God. 1955.
The Wild Swan. 1957.
The Outlaws on Parnassus. 1958.
A Night in Cold Harbour. 1960.
The Forgotten World. 1961.
Not in the Calendar: The Story of Friendship. 1964.
Women at Work. 1966.

MARY LAVIN

1912–1996

MARY LAVIN was born on June 11, 1912, the only child of Tom and Nora Lavin, Irish immigrants living in East Walpole, Massachusetts. When Mary Lavin was nine, the family returned to Ireland, where she was educated at the Loreto Convent in Dublin. After earning her master's degree at University College, Dublin, Lavin taught French while working on her dissertation on Virginia Woolf (which she did not, however, complete). Two poems and her first short story, "Miss Holland" (written on the back of the typed thesis pages), were published a year later in *Dublin Magazine*. In 1942, *Tales from Bective Bridge*, a collection of stories, was published. It won the James Tait Black Memorial Prize and was followed by a second volume, *The Long Ago*, in 1944.

At 30, Mary Lavin married a friend from University College, Dublin lawyer William Walsh. After her father died, they bought her childhood home, Abbey Farm in Bective, and had three daughters. But a year after the birth of their third child, Walsh died, and Lavin's focus shifted from writing to caring for her young children and running the farm. By 1959, the pressure had waned. With a Guggenheim Fellowship, she reexplored her artistic capability, producing the collection *The Great Wave* (1961) that brought her the Katherine Mansfield Prize.

Mainly a writer of short fiction, Lavin commented provocatively in an interview with *The Irish Times* on the genesis of her ideas: "I carry around a question in my mind, a question that teases and torments me for an answer, and then one day I think I see the answer in a person or an incident. But even then I don't rush to write it, it is only after I have encountered it a few times that I take the risk of inventing the story." Her stories describe ordinary people in provincial Irish settings and are written with a reflective irony that suggests her wish to improve society without passing judgment on it.

In addition to her numerous short stories, Lavin wrote two novels, *The House in Clewe Street* (1945) and *Mary O'Grady* (1950), the latter remarkably written in one month during her father's fatal illness. Two of her stories, "Cuckoo-Spit" and "My Vocation," were made into teleplays by the BBC.

Lavin has received numerous honors and awards. In addition to her Black Prize, Guggenheim Fellowship, and Mansfield Prize, she has been honored with a D.Litt. from University College, Dublin; an Eire

Society Gold Medal in 1974; the Gregory Medal in 1975; and the American Irish Foundation Literary Award in 1979.

Lavin married another University College friend, Michael MacDonald Scott, in 1969. She continued to write until failing health forced her to move into a Dublin nursing home, where she died on March 25, 1996.

CRITICAL   EXTRACTS

LORD DUNSANY

I have never had much to do with the classifying of writers, my attitude towards art having always been that of a child to a butterfly rather than that of an entomologist, that is to say a greater interest in its flashing beauty than in its Latin name; so that others will classify Mary Lavin's work, if it is necessary for it to be classified. To me she seems reminiscent of the Russians more than of any other school of writers and, with the exception of the gigantic Tolstoy, her searching insight into the human heart and vivid appreciation of the beauty of the fields are worthy in my opinion to be mentioned beside their work. Often, as I read one of her tales, I find myself using superlatives, and then wondering if such praise must not necessarily be mistaken, when applied to the work of a young and quite unknown writer. And yet are not such doubts as these utterly wrong-minded?

⟨. . . R⟩ead these stories ⟨in *Tales from Bective Bridge*⟩ for yourselves, and see if again and again you do not find sentences which, if they had been translated from the Russian, would make you say that they do indeed show us that those writers understood life. I am reluctant to quote, because anything I would quote lies before you in this book, and because there are quotations which I might make from those tales which would seem to prove my point with almost unnecessary violence. But I suggest that a page should be taken at random from "The Green Grave and the Black Grave" and compared with a random page of any novelist of the present century, to see which page evokes with vividest pictures. ⟨. . .⟩

She tells the stories of quite ordinary lives, the stories of people who many might suppose to have no story in all their experience; and when she tells these stories there may be some whose ears, attuned to the modern thriller, may suppose that they are not stories at all. The pivot of one of them for instance is where a fly thrown out of a cup of tea, "and celebrating his release a little too soon by sitting on a blade of grass rubbing his hands," is killed by a small dog. It may seem too tiny a thing to notice, and the man's life, which turns in another direction from that moment, may seem tiny and unimportant too, to any who may not reflect how hard it is for any of us to say what is important and what is not. Browning speaks of the gnats

> that carry aloft
> The sound they have nursed, so sweet and pure,
> Out of a myriad noises soft,
> Into a tone that can endure
> Amid the noise of a July noon,

and many an ear must miss that tone, and many may miss the work of Mary Lavin. The bold plots and the startling events of the modern thriller are to these tales what a great factory is to the works of a gold watch. Those looking for great engines running at full blast might overlook the delicacy of the machinery of such a watch.

—Lord Dunsany, "Preface" to *Tales from Bective Bridge* (1942), excerpted in *Twentieth-Century British Literature*, ed. Harold Bloom (New York: Chelsea House Publishers, 1985), 1618

DAVID MARSHALL

⟨In *The House in Clewe Street*⟩ Mrs. Lavin has drawn for us a portrait of Trim. She calls it Castlerampart, but it's Trim all right; and it's Trim without false coloring matter. It's Trim under a pale sun when the weather is fine, and under wet, windy skies all the rest of the time. It's Trim seen in a cold gray light—which is, after all, the authentic light of Ireland. And don't let anybody tell you that Mrs. Lavin, who was born in Massachusetts, looks upon the Irish scene with alien eyes. With this distinguished novel she takes her place among the best writers Ireland has produced in a hundred years.

She has drawn for us a sensitive, honest picture of Trim, and of the family who lived there in the landlord's home in Clewe street: the father, who made each penny count though he had outlived the necessity for doing so; the son-in-law, a solicitor, who breaks his neck the minute he sets up as a gentleman and tries riding to hounds; the married daughter, who dies young; the orphaned grandson, who is raised (so perilously close to the castle park) by his two maiden aunts; and Onny, who works in the kitchen by day and goes home o' nights by way of the castle park. You may not like Onny, but you won't easily forget her.

As a novel, "Clewe Street" is probably too long; it runs to 530 pages. But tragedies told briefly are six for five cents in your daily newspaper. Again, time passes slowly in Trim, and how else than by a piling up of detail is a novelist to convey the sense of slowly passing days? How else, indeed, can one give power—as Mrs. Lavin certainly succeeds in doing—to what must otherwise have been a rather trivial story? There are moments in this book when the story has the intensity and some of the nobility of the highest drama. ⟨. . .⟩

Just the same, I wish a hundred pages of this book had been weeded out. For example, the race of the two funeral corteges to the cemetery contributes nothing to it; and if the same story has not been told twice before, by Carleton and again by William Sharp, I'll confess my memory has played me tricks.

On the other hand, I must pay tribute to Mrs. Lavin's quite exceptional talent; here is some of the finest writing that has come out of Ireland in many a year, and though there is great and laudable honesty, there is no vulgarity in this book. Other reviewers, I am aware, have thought the characters wooden, but that, I think, is a very wrong idea. I have not in years come across a portrait so appealingly true as that of Aunt Theresa. It is the case, however, that the lyrical note is strong in Mrs. Lavin's prose; and her characters, though sharply and firmly conceived, are infused with a kind of poetic intensity that carries them, I suppose, to the point of verging on abstractions; so that you can, perhaps, forget at one moment how real these people were the moment before.

—David Marshall, [Review of *The House in Clewe Street*], *The Commonweal* (20 July 1945): 340–41

FRANCIS HACKETT

Most novels are lit by electricity, bright, rational, social, sociological. Miss Lavin's is lighted by candles and lamps and the moon. It is as pre-sociological as a Brontë novel. There is a coldness in it that the Brontës, exiled to the wilds, were wholly incapable of. Miss Lavin does not feed on her own heart for the sustenance of her ravenous romance. But *The House in Clewe Street* achieves the triumph of disclosing the resources of a superb temperament. And a story ostensibly realistic, written to satisfy a dominating imagination, has a quality denied to all rational novels. It takes courage to spread wings and lift with them the weight of reality. ⟨. . .⟩

⟨. . .⟩ In *The House in Clewe Street* Miss Lavin levels her unsparing and at times supercilious gaze on the fat and sloppy Irish matron of a hotel, on the mother of a brood that in East Walpole would be "shanty Irish," on the neat and nipping bank manager's wife, on the go-getter who means to marry the daughter, any daughter, of the local plutocrat, and on the frustrated sisters who become pious. Miss Lavin does not evade the sordidness common to all stagnant communities. Her imaginative demands are too resolute, too independent, too fortified by inner dignity, to permit either evasion or submission.

Humor of a withering detachment is her weapon, and a steely refusal to be enlisted by the community. Even the minor character who prepared her shroud and her mortuary cards is held at arm's length as comic—though it was never comic when a poet like John Donne did it.

But Miss Lavin's Irish heartlessness is not penury. She hoards her emotions to buy dreams with them, and even an unfeelingness that gives Gabriel's mother the insubstantiality of a myth comes from a preoccupation rather than a dearth of nature. What she spends on, with royal profusion and Proustian indulgence, is a succession of incomparable emotional moments for which her novel has come into being. In these moments she is a great writer, as in the twilight magic of the garden that brings together the couple who are to be Gabriel's father and mother, or in the mad race of two funerals for precedence, or in the thunderstorm that reveals to Gabriel in a grimy Kildare Street studio the animal superstition of the Tinker's daughter he has eloped with. Miss Lavin lays it on thick, just as thick as Thomas Hardy, but she does it for the same reason—to give majesty to what would otherwise be base embroilment, and thus she can re-create Stephen's Green in Dublin, that handkerchief of a park which she picks up with the tragic gesture of a Duse.

But in the novel we expect a logic of events, and it is idle to pretend that her experience of people is quite adequate to the situations which she so grandly imagines. Psychologically her makeshifts in *The House in Clewe Street* are tolerable because the texture is so rich and the power is so deep. Only a young Chopin could find music for such a love scene as that in the garden, and it scarcely matters that it is bestowed on a couple flimsily propped into place. But it is serious that no preparation is made for Gabriel's economic helplessness and Onny's moral looseness in Dublin. Gabriel, the heir to a fat property, would have been induced to borrow on it in Dublin. He would never have tried for a literary job at Onny's urging. The compulsions in a novel, as *The Old Wives' Tale* exhibited, have to be underpinned; if Miss Lavin masters this in an art so endowed as hers is, all else will be added unto her. Meanwhile *The House in Clewe Street* offers the rare delight of a proud, spirited, lovely talent coping with a theme of magnitude.

—Francis Hackett, *On Judging Books: In General and in Particular* (New York: The John Day Company, 1947), 272–74

Frank O'Connor

⟨An⟩ Irishman, reading the stories of Mary Lavin, is actually more at a loss than a foreigner would be. His not-so-distant political revolution, seen through her eyes, practically disappears from view. She has written only one story about it—'The Patriot Son'—and from a patriotic point of view that is more than enough. It describes two young men, one a revolutionary, the other a mammy's boy who, despite his mother's scorn, admires the revolutionary from afar.

When the revolutionary attempts to escape from his enemies the mammy's boy tries to shield him, but all that happens is that he rips himself on some barbed wire and meekly returns to the authority of Ma and the local police. What it was all about was apparently the attempted overthrow of the Irish matriarch, a type Miss Lavin seems to dislike, and we may consider it a failure as the matriarch persists. The point of view is perhaps too exclusively feminine, for as the story unfolds a man may be excused for thinking that the mammy's boy is a far better type than the revolutionary, Mongon, and might even feel inclined to pity any matriarch who in future tried to bully him.

But here, at least, the Irishman is on familiar ground, the ground of O'Flaherty and O'Casey. It is only when he turns to the other stories that he gets the real shock, for, though names, details, dialogue seem all of unimpeachable accuracy, he might as well be reading Turgenev or Lyseskov for the first time, overwhelmed by the material unfamiliarity of the whole background, versts, shubas, roubles and patronymics. First, there is the sensual richness, above all in the sense of smell. 'There was a queer pleasure, too, in smelling the children's soiled clothes and Tom's used shirts. Even the smell that would have turned her stomach as a girl had a curious warm fascination for her now, and in the evenings when the diapers were hanging by the fire to dry, with a hot steam going up from them, she shut her eyes and drew in a deep breath, and felt safe and secure and comforted.' Even the word 'diapers' in an Irish story is not more foreign than the feeling of that passage from 'The Inspector's Wife.' And surely, when one first read Russian fiction, there was nothing in it more startling in the way of psychology than this from 'The Nun's Mother':

> Women had a curious streak of chastity in them, no matter how long they were married, or how ardently they loved. And so, for most women, when they heard that a young girl was entering a convent, there was a strange triumph in their hearts at once; and during the day, as they moved round the house, they felt a temporary hostility to their husbands, towards the things of his household, towards his tables and chairs; yes, indeed, down even to his dishes and dish-cloths.

As the last Emperor of Russia wrote in his diary on hearing of the Revolution, 'Nice goings-on!' I remember my dear Lady Gregory, and the mighty end of 'The Gaol Gate' and ask myself if this is indeed how most women feel. But then I remember the girl from the North Presentation Convent who came to the real gaol with the cake she had freshly baked, in the shopping bag on her arm, and, though she has been practically left out of modern Irish literature, I wonder if in fact this is not precisely how she does

feel, and it seems as though a new dimension had been added to Irish literature. 'O'Flaherty, L. *see also* Lavin, M.'

A woman cannot afford to caricature herself as a man may do, and if she
does, she is made to pay for it. It is a drawback to the Irish woman writer. But,
on the other hand, a woman's ideas of success and failure need not necessarily
be the same as man's. No man need regard himself as a failure if he has failed
with women, but a woman does so almost invariably if she has failed with men.
All through Mary Lavin's stories one is aware of a certain difference in values
which finally resolves itself into an almost Victorian attitude to love and marriage, an attitude one would be tempted to call old-fashioned if it did not make
the attitude of so many famous modern women writers seem dated.

—Frank O'Connor, "The Girl at the Gaol Gate," *Review of English Literature* (April 1960),
excerpted in *Twentieth-Century British Literature*, ed. Harold Bloom (New York: Chelsea House
Publishers, 1985), 1618–19

Thomas Whitaker

Mary Lavin has had long experience in adjusting ⟨. . .⟩ incongruities of voice
and vision; and in reading *The Great Wave and Other Stories* I find myself now puz-
zled, now disturbed, now delighted by the results. Sometimes ("What's Wrong
with Aubretia?" or "Second-Hand" or "The Yellow Beret") the story lacks
impact, perhaps because of mechanical development. In "Lemonade" one can
almost trace where direct experience (a deeply known childhood uprooting)
leaves off and postulated development begins; and the structural symbol of
lemonade as the pathetic offering of insensitive adults to wounded children is
not enough to save the story. Even in "Bridal Sheets" I am bothered by the
lengthily mechanical development of that macabre anecdote, which would
require the prose of Synge himself to sting it into life. But the structure apparent here, in which the characters' limited voice and vision serve as means for
the unobtrusive amassing of data which then may be charged by one last quiet
detail—that is perhaps Mary Lavin's most interesting technique. In "The
Mouse" that detail is the gesture of the "mouse" itself, which remains a puzzle
for the story's second narrator: " 'Did you ever hear such a rigmarole?' she said.
'Could her mind be affected; that's what I want to know! Or can *you* make anything out of a story like that?' " But an intelligible story is all there, quite subtle in its psychology, and all presented before we were quite sure that there
really was a story. Something similar, though with less surprise, happens as we
see beyond the rather uncomprehending voice which recounts "My Molly."
And the power that may break through even the most commonplace modes of
vision when that crucial detail settles into place is rendered quite variously in
the parabolic tale "The Great Wave" and in the more realistic stories "In a

Cafe" and "The Living." We may underestimate the latter two until their closing moments, and not simply through inadvertence. Without the somewhat
plodding and anecdotal flavor appropriate to the consciousness of widow or
child, the very last sentences (which return from the shock of experience to an
earlier tone) would lack their effect: the immanence of the miraculous or the
terrible in the random texture of the ordinary.
  —Thomas Whitaker, "Vision and Voice in Some Recent Fiction," *The Minnesota Review* 2,
  no. 2 (Winter 1962): 247–48

AUGUSTE MARTIN

In her work there is a whole range of characters who recoil from the more full-
blooded implications of life and settle for a cool cloistered compromise; over
against them stands an equal rank of figures who are characterized by their
energetic commitment to the hot realities of living. Several of her stories enact
the conflict between these two basic life attitudes and it is especially significant that in one of her very earliest stories 'Love Is for Lovers' the tension is
quite clearly epitomized. Here Matthew, a character of the first type, is almost
tempted from his ordered, emotionally tepid existence by a stiflingly full-
blooded widow, Mrs. Cooligan, but he retreats quite deliberately into the cool
cloister of his bachelorhood. As it is an early story the author presents the
issues less subtly than in her subsequent work and the contrast is quite aggres-
sively deliberate:

> Life was hot and pulsing and it brought sweat to the forehead. He
> didn't know anything about marriage, but it must be close and pulsing
> too . . . Life was nauseating to him. Death was cool and fragrant. Of
> course, he had a long way to go before its green shade lengthened to
> reach him. But in the meantime he could keep away from the hot rays
> of life, as he had always done before he had got familiar with Rita.

Surely this is the death wish presented in a most assertive, not to say
unnerving form. If it cropped up only in one early and rather clumsy story, one
might dismiss it as a transitory if curious tangent of the author's creative imagination. But it reemerges inexorably though more subtly through her later
work: in the contrast between Miss Holland and her fellow lodgers; in the
contrast between the prim and pathetic spinster and her father in 'A Single
Lady'; in Daniel's rejection of the little servant girl in 'Posy'—where even the
heroine's nickname is redolent of the life principle; in the disparity between
the vigorous and sweating Magenta and the two pallid old maids; and more
subtly in the contrast between Mamie Sully and Naida Paston in the two stories in which they appear. This persistent dichotomy could be expanded and

developed. There is little doubt that the author is on the side of life despite
the fact that many of its protagonists in her work are little short of repellent—
Mamie Sully, Annie Bowles, Rita Cooligan—and many of its deniers are sym-
pathetically, almost tenderly evoked—Naida Paston, Miss Holland, Matthew
and Daniel. Again it is difficult to be sure whether the author is—however
unconsciously—presenting the death wish as something central in the human
condition or merely posing the question of its peculiar relevance to Ireland. It
is sufficient here to note that the psychological tensions which surround it are
a constant principle of energy in her creative consciousness.

   The centre of her focus is the 'vagaries and contrarieties' of the human
heart as seen in its small-town habitat. This is her objective correlative and it
is on this murky prism that she concentrates the strongest creative light; it is
here that her human concern is most sustained and urgent.

   —Auguste Martin, "A Skeleton Key to the Stories of Mary Lavin," *Studies* (Winter 1963),
   excerpted in *Twentieth-Century British Literature*, ed. Harold Bloom (New York: Chelsea House
   Publishers, 1985), 1619

ROBERT W. CASWELL

The importance of Miss Lavin's first volume of stories, *Tales from Bective Bridge*
(1943)—the year of the censorship debate over Eric Cross's *The Tailor and
Anstey*—is due primarily to the way in which she retains certain ideas of Irish
life with which we are familiar from the work of Moore, Joyce, and others,
while at the same time she transforms these ideas into conceptions of a more
than Irish value. In fact the transformation is so successful that, as she herself
has said, her stories could take place anywhere. By not adhering to the "reality of politics," and by not exploiting nationalism in its widest sense, she risks
losing the force of a specific Irish identity. So far she has not done so.
Moreover, her approach enables her, even at the beginning of her work, to
keep from coming enmeshed in certain images of Irish life that by now have
become clichés.

   To illustrate. The conflict in "Lilacs," the first story in *Tales from Bective
Bridge*, arises from the desire of the daughters of Phelim and Rose Molloy, Kate
and Stacy, to get rid of the dung in which their father trades. To Phelim as a
young man, the dung is a source of income which will enable him to marry
Rose. Later, it is a source of income for giving a fine education, including
music lessons for Stacy, to his daughters. Moreover, to Phelim there is at times
a natural beauty in the dung. ⟨. . .⟩ However, Rose "didn't like the smell of
manure, then, anymore than after, but she liked Phelim" (p. 16). The remark
helps to explain the title: the ideal, in this case love, and the real, in this case
the wherewithal to support the love, are inextricably bound together; both, if

life is to be something rich, must be accepted. Neither Kate nor Stacy ever realize this fact. After the death of the parents, Kate decides to expand the dung business so that she can make enough money to escape from the house she detests with a large dowry. Kate recognizes the necessity of coming to terms with the reality of the manure, of the necessity of using it to get the lilacs of freedom from the house and of marriage. However, she has no intention of coming to terms with the perennial fact of what is, to her, disgusting in life. It is something that she recognizes must be faced, made practical use of, and then put aside. ⟨. . .⟩

If life for Phelim and Rose is an indissoluble union of lilacs and dung, and if life for Kate is a task of making use of the dung to get the lilacs, however impaired they may be as a result of her attitude, for Stacy life must be all lilacs. She is less bothered by the social stigma of the dunghill than Kate is, but the odor from the manure, especially on the days when fresh manure is delivered, causes severe headaches. Because of them she can seclude herself in her room delivery days where at least she does not have to see the dung. It is Kate who notices Stacy's propensity for withdrawal from facing the unpleasant. At the time of Rose's death, Kate comments:

> No wonder Stacy had no lines on her face. No wonder she looked a
> child, in spite of her years. Stacy got out of a lot of worry, very
> neatly, by just flopping off in a faint. Poor Rose was washed, and her
> eyes shut and her habit put on her, before Stacy came round to her
> senses again. 'It looks as if you're making a habit of this,' said Kate,
> when Stacy fainted again, in the cemetery this time, and didn't have
> to listen, as Kate did, to the sound of the sods clodding down on the
> coffin. (p. 27)

Earlier, during one of her headache spells, Stacy has the following fantasy:

> . . . she lay in bed and thought of a big lilac tree sprouting up
> through the boards of the floor, bending the big bright nails, sending
> splinters of wood flying till they hit off the window-panes. The tree
> always had big pointed bunches of lilac blossom all over it; more
> blossoms than leaves. But the blossoms weighed down towards her
> where she lay shivering, and they touched her face. (p. 26)

There is a strangely erotic note in this passage, and the immensity of the somewhat phallic lilac tree here might suggest barrenness of physical love in her life. She is never paired with any male in the story. But however suggestive the fantasy may be along these lines, the main thrust of the story renders such an interpretation peripheral. More to the point is the destructiveness of the lilac tree and the unnaturalness of the blossoms outnumbering the leaves.

It is the dream or ideal unhinged from the reality of the manure. This point is made final in the closing scene of the story. After Kate marries and moves out of the house, Stacy informs Jasper Kane, the family solicitor, that she is at last going to get rid of the dunghill. "But what will you live on, Miss Stacy?" he said (p. 32), and the story ends.

The implications in the line are various although they do not focus the entire story. Practical Jasper Kane literally points out a detail that the sensitive and impractical Stacy has simply never thought of, and the moment he does so the humor is delightful. The reader's answer to the question is, almost involuntarily, that she will live on lilacs, figuratively, of course, her day dreams—or perhaps her unused violin and piano? Impossible, and no doubt Jasper, as well as the reader, knows this even if Stacy does not. Clearly the course of Phelim, in making a living from the manure, which enabled him to marry Rose, and the course of Kate, in doubling the intake and sale of manure to insure a large dowry so that she could marry Con O'Toole, is preferable to Stacy's alternative. The sane thing for her to do is to deal in enough manure to make a living. The story, however, is more than a criticism or gentle mocking of the dreamer who gets unmoored from reality; the word "live" in the final sentence can carry more meaning than simply to make a living. Implicit in the word, although neither Jasper Kane nor Stacy seem aware of it, is the necessity for Stacy, if she is to have a life as meaningful as that of Phelim and Rose, with whom she is temperamentally akin, to find for herself the relationship, the abiding and necessary union, between the lilacs and the dung. Only in this way will her life, unlike that of Kate and Con, be a thing of beauty.

Had Miss Lavin fashioned the dung heap as an image of Ireland, and had she fashioned the lilacs as an ideal that was incompatible with life on the Irish dung heap, the story would be a variation on a familiar theme; presumably it would also be considered a work that adhered to the "reality of politics." What we have instead is a story that adheres to reality, Irish or otherwise.

—Robert W. Caswell, "Irish Political Reality and Mary Lavin's *Tales from Bective Bridge*," *Eire-Ireland* (Spring 1968), excerpted in *Twentieth-Century British Literature*, ed. Harold Bloom (New York: Chelsea House Publishers, 1985), 1622–23

ZACK R. BOWEN

Both Lavin and the critics agree that *The House in Clewe Street* is too long and disjointed, a criticism justified to some extent, at least in the first section, which deals with Gabriel Galloway's origins. However, as David Marshall points out, this is a family tragedy spanning generations, the sort of story that needs room to develop. The novel is in a sense the profile of a town. Like the villages of Lavin's short stories, the town itself may collectively be regarded as a character, so predictable are the strictures and responses of its code. ⟨. . .⟩

The book hinges on an understanding both by the readers and characters of the town's code of unspoken social rules or graces. There are three daughters to marry off, and, like Mr. Bennett in *Pride and Prejudice*, Theodore Coniffe must get busy and find someone, preferably for the eldest first. The courtship and marriage in the first section of the novel work in a tight framework of ritual procedure which renders acceptable only marginal deviations from accepted practice, such as Cornelius' falling in love with the youngest daughter instead of the eldest. Everyone knows that a marriage is inevitable. Indeed, to enforce the inevitability of the event, the first section begins in *medias res* with the father, Theodore, waiting for his daughter and her husband to return from their honeymoon. The question of which daughter got the man is all that remains unanswered.

In the last section of the book, Gabriel will violate the accepted morality of the town and the family by running off with a servant, but impulsiveness will lead to heartaches and the moral code will be redeemed, as Gabriel admits his part in the death of the servant girl, Onny. The novel draws its meaning from this code and the deviations and desperate attempts of Gabriel and Onny to escape from it. Pure submission to the tyranny of the code is exemplified by the second sister, Sara, while the utilitarian use of the code to justify her dictatorial personality is illustrated by the eldest sister, Theresa. Lily, the youngest and the Cinderella figure in the Coniffe family, is given one brief moment of happiness within the social framework of the novel, her marriage to Cornelius and her moment of independence from her eldest sister, before she, like her other sister, Sara, is doomed to a life of servility to the social ethic and Theresa's tyrannical interpretation of it. Of course, all this leads to Gabriel's desperate attempt to escape to the more cosmopolitan world of Dublin.

The sense of rigid social order is augmented by an intense awareness of social class as an irrevocable factor shaping the events of the novel.

—Zack R. Bowen, *Mary Lavin* (Cranbury, NJ: Associated University Presses, 1975), 62–64

JANET EGLESON DUNLEAVY

Mary Lavin, whose fiction reflects the sights, smells, and sounds of places where she herself has lived and presents characters who follow patterns of life familiar to such places, has been called both a naturalist and an autobiographical writer. Because each of her stories is built around events that have a discernible beginning, middle, and end, she also has been described as an old-fashioned storyteller, comforting to readers who like to be assured that the universe is, after all, an orderly place. But Mary Lavin is also the writer who fascinated Frank O'Connor, because of her early capacity to suggest that she had not said all that she had to say. And V. S. Pritchett, intrigued by her "extraordinary sense that what we call real life is a veil", has described her as an artist who presents "the surface of life rapidly, but as a covering for something else."

All these statements about Mary Lavin's work are true. The surface of her fiction faithfully records details of an exterior reality through which men, women, and children who resemble people she has known move from yesterday to today to tomorrow. Hidden in their words, gestures, and observations, however, is that which extends beyond the limits of time, place, and individual character. What seems so solid and permanent in her stories is revealed, in afterthought, as fluid and temporal—the moment immobilized by the reader's willing suspension of disbelief in response to the artist's power to recreate milieu. What seems so fleeting and illusory is revealed as timeless—a fragment recognized, in afterthought, as essential human nature: The resulting interplay of universal sensibility and particular experience is what makes her work disarmingly simple on first reading, disturbingly complex on recollection, elusive, tantalizing, and seductive.

—Janet Egleson Dunleavy, "The Fiction of Mary Lavin: Universal Sensibility in a Particular Milieu," *Irish University Review* (Autumn 1977): 222

A. A. KELLY

It is through ⟨. . .⟩ apparent trivia that the revelation in Mary Lavin's stories most often comes, and her later work demands even more of the reader's percipience. 'Heart of Gold' is another such story showing narrative subtlety. The narrative line alternates between scenes in Lucy's mind, Lucy acting out her ideas with others in dialogue, and Lucy fabricating scenes from the past and acting them out in her own mind as a form of interior dramatic narration. Occasionally a neutral omniscient passage is inserted as a narrative bridge between the two dialogue passages separated in time, but for the most part the author enters deeply into the mind of Lucy through the latter's interior monologue, which the reader interprets in relation to what has been revealed of Lucy through her exterior action. Lucy's self-awareness grows as the story progresses and comes to its crux in the train bearing her away on her honeymoon.

As Mary Lavin thus enters more subtly into the thoughts and feelings of her characters through the multiple viewpoint, the complicated articulation of their reactions reveals them as spiritual beings faced with ultimate meaninglessness, as moral beings faced with social condemnation and as biological beings faced with the annihilation of death. These three threads of uncertainty affect feeling, and with it the concept of reality. They are woven into the fabric of her stories using the shuttle of time, the colours of different narrative tones and the pattern of descriptive language.

Within the dominant tone Mary Lavin may be using in a particular story, descriptive language has always played an important part. She may convey feeling by an occasional motif representing the abstract, such as the snow-drops Sam and Lucy in 'Heart of God' wear for their winter wedding; the symbolic kernel of the story may be revealed by its title, as in 'The Lilacs' or, less obviously, in 'The Cuckoo-Spit'; by the naming of characters as in 'Love is for Lovers' or 'The Pastor of Six Mile Bush': descriptive metaphor may adhere to concrete image, like the worm impaled on the fork prong in 'The Lost Child'. For the sight of this image on the retina of the pregnant Renée reacts at an intuitive level and connects, for the perceptive reader, with Renée's previous thoughts about her unborn child. Feeling is sometimes conveyed by simile, as Lally's prayer in the train ('The Will') described as 'rapid unformed words, that jostled themselves in her mind like sheaves of burning sparks'.

This is a language of the blood, or senses, of which Mary Lavin's later work shows increasing use. The multiplication of echo within Mary Lavin's stories is something at which she has become ever more adept. The reader has to be on the alert as he moves from the simple comparison of Mr Parr's pursed lips to a chicken's vent ('The Mock Auction'), to the more complicated image of 'their mouths like swinging censers spilling song to right and left', ('Tom'). Mary Lavin, from the first, aims to stimulate awareness, and with it an enlarged concept of reality, in the minds of her readers. As she has matured herself, her desire to do this has not diminished. ⟨. . .⟩

A writer whose principal subject matter is states of feeling must incorporate all levels of consciousness and Mary Lavin's mythogenic faculty cannot ignore the subconscious state. She claimed in her *Sunday Press* interview with Brid Mahon that she had 'almost total subconscious recall'; a statement which she would need to explain herself, for can anyone claim to have this? But that she said such a thing means the subconscious is important to her. She writes about reality of outward representation, based on the happenings in individual lives. This is surface reality, behind lies an inner reality. Memory is crystallised from an amalgam of the two which are mutually dependent. This enduring core of human experience is not something which can be categorised. It can only be hinted at through the patterns language uses to convey meanings: the paradox being that the conscious act of writing overlays and limits the conveyance of subconscious expression.

—A. A. Kelly, *Mary Lavin: Quiet Rebel* (New York: Barnes & Noble, 1980), 128–31

B I B L I O G R A P H Y

Tales from Bective Bridge. 1942.
The Long Ago and Other Stories. 1944.

The House in Clewe Street. 1945.
The Becker Wives. 1946.
At Sallygap. 1947.
Mary O'Grady. 1950.
A Single Lady and Other Stories. 1951.
The Patriot Son and Other Stories. 1956.
A Likely Story. 1957.
Selected Stories. 1959.
The Great Wave and Other Stories. 1961.
The Stories of Mary Lavin (Volume One). 1964.
In the Middle of the Fields and Other Stories. 1967.
Happiness and Other Stories. 1970.
Collected Stories. 1971.
A Memory and Other Stories. 1972.
The Second Best Children in the World. 1972.
The Stories of Mary Lavin (Volume Two). 1973.
The Shrine and Other Stories. 1977.
A Family Likeness. 1985.

DATE DUE

GAYLORD			PRINTED IN U.S.A.